WAYNE BENNETT

WAYNE BENNETT
THE MAN IN THE MIRROR

with Steve Crawley

ABC Books

Published by ABC Books for the
AUSTRALIAN BROADCASTING CORPORATION
GPO Box 9994 Sydney NSW 2001

Copyright © Wayne Bennett and Crawley & Associates Pty Ltd 2008

First published November 2008

All rights reserved. No part of this publication
may be reproduced, stored in a retrieval system or
transmitted in any form or by any means, electronic,
mechanical, photocopying, recording or otherwise,
without the prior written permission of the
Australian Broadcasting Corporation.

National Library of Australia Cataloguing-in-Publication entry

Bennett, Wayne, 1950-
    Wayne Bennett : the man in the mirror / Wayne Bennett and
    Steve Crawley.
    ISBN 978 0 7333 2428 4 (hbk.)
    Includes index.
    Bennett, Wayne, 1950–
    Football coaches – Australia – Biography.
    Brisbane Broncos (Football team) – History.
    Rugby League football – Australia – History.
    Other Authors/Contributors:
    Crawley, Steve.
    Australian Broadcasting Corporation.
796.3338092

Jacket design by Luke Causby at Blue Cork
Front cover photograph by Tony Phillips / AAP Image
Back cover photograph by Colin Whelan / Action Photographics
Typeset in 12.5 on 16pt Perpetua by Kirby Jones
Edited by Justine Crawley
Edited and produced by Geoff Armstrong
Colour reproduction by Graphic Print Group, Adelaide
Printed in Australia by Griffin Press, Adelaide

10 9 8 7 6 5 4 3 2 1

To the 163 men who played first grade for the Broncos 1988–2008, their loyal fans and all the staff who worked so wholeheartedly with me over these 21 years.

CONTENTS

The Man in the Mirror		ix
1.	Early Days	1
2.	The Big League	16
3.	Uncle Eddie	34
4.	The Little Things	39
5.	It Wasn't a Dream	54
6.	Same Old, Same Old	57
7.	On the Right Track	74
8.	The One You Feed	89
9.	Whatever It Takes	92
10.	The Making of Us	98
11.	Talk About Tough	108
12.	Cyril	117
13.	Even Champions Get Into Ruts	123
14.	Super League	129
15.	Four Good Men	138
16.	Who Are the Broncos?	143
17.	Justin	156
18.	Coaching Tough	161
19.	Ribes	172
20.	The Will to Win	176
21.	Women in my Life	187
22.	Farewell to Alf	194
23.	To a Man They Were Magnificent	206
24.	No Way Was He Going To Fail	217
25.	Singo	231
26.	Turning Up, Ready to Play	236

27.	It's All About the Team	247
28.	Couldn't Buy a Win	252
29.	Operation Successful, but the Patient Died	258
30.	Doing What's Right	273
31.	True Believers	286
32.	Three Amigos	303
33.	A Succession Plan	308
34.	Three Priorities	316
35.	Together We Worked On It	320
36.	21 Years	325
37.	Mass	338
38.	You Can't Always Win	342
	There Is No Indispensable Man	353
	Coaching Record	355
	Index	361

THE MAN IN THE MIRROR

I was introduced to this wonderful poem quite a few years ago. In my mind, it's called *The Man in the Mirror*, but when it was first written, back in 1934 by an American named Peter 'Dale' Wimbrow, it was titled *The Guy in the Glass*. It's had many adaptations over the years, and this version isn't quite as Dale Wimbrow originally wrote it, but the message is always the same ...

When you get what you want in your struggle for self
And the world makes you king for a day.
Then go to your mirror and look at yourself
And see what that man has to say.

For it isn't your father, your mother or wife
Whose judgement of you — you must pass.
The fellow whose verdict counts most in your life,
Is the guy staring back from the glass.

He's the man you must please, never mind all the rest,
For he's with you clear up to the end.
And you've passed your most difficult and dangerous test
When the man in the glass is your friend.

You may be like another and chisel a plum,
And think you're a wonderful guy.
But the man in the glass says you're only a bum,
If you can't look him straight in the eye.

You can fool the whole world, down the pathway of years,
And get pats on your back as you pass.
But the final reward will be heartaches and tears
If you've cheated the man in the glass.

CHAPTER ONE

EARLY DAYS

I HAVE ALWAYS MADE SURE if I had nothing to say — nothing that would make sense — then I'd keep my mouth shut. Cut the lecture short, Wayne. Get out of here. And leave the way you came in — quietly.

When you are deficient in areas like education and formal training but still want to make your way in life, you have to get the smarts about you, think on your feet and do the things you have to do.

I have to assume my upbringing helped out in this area. With my upbringing I always had to be street smart, because I was in a lot of situations as a little boy that required good decisions, and fast ones. Bad decisions could have cost me enormously, whether it was around drunks who were beginning to lose it, or around domestic violence, or around not being able to pay the bills. As a boy I walked on egg shells, forever having to handle delicate situations. So street smarts have always been important.

The other thing I've always been conscious of is your feelings, the feelings of others. I've never wanted to hurt somebody's feelings ... not deliberately, anyway. I'm very sensitive about people, about how they may feel and how they'll react. I watch everything, and always have. I go back and relive situations and ask, 'Could I have handled it better?' And I've been doing that all my life.

My greatest experiences growing up wouldn't have happened if someone hadn't come in and coached the footy team. Because all the special people I knew emerged from football: my friends and my mentors, the many opponents who made me feel stronger and better. They were the people who handed me opportunity. If we didn't have a coach we wouldn't have had a team, and without a team everything in life adds up to nought.

ALL I WANTED TO DO was give something back, so in 1974 I became a coach. I was 24 then, playing first grade at Brisbane Brothers, and stationed at Petrie, in Brisbane's northern suburbs, as a policeman.

Already I'd played for Collegians in Warwick, for Toowoomba All Whites, for Queensland, Australia and Huddersfield in England, along the way completing three wondrous years with the Queensland Police Force as a cadet.

In the early 1970s they changed the whole culture of cadetships and built an Academy for 300 boys. They were being represented in the Under-20 Brisbane church league and had just lost their coach. So they approached me. I remember the three of them walking in: Gary Hutchinson, Tony Cross and a guy named Wockner. Trevor Wockner. It was the middle of the season and I was heavily committed, playing for Brothers and working shifts at the station at Petrie, on the other side of town.

For those three years as a police cadet, which I loved, I'd go home to Warwick every weekend to play football, and I remember thinking how good it would have been to stay put and play for the cadets' team — being mates, living in dorms together, playing as one. But no one ever put us together like that. We'd work, sleep and then go our separate ways on weekends.

This was a wonderful opportunity to put to rest something that had played on my mind. I wanted to make a difference with these young men and I had always believed I could do that.

History would remember no big names among them. They were just a great group of kids trying hard and loving their rugby league.

We won the competition.

That was 1974, and winning that grand final felt the same as winning any grand final since, no matter the level. What is important to me has never changed much, I don't think.

But it was only the beginning. In September of that year, Les Allan, a chief instructor at the Academy, approached me about going on his full-time coaching staff instead of being out on patrol.

I remember the sergeant at Petrie station saying, 'Wayne, I wouldn't be doing that — that's not what you want to be.' I said, 'Yes, that is what I want to be. That's an opportunity to work full-time with young men. I want to do that. I want to take this opportunity.' It was a huge turning point in my life.

There were 300 cadets and 150 probationaries. I spent the next 12 years there, working with some of the finest men I've ever worked with in my life. All very dedicated to the education and training of police officers.

It was a great place to work and learn.

I LOVED BEING AT THE Academy because you were coaching every day and that's how you learn things ... things like how to speak better.

My first day in the classroom was woeful. You had to go in there and address a group of trainees — and we were doing probationaries as well that day — so men and women between 18 and 40 years of age. Les Allan would say, 'Wayne, you have to go in at the deep end — make sure you do your preparation. Get in that classroom and present your lecture.'

I had no formal training. I was nervous, introverted and hated putting myself out the front. These were huge obstacles for me to overcome. Again it was all about street smarts — knowing when to open my mouth, and when to shut it too. To be prepared and stick to my subject. These lessons were to serve me well for the rest of my career.

I was being challenged and that is when I found I learned and improved the most.

BEING ON PERMANENT STAFF, I soon took over coaching the Queensland Police Academy for its annual match against the NSW Police Academy, and weren't they wild affairs.

True, I've always been against fighting on the football field, but I've forever been into sticking up for myself — been big on that. I hate bullies with a passion. The only fights I've ever had in my life have been when seeing other people being bullied. I'd go straight over and buy into it. I'd rather get a black eye than excuse a bully because I just hate bullies. Never had any time for them.

We had a great run against New South Wales. It was war. The first time we played them with me as coach was at Cronulla in Sydney — before a Sharks club game in 1975 — but from then on the games were played at the Sydney Cricket Ground or Lang Park, as curtain-raisers to the main Queensland–New South Wales interstate matches, and it was a big deal for us. Something huge.

The whole Academy kind of stopped and it built a great spirit, even though you'd get plenty of criticism from certain staff who were anti-football. But my players were committed, which was all I needed. The critics did not matter — another lesson for later in life.

They were training at half past six in the morning, had a whole day's work in front of them at the Academy and then they'd turn up to play. They paid a huge price, those kids, to be in these teams and as a staff member I gave up a lot of time as well.

Ray Whitrod was the Queensland Police Commissioner at the time — Commissioner Whitrod — and he was against the interstate games. But we somehow convinced him to come along to the game at Lang Park. It turned out to be a great game and Queensland won. Well, you should have seen Commissioner Whitrod. They were suddenly *his* boys: 'What a great team *my* boys are ...'

The superintendent in charge of the Academy was Frank Clifford and he was very supportive of what we did. In 1975, our Under-20 team went through the competition undefeated, without a try being scored against them.

It was a hell of an effort, but come grand final day I couldn't go. I was playing first grade for Brothers against Wynnum-Manly on the same day. The Brothers–Wynnum match was broadcast throughout Queensland and I still remember relatives telling me how one of the commentators bagged the hell out of me. And I did play terribly. I didn't want to be there. It was Brothers' last game of the season and we couldn't make the play-offs, and I wanted to be with the young men I coached, because that was more important to me.

I had written a note to each of them and my mate Greg Petrie handed them out one by one before they played. They won easily, still without a try being scored against them.

EARLIER IN 1975, WE'D PUT on our best shirts and shorts for induction day, when 100 new cadets come in with their parents. Being their first day at the Academy, it dragged on and on, so to help entertain them we asked, 'Who wants to play touch footy down on the oval?'

A stack of them cantered down the hill and I went out to referee and supervise the game. And there he was — this wonderful athlete. He just stood out. Like nothing I'd ever seen before.

EARLY DAYS

Tremendous build. Great ball sense. Speed to burn. Wonderful touches with the ball. I had never heard of him. He'd come to be a policeman, but would turn out to be a footballer for the ages. He was one of the few people I've ever seen at that age who just had it all.

I remember being excited inside. I didn't say much at all that day, but at the end of it whispered to the staff we had somebody pretty special in the place.

His name was Mal Meninga.

IN 1977, I WENT to Brisbane Souths to play football. They had a coach there named Tom Berry who kept quitting every time he couldn't get what he wanted.

Tony Testa was the new club chairman and he was a good guy. 'Every time Tom doesn't get his way,' Tony said one day, 'he resigns as coach only to turn up the next day with his clipboard for business as usual.'

'Next time he resigns,' said Tony Testa, 'I'm going to tell him, "Fine, that's it."'

So sure enough, January rolls around and Tom Berry resigns. 'That's fine, Tom, see you later,' says Tony.

Next day, Tom rings up wanting to withdraw his resignation. 'Not on your life,' says Tony.

Tony comes to me and asks whether I want to be captain-coach. I tell him I'm not ready, I'm only 27 years of age — still a young man.

'Wayne,' he says, 'you're ready.' I was anxious. I knew I wanted to coach but I also knew I wasn't ready. But when are you ready?

Bob Bax, the great Queensland rugby league coach, was quoted in the paper as saying, 'Wayne Bennett, like Bunny Pearce, is too nice a guy to coach a football team.' And there was a lot of anxiety in my life at that time. I had married Trish and Justin was just a little boy, a baby. I was still coaching the Queensland Police Academy rep team and the Under 18s — and they were playing in the Brisbane competition against guys like Paul Vautin, Paul McCabe and Wally Lewis, a bunch of young guns.

But I said yes. Suddenly I was captain-coach at Souths. In hindsight, I did a lousy job.

Halfway through the season I gave up playing because I couldn't handle being captain-coach. I couldn't live with myself telling guys they were doing things wrong when I was playing poorly myself, and part of the reason I was playing poorly was because I was too worried about them. I couldn't help but think about them on the footy field. The choice was either drop myself to reserve grade or retire.

Less than bravely, I chose retirement.

At the end of the year I was pretty lucky to hang on to my job. The players were disgruntled — and so they should have been. I made a lot of mistakes. On the other side of town I was still coaching police cadets, which was different to coaching grown men.

A good mate told me to stop acting like a school teacher at Souths and start being myself. This was just one of many changes I would have to make to myself. We had a really good forward named Marshall Colwell who at the end of the season decided to go back to Townsville. His parting words were: 'Wayne, you never really taught me anything or showed me many things.'

And he was right. I felt terrible because I knew I had failed him and all the others. So I made changes. From 1978 onwards I set out to be different, to be a better coach.

BEFORE THE 1978 SEASON BEGAN Tony Testa told me Souths were broke and there would be no sign-on fees or bonuses. All the club could afford to pay players was $200 a win and $50 a loss. Straight away, we lost 13 players who'd played first grade the previous year.

I'll never forget Pat Phelan, brother of the better known Chris and a wonderful player in his own right, standing up and staring down at Tony. Pat was a hard worker, a brickies' labourer who'd proudly do the work of two fellas. He was just a special guy. He stood up and said: 'I'll stay. I've got no problems staying. But if I hear of you paying one player $1 more than $200 a win I'm going to come looking for you.'

And that's what we built the team on — honesty. And good people. Workers. We built it on police cadets. I brought them from the Academy across to Souths and we rebuilt the whole place. Playing for $200 a win.

The following year we made the grand final. It was three years in the making.

TONY TESTA WAS VERY, VERY disappointed with me when I left Souths after the 1979 season and, in hindsight, I don't blame him.

The Supercoach, Jack Gibson, was one of my idols and I'd noticed every three years he'd move clubs. By the end of 1979 I had been three years at Souths. I knew how far we'd come and what we'd been through, and just didn't know if I could replicate that again. So I decided to leave.

Years later I found out from Jack's great friend Ron Massey, a man who has had a huge influence on my life, that the Supercoach had to go every three years because he'd run out of friends. He had upset that many officials. I hadn't realised that's why he kept moving. I'm not in the business of upsetting people that badly and probably could have stayed longer.

Anyway, I went to Brothers, and it felt like going home. Frank Dolan was the club boss and a good friend. That first year Brothers lost 24–17 to Norths in the knockout semi-final but Frank took ill and had to resign. To this day it was a great reminder about the importance of the front office. If the front office is not in great shape, the business — any business — is doomed.

I left at the end of 1982 with no fanfare ... and not much else either. With four or five games remaining that season, the players had a real opportunity to make something of themselves but instead of lifting they played terribly. I was part of the problem, I had no doubt about that.

What I didn't fully understand at the time was a quote from Bobby Bax. He said in the *Sunday Sun*: 'If anything, Wayne is before his time and is going to have problems because Queensland players lack the professional approach he requires.'

I didn't know what my time was. I couldn't work that out. All I knew was that from the moment Frank left, I'd been surrounded by football politics and I wasn't strong enough and big enough to handle it well.

I WAS THINKING, MY COACHING career could be over ... I'm in a fair bit of trouble here.

I'd had three years at Souths and made one grand final. I'd had three years at Brothers and we'd done bugger all. I wasn't the flavour of the month like Johnny Lang and Des Morris, who'd coached with success at Easts and Wynnum-Manly respectively.

But Jack Astill, the man who built Souths Juniors, threw me a lifeline as Souths' director of coaching. Put this down as a fill-in time, because that's how I saw it.

Bob McCarthy was running out of gas as the first-grade coach at Souths seniors. They'd played three straight grand finals, winning one and losing two. In 1983 they missed the play-offs altogether. They were talking change.

Tony Testa declared publicly they would not have me back, but privately he was a softie and he knew I badly wanted to come back.

Many of the police cadets and some of the guys I had coached were still there, and on 20 September 1983, I was appointed Souths coach for the following season. But within 30 days Tony was at it again, declaring the club fly-blown and busted. When we won the Woolies pre-season competition the following March, beating Wynnum 18–11, I remember saying, 'Wait until we start playing for money!' The $10,000 prize money went to paying players from the season before.

Souths finished the 1984 competition proper second on the ladder to Wynnum, losing 46–22 to them in the major semi-final before beating Ross Strudwick's Valleys 18–8 in the preliminary final and ultimately being whopped 42–8 by Wynnum in the decider. Des Morris was still coaching them. Wally Lewis was there, plus Gene Miles, Rod Morris, Greg Dowling. It was a wonderful, wonderful football team.

And that was that.

WELL, ALMOST. THE FAMILY packed into the one car straight afterwards — me not wanting to talk and slumped in the back seat — and my mother-in-law, Jeannie Veivers, turned from the front seat and said, curiously, the way mother-in-laws do: 'Wayne, why do you keep coaching? Why don't you give it up?'

I just said, 'I'm not going to give it up. I know I'm better than that. I know my players are better than that. I'm not going to give it up.'

I don't think I said another word for the next 24 hours. I was in my cave.

Why wouldn't I give up?

Because I believed in myself. I believed in what I was doing and believed it was right. I always have. There were times when I'd get something wrong and in those situations I knew I had to change, but I also knew what I did and what I believed and what I coached was right for the young people I did it for.

Other coaches weren't doing what I was doing. I didn't want to be like them, anyway. I wanted to be me, different. Not different for the sake of being different. But I never wanted to be a normal rugby league coach or a normal coach per se.

I didn't want to coach my players the way other successful teams were being coached. So I had to stay strong with myself and surround myself with people who believed in me, because only time would get me there.

My mother-in-law said, 'That's all very well, Wayne, but you're stone mad.' By then she knew my stubborn ways well enough to know she wasn't going to change anything.

THE FAMILY CAR ENGINE hadn't cooled before I got wind the Souths board was going to appoint Barry Muir as coach.

I was still young and I was not going to let these bastards beat me. Tony Testa was still the chairman and still a supporter but he told me straight that others on the board were not so supportive and I was going to have to come down and give a presentation to save my rubbery skin.

Well, I just told them about the vision I had and my plans and beliefs ... I stuck up for myself. I'm not big on that but I stuck up for myself and I made the sale. When I get passionate about something, I can sell you anything.

Actually, no, not anything. I couldn't sell you a car. I couldn't sell you life insurance, but I can sell you on football. I can sell you on, you know, what drives me.

So I got the job back. The other significant thing that happened to me in 1984 was the advice of a close mate. He said: 'Wayne, if you were a racehorse trainer you'd finish up running second in everything. Why? Because you keep picking the wrong horses.'

That's all he said.

I got to thinking about it and he was right. I kept picking the players who looked good at training and had good flair, because I love that in a player. But not everyone has those qualities.

What about toughness, strength of character and desire? The bloke who doesn't look great but within the team is great value. The bloke you win with. The guy who has to play his heart out every week just to make the team. If he doesn't play his heart out, he knows he's gone. He's the man you want. Most stars won't do all that stuff: the little things, the little–big plays few people notice.

So this was the go for 1985: we kept four players from the grand final team, put nine new guys alongside them and thought Wynnum-Manly, Wynnum-Manly most waking hours.

Every game we played we would practise how to beat Wynnum. Every opposition centre was Gene Miles. Every opposition five-eighth Wally Lewis. Dowling and Morris were the props. Eventually I devised a game plan that would beat Wynnum and sold the players on it.

Johnny Elias had turned up. He'd come from South Sydney. I remember contacting one of the Brisbane media men to sift out some information on Elias, and he returned with the message Elias was a tough guy, and very hot-headed. My reaction: good, he'll do me. Chris Phelan and Norm Carr. Wayne Cullen was on his way to talk with Norths when he called into David Bourke's family service station and ended up with us. Blokes who did the little-big things right by playing their hearts out.

Chris Phelan had been to Parramatta — they'd won three premierships in a row — and he came back to Souths to repay a debt of family honour after his brother Pat, the brickies' labourer, had been killed in a boating accident. He was the rock we built that team around. Something special. Wherever Chris went, teams won.

We believed if our game plan was good enough to beat Wynnum on 22 September 1985 it would be good enough to get us there.

What each and every team member knew was that between the beginning of the season and grand final day, we were to play 27 trial matches — trial matches for D-Day.

It was one of the great upsets. Souths 10, Wynnum 8.

I HAD LEFT THE POLICE force in February of 1985 after Senator Ron McAuliffe, the President of the Queensland Rugby League, approached me to be the QRL Coaching Director.

Together with Bob Bax, I had been involved in the setting up of the QRL Coaching Panel. The other codes of football were getting a bit of a leg up in Queensland and Senator McAuliffe and QRL Chief Executive Ross Livermore convinced me I should leave the police force, which was very hard to do, and take up this role.

So I took the job, realising the insecurity of it, simply because I wanted to make a difference in the game. I didn't want to be hiding around corners whingeing about the game's lack of direction while doing nothing about it.

Part of the deal was I could continue to coach Souths in 1985 but McAuliffe did say we had better have a good season because he didn't want the Queensland director of coaching telling people how to coach when his own team was failing.

After winning the grand final I was even more excited about 1986 and Souths, and then McAuliffe and Livermore told me I couldn't coach at club level any longer. They wanted all my focus on one thing, that I could be doing more hours at headquarters. What they didn't understand was that the club coaching gig was not only relaxation but kept elevating my skills daily — and I didn't need to do more hours at the top end of town.

I wanted to resign from the Queensland job then and there, but I had a family and didn't want to cut my nose off to spite my face.

At the same time, there were problems at Wynnum, and one of the consequences was that coach Des Morris had a falling out with his captain, Wally Lewis, which led to Lewis taking over there as captain–coach. Morris had been Queensland State of Origin coach in 1985 and there were rumblings. I didn't know the issues and still don't, but I do know McAuliffe was worried what had happened at Wynnum meant the coach and captain couldn't work together again at Origin.

I was in a pub in Rockhampton, doing a QRL coaching course, when the phone call came. Ross Livermore didn't stay long on the line, but in the few minutes we talked he offered me the Queensland coaching position. I'd already done a few things with the Maroons. When Arthur Beetson was coach (1981–1984) he had asked me along to training a couple of times, just to help out on rules and that type of stuff. So I was familiar with them all and had coached a few of them, like Mal and those guys. I took the job.

We were beaten 3–0 in that 1986 Origin series, but never by more than six points — by six points in the first game in Brisbane, by four in the Sydney game, and by just two back in Brisbane for Game 3. It was a great effort by the Queenslanders. We introduced a number of new players and started to change the direction of our play. I was so proud of them.

But what I also remember is a conversation with our halfback Mark Murray after the second game, when we were flying home to Brisbane.

'Wayne, you don't respect the players well enough,' he said. 'We have great players like Wally Lewis in this team and you are too hard on us. These guys have great records. Picking out our faults, you criticise us and a few of the boys aren't real happy.'

Queensland had just lost its second Origin series in two years. I told Mark we had to get better if we wanted to win again and I didn't know any other way than to highlight what we were doing wrong and then to work on correcting it.

I admired that little bloke's courage in fronting up and telling me, because he was obviously speaking the sentiments of more than himself, and was doing something about it instead of whispering around corners.

'Are my criticisms relevant?' I asked.

'Yes,' he said, 'they are.'

And we were on our way.

CHAPTER TWO

THE BIG LEAGUE

I'M GOOD AT SELLING WHAT I believe in but I'm not good at selling myself.

So I'm sitting in the Canberra Raiders waiting room. Coach Don Furner and club boss Les McIntyre have the door shut in the main office and big Peter Jackson is sitting beside me. Jacko had long been wanted by a stack of Sydney clubs but until now had stayed at Brisbane Souths.

I said, 'Pete, what are you going to do today? What are you going to ask for?'

'Seventy thousand dollars, Wayne.'

'Are you serious?'

'Bloody oath I am.'

He said, 'I know I can get that. What are you going to ask for?'

I said, 'I don't know. I was going to ask for about $40,000.'

He said, 'You're kidding me. You get in there. You're worth as much as I'm worth.'

So he talked me up, started pumping me up. I went in there and asked for $65,000 and they said, 'That's fine, mate.'

I came out and gave Jacko a big hug. I said, 'Seriously Jacko, thanks — I would have gone for $40,000.'

There was no debate, no argument and it probably wasn't an over-the-top price, but Jacko had given me the courage I needed. So the deal was done. I was co-coach of the Canberra Raiders. The Big League.

WHEN IT COMES TO FOOTBALL, I've always had an inner belief. Not so much that I'm right, but that the things I'm doing are right. I'm doing it for the right reasons.

That's given me great strength all my life. I've never made a decision just to make someone happy. Whatever I've done, I've done it for the right reasons. At times I've been wrong, but I didn't do it for the wrong reasons.

I went to Canberra because the QRL had ruled I couldn't coach any more at club level. But that's what I wanted to do — coach. I knew I was going to Canberra for the right reasons. It was an opportunity to be a full-time coach.

When I went to the Police Academy and when I went to the QRL I went because I wanted to help ... to be involved with young people and make a difference. My chance to make a difference was in coaching. Coaching rugby league. It was the one thing I believed in.

Always, though, there has been doubt in my mind. By nature I'm conservative, and I'm extremely introverted, so I'm always going to have doubts. I'm not a negative person, but I have to at least have a look at the downside. That's why moving to Canberra was such a big step.

For starters, Trish and I had three kids and we were moving away from the support of family and friends for the first time.

And I was anguishing about leaving the Academy. I loved the police force — all the things it had taught me, and the wonderful people I worked with. People like Frank Rynne, Les Allan and Greg Petrie.

Frank was friends with my uncle, Eddie Brosnan; he'd been a policeman with him. When I went to the Academy, Frank was an instructor. He was also a senior sergeant in the force and went on to be superintendent. He always gave me wise counsel and had great belief in me, could see things in me I couldn't see in myself. One of the things I marvelled at was his wonderful gift as a speaker — and he never used notes. Ever. At assemblies and functions I would sit in awe of him, listening and wondering if I could ever be so blessed.

I was born a football person and all the great influences on my life have been football people, yet there was a time when many football people did not do themselves justice. The coaches I saw when I was a kid growing up, or the players, would embarrass themselves by not being able to communicate well publicly. So it was a real driving thing for me. I didn't know I was going to do the things I ended up doing in coaching, but watching Frank made me want to make sure that when I did get up to speak I could do it without notes and I could do it properly so as not to embarrass our game.

Les Allan, another influential figure at the Academy, was in the grand final of outstanding men. He was a former first-grade rugby league footballer who continuously challenged me and would never accept my second best. He made a real difference to the way I worked and lived my life.

Greg Petrie was a civilian when I arrived at the Academy. He'd played first-grade cricket in Brisbane and would later become the manager of my football teams. Most of all he was a great dreamer. I remember early on I had to stop him writing letters to Ron McAuliffe about how the QRL boss should appoint me Queensland coach.

Greg was an eccentric in a lot of ways and had a cliché for everything — such powerful sayings.

He used to embarrass me when he'd tell people what a wonderful coach I was going to be; he just had this great belief in me. He challenged me, and would never take no for an answer. You could never satisfy him yet you knew he was satisfied ... he kept throwing challenges at me and extending me.

THE HEADLINES WERE CALLING THE Canberra Raiders a Banana Republic. Gary Belcher and Mal Meninga had gone down the year before. Kevvie Walters was just 18 and I'd been coaching him in Queensland teams since he was 17. Les Morrissey, David Paterson, Jay Hoffman, Steve Jackson, Andrew Fox, Gary Coyne, Rowan Brennan, Peter Jackson, Steve Walters, Sam Backo and Mitch Brennan were all Queenslanders ... and Raiders too.

Dean Lance had come from Newtown — he was an inspirational player. And we had 'Chicka' Ferguson, though he'd do his cruciate early that season. Chris O'Sullivan was an absolute legend in the place. We had Ivan Henjak, and my big second-row mate Ashley Gilbert. Brent Todd had come over from New Zealand. Terry Regan was there, and he was quite a legend. So there was the nucleus of a pretty successful organisation.

And there was Don Furner. I liked him straight away. He was a lovely guy. On the game and how it should be played, he is one of the best. Him, Cyril Connell and Bob Fulton I would regard as the best guys I have ever talked to about identifying talent. Don had a great eye for who could play the game and who couldn't. The Raiders had come into the premiership in 1982, with Don as their coach, and in the next six years he'd built up a hell of a football team.

We had a great relationship from the very beginning, because Don allowed me to concentrate on the football team while he looked after the media and team selections.

I HAVE NEVER HAD A great relationship with the media. I have never felt comfortable — and never enjoyed — dealing with them. The hypocrisy of it all. Long before I went to Canberra, I'd seen players I played with become media darlings and I'd seen other guys I played with who were really good and valued players, but no one in the media gave a damn … they never recognised them.

Generally, people seem to feel they can trust me and when they tell me something I always keep that trust. It's not easy for me to come out and say things publicly that someone has told me. I'm not one to want to give out information I either think is not important or should not be given out.

I've always been like that. I remember as a young coach having stand-up bust-ups with journalists like Lawrie Kavanagh, who was a highly respected writer for the *Courier-Mail*, and Barry Dick, who is now a very good mate of mine.

Given my terse relationship with a number of journalists, I know it's a contradiction for me to claim I have friends in the media, but a lot of them have been very good to me in many ways. Particularly long-term journos, the ones who have been around for a long time — I have strong relationships with them.

Others, though, are always looking for the downside in what we do and I don't live like that. I'm always looking for the upside. I'm always looking for the good. Even in the carnage I'm still trying to pick the good out so we can get back on our feet and move forward. These people never see that. It's not part of what they want to write about.

Channel 7's Patty Welsh tells a story of how, as a young reporter, he came to interview me and I just kept giving 'yes' and 'no' answers. In the end he said, 'Can you put a few more words into your answers? Because I'm running out of questions.' I trust Patty completely. He is a long-time friend. But that's the way it is.

So 1987 was my happiest year in coaching because Don took all that away. I didn't have to worry about it. Wasn't under the pump with it. I could concentrate on coaching and just be with the players and not have to worry about a press conference, not worry about what I'd said, not wake up and find something I said a headline. I have never enjoyed reading about myself.

BEING A QUEENSLANDER, YOU are brought up to believe New South Welshmen think they are better. I've always been on a mission to prove you don't have to be born in New South Wales to be good at something and you don't have to be born in New South Wales to have all the original ideas. That's part of a Queenslander's psyche — that's what we are born with. You hear your parents talking about it, and you just pick it up. It's like the dirt on the ground you get in your feet: you just pick it up as you are growing up, that's how you feel. I've always been on a mission to say you don't have to live in Sydney to be somebody in life.

The laidback attitude of the Queenslanders and the competitiveness and toughness of the likes of Dean Lance, Ashley Gilbert and Brent Todd took a little time to gel at the Raiders, but Canberra was definitely an ideal place for them, because the only thing the players had to do was play football and be with their mates. Their families didn't live there so all they had were their mates and it somehow made it more special. It was never a case of getting in your car and visiting mum and dad. Mum and dad weren't there. You went to see your team-mate, because that's all you had.

It took me until about seven weeks out from the finals to realise we were a real shot. I was away at Origin with four or five of our key players, sitting in the Gazebo Hotel in Brisbane, really excited. Ivan Henjak did a great job that day. We beat Cronulla at Cronulla in a really gutsy effort. It wasn't a big score, about 12–10 or something, but I thought, there's something about this team. It had taken us quite a few months to get to that point because until then we were winning one week, losing one week.

When we'd played Parramatta, for instance, we'd led 22–0 at halftime. That was the day Don made the famous statement he coached them in the first half and I coached them in the second. We got run down and beaten 30–22.

We came home from Origin and played Canterbury on a fairly nice winter's day for Canberra. The Bulldogs were on the brink too. They'd been grand finalists the previous year but were having an up and down year as well. Warren Ryan was coaching them. He was already a legend coach. I kept reading about 'Wazzaball' and 'Wokball'. But we beat them in Canberra. Got a little self-belief that day and thought we could really do something.

IT WAS A HELL OF a year, 1987. My mouth was full of ulcers. Over the years I've had a few ulcers, but that year my mouth and throat were full of them. I'd never been that bad before and I've never been that bad since. I have no doubt at all it was tension, and I went to see the specialist and he agreed. I don't think the time I had that year has been paralleled in the coaching field, actually.

The call came out of the blue. It was half past six, quarter to seven in the morning, and it was cold. It was Steve Williams, a bloke I knew from my playing days. We'd played together for Queensland and against one another in club football after he'd come from North Sydney to Wests in Brisbane. He was a good five-eighth. He was also one of the four part-owners of the Brisbane Broncos, who'd just been given a ticket to play in the 1988 NSWRL competition.

'We've just been down to Sydney to see Jack Gibson,' Steve said. 'Jack says you're the coach we've got to get. We want you to coach the Broncos.'

I told him I didn't need to hear that. I said I was committed to Canberra for four years. 'Wayne,' he said, 'have you ever heard of a guy called Tom Landry?'

I said yes, I'd heard of Tom Landry. He said, 'Landry coached the Dallas Cowboys for 27 years. You can do that.'

I said, 'Steve, don't start talking rubbish to me. That ain't going to work with me, you know.'

Anyway, I flew to Brisbane without anyone knowing and met them at the Bonaparte Hotel. It was me, Paul 'Porky' Morgan, Barry Maranta, Gary Balkin and Steve. Porky had a bit too much red wine in him, so he was in a pretty boisterous mood, but he wanted me right or wrong. They'd interviewed a number of coaches but Jack Gibson had anointed me and that was that for them.

Then I told them what I was on in Canberra and they nearly fell off their chairs — they obviously weren't in touch with what the market was paying. I said, 'I've got a four-year contract with Canberra.'

They said, 'Have you got it written down?'

I said, 'No, I haven't got an official contract, just a piece of paper I wrote myself. A foolscap piece of paper with three or four points on it and signed by me.' Les McIntyre was supposed to sign it but hadn't got around to it. 'Regardless,' I said, 'whatever they told me they were going to do for me they've done, and there've been no dramas ... they've been totally spot on with everything. I know what I have committed to. So I'm going to need some legal advice. I'm going to need you to pay my legals because we're going to have a fight here. But if you're prepared to back me ... well, you know, I'll go and talk to Trish.'

The Broncos were going to be a genuinely Queensland team in the Sydney premiership. There was also going to be a side from the Gold Coast starting in 1988, but in my mind the Brisbane team was the real 'landmark' set-up. I liked the idea of being part of that. Plus there were the kids. The girls were unhappy in Canberra. Katherine had only just started Grade 1 and Beth hadn't settled down there. She wasn't happy. It didn't worry Justin. We just had so much more support at home in Brisbane, support we knew we were going to need. Nothing was said anywhere, and I went back to coaching.

We took a Queensland team on a 10-day tour of New Zealand to prepare for Origin. Allan Langer was on that tour. At this stage, I wanted Easts' Laurie Spina at halfback and Kevin Walters at five-eighth because they were both playing great in the premiership, and I'd seen Alf play a Panasonic Cup game for Combined Brisbane against Penrith, his first major rep game, and he'd been outplayed. So there were lots of questions about him, but Dud Beattie, a former Test forward and one of the Queensland selectors, had talked to Tommy Raudonikis, who was coaching Alf at Ipswich, and he said, 'Mate, this bloke is going to be a champion, give him a go.' That's how I got overruled in the selection process, which was fine because, on reflection, it was the making of the great Allan Langer.

The only time Alf ever played well for you was when he felt totally comfortable in the team environment. Back then, before that tour, we didn't know his personality, that he was intimidated by Wally and Gene Miles. Me and Greg Dowling. But there was not a lot of pressure on us in New Zealand, which allowed Alf to be Alf. They all gelled to him, and as soon as he sensed they liked him he was a transformed boy. Alf hates to think you dislike him. He just can't handle that. I often wonder what might have happened to his playing career had it not been for those 10 days in New Zealand.

We came back to prepare for Origin I and Porky was overseas, so I rang Steve Williams. 'What's your legal advice? Where do I stand, what have you guys done?'

He said, 'We've done nothing.'

I said, 'You've done nothing?'

He said, 'No, nothing's happened.'

I said, 'In that case, Steve, don't worry about it. I won't be coming. I asked you to do certain things and they haven't been done. If that's the joint I'm going to work for, mate, don't worry about it. You can ring Porky up and tell him.'

Steve went into a flap and rang John Ribot — they had just appointed John Ribot CEO of the Broncos football club. So Ribes came around to see me and I said, 'Ribes, I ain't coming … it's all over.'

INTO CAMP FOR ORIGIN I. It's 16–all and everyone's waiting for the hooter when the Blues Mark McGaw scores in the corner and the Channel 9 cameras catch me screaming 'Oh no!' in the stands. Oh, no, all right. So now I'd coached a grand total of four Origin games, and we'd lost them all.

To this day, people think I walked back to the hotel alone that night in disgust and total bewilderment. I was so despondent, and when I wasn't on the bus that's what everyone figured — that I'd walked home alone.

The truth is, a few days beforehand Bruce Hatcher had called. I'd played football with Bruce in the early 1970s; we were long-time mates and he was my accountant. He was also mates with Porky Morgan.

He said, 'Porky's coming back from overseas and he's really pissed off about what's happened. He wants you for coach. He doesn't want anyone else; he says he wants you.'

I said, 'Tell Porky I ain't coming. It's all over. I've made up my mind, I ain't coming.'

He said, 'Well look, he's going to want to talk to you.'

I said, 'He can come and talk to me but he's wasting his time.'

In the aftermath of Origin I all I said was, 'I won't be on the bus.' I didn't say anything else to anybody. I walked around the back and jumped into Bruce Hatcher's car. He took me back to the hotel. I got the key, we walked into my room and Porky Morgan was sitting there. Large as life. Sure, I'd won a premiership at Souths but I hadn't won much else, and less than an hour ago I'd lost my fourth Origin match in a row. He was still adamant he wanted me. The guy's stone raving mad.

Porky was finger pointing and carrying on. 'You're not pulling out of this,' he roared. 'You are going to be the coach of the Broncos.'

I said, 'Hey, Paul, your guys didn't do what they said they'd do. It's a big issue for me and my family, you know how it all stands.'

So we argued for an hour. I just kept saying, 'No, no, no.' I had the dirts big-time. I said, 'Mate, it's all over. See ya.'

I was walking out of the room. I said, 'I have to go to this team function. He said, 'I will wait until you come back.' I said, 'Don't.'

Bruce followed me out the door and said, 'Porky wants to fly to Canberra to talk some more.' I said to tell Porky to forget about it — it's over. Bruce asked me to promise him one thing: that I'd ring him in the morning from the airport, just to touch base.

I was on the six o'clock flight — Brisbane to Sydney — and before I boarded I went to the public payphone at the airport. I rang Bruce.

I said, 'Mate, how did you finish up?'

'Oh,' he said, 'he's pissed off. He said he wants you, right or wrong. He said he'll do anything to get you.'

I said, 'Mate I'm not coming, I'm just ringing out of courtesy.'

He said, 'Can you do me a favour?'

I said, 'What?'

He said, 'I've never been to Canberra. Porky wants to come down and meet with you, with the family, Trish and that. I haven't been down.'

I said, 'Oh Jesus Bruce.'

He said, 'I'd really love to go to Canberra. And he's paying.'

I said, 'Well Bruce, if you want to come down, mate, come down, but nothing is going to change.'

The next day, they were there, the two of them. There was a knock on the door but I already knew who it was. I opened the door and there was Bruce and there was Porky, and Porky was carrying a suitcase. A big suitcase. A bloody big suitcase.

I said, 'What have you got that for?'

He said, 'I'm going to stay here until you sign.'

I'm thinking to myself, this is not going to be much fun. He meets Trish for the first time and within five minutes she's in love with him because that's the guy he is. My sister-in-law Helen was there. She was down visiting. So he's got them both in the palm of his hand. I hang around for the best part of four hours before it gets too much.

I said, 'Paul I've got to go for a run. When I come back I'm going to give you an answer. It's going to be the final answer. But I have to run to sort my head out.'

Anyway, I went out and ran. A number of things went through my mind. Porky was back, and in control. And a month beforehand I'd been happy to do it. So I came back and said, 'OK Paul, I'm coming home. Mate, I couldn't put up with you being here any longer.'

He said, 'Fine, let's jump in the car now and go and see Les McIntyre and Don Furner, tell them what's going on.'

I thought, do we have to? I said, 'Paul I don't want to do that, not today.'

He said, 'Mate, we have to do it now'

I get in the car and in we go. Les is in his office. It was about lunchtime.

Les McIntyre is one of the finest men I've met, a very passionate guy. He loves his Raiders and he was wonderful to me during my time at the club. Porky introduces himself and just says to Les, quite openly and bluntly, 'I'm taking your coach off you. He said he's going to come back to Brisbane.'

Les said, 'Is that true, Wayne?'

I said, 'Yeah Les, that's true. I've got an opportunity, Les, and I know I've got a deal here, I appreciate all you've done for me, but I would like to be released. I'd like to go back to Brisbane.'

As I'm finishing Porky says, 'And I'll tell you something, Les, I've interviewed a lot of coaches lately. I've got a couple of good ones for you.'

I couldn't believe it. I was so embarrassed. I said, 'Jesus, Porky, don't do this to me.'

Les handled it beautifully. He said, 'Paul, I can tell you one thing. I do not need you to tell me who we need as a coach at the Canberra Raiders.'

I grabbed Porky by the shirt and said, 'Come on, mate, let's get out of here.' I was so uncomfortable, because it was tough. So we just got up and we walked. Then I rang Don Furner. I went and saw him and told him what was going on.

Of course, Les's first reaction was to sack me, get rid of me, on the spot. He was cranky and I understood why. There had already been speculation about me going to Brisbane and I had gone to see him to tell him I was staying — because at that time I believed I would stay.

It was a bloody tough time. Within the next 24 hours I went to training and told the players I was going, and I wasn't sure what the club was going to do. 'If you don't want me to be here for the rest of the season, if you want me to leave now, just tell me and I'll do that,' I said to them. They had a meeting in the sheds and I waited outside.

It seemed an eternity before Peter Jackson emerged alone. He just grabbed me and said, 'Mate, we want you to leave, and now.'

That was nearly the worst moment of my life, I reckon, or close to it. I just felt so hollow inside.

Then Jacko burst out laughing and said, 'It's a wind up, mate. Just lead us through the season.'

All the blood went out of me. I felt like fainting. All this might have swayed Les McIntyre, I don't know, but in the end he changed his stance and allowed me to stay. But there was still the matter of compensation.

In between coaching the Raiders and preparing for the next Origin, we went to Sydney for mediation with John Quayle and Ken Arthurson at the NSW Rugby League. Quayle says to me, 'You've signed a contract, Wayne.'

I said, 'Well, I signed a contract. I don't think Les or Don signed it, but I'll tell you this much, John, I agreed to four years at the Raiders. I don't need a contract. I know what I've got to do, I know I'm in breach of that. I made a decision I'm going back to Brisbane, and if that doesn't work out today and Canberra hold their ground, well, I obviously won't be coaching.'

Porky is sitting there. John Ribot is sitting there. Les McIntyre. Their solicitor. Porky says, 'Well, what do you want, fellas? What is it that will satisfy you to release Wayne Bennett?'

The solicitor says, 'We want compensation of at least $100,000.'

Again I went cold. It was a lot of money, $100,000, back then. It's still a lot of money today. I thought, Porky, we're in all kinds of trouble.

He just said, 'That'll be fine. If that's what you want, that's what we will give you. We'll pay you $100,000 cash. Just give me a couple of minutes with the coach, will you?'

He walked into the back room with me and Ribot. He said, 'The board's probably going to be filthy with me but you're worth it. I'll ring them and tell them once we've done the deal.' At the same time the Broncos were paying hefty transfer fees for Wally Lewis, Gene Miles and company, but I turned out to be the dearest.

ORIGIN II WAS TO BE played at the Sydney Cricket Ground, so we booked into the Travelodge at Rushcutters Bay, which was a great place to stay. The night before the game I took a walk through the park with Dick 'Tossa' Turner, the great Queensland team manager and an icon of Origin football. He would have been sussing me out; I knew that's how he worked. I said, 'Tossa, if we don't win tomorrow night I'll resign at the end of this series. I've had two years at it and I don't want to put people under pressure. I don't want people debating whether I should be coach or shouldn't be coach. I'll do what's right: I'll resign.'

He said, 'I agree with you, that's how it should be.'

I felt pretty calm about it all because I knew I'd done the best I could. I wasn't angry with myself but that's not to say I wasn't feeling cut up.

On the morning of the game it started raining and it poured all day. The SCG was a bog, an absolute bog. We get out there, NSW score early and then about 20 minutes into the game Paul Vautin went on what I still regard as one of the most courageous runs I've ever seen. He just picked the ball up somewhere near the halfway, might have been a bit further out, then he just ran into every NSW player he could and kept going and going. His legs just kept pumping. I don't know how the hell he did it but it was so inspirational — and Queensland never looked back.

We were to win the next eight Origin games straight over a period of three years. Everybody went up another gear. Gene Miles, Wally ... everyone. We came home for Origin III in Brisbane — a classic game of football. To me it was one of the great Origin games. Queensland won 10–8 in a very low-scoring game, in which the scoreboard didn't change after halftime; it was the tightest, toughest second half you'd ever see. Afterwards, I kept thinking about that chat with Mark Murray — and how we'd stayed on course. In those last seven minutes, with the game in the balance, we did the things I knew we had to do to win Origin. For seven or eight minutes we contained them in their half. They couldn't get out. I was so proud, because all the things I'd pushed into them, the things I'd convinced them we had to do in tight and tough games to win, all unfolded in front of us.

THE LEAGUE DECIDED TO take Origin to the world and we played a one-off exhibition game in Los Angeles. It was a wonderful concept and one of the best times I've been involved in during my coaching career.

New South Wales sat up the pointy end of the plane, where players had their special dietary needs catered for and weren't allowed to drink. Queensland sat up the back and we had a few beers and ate anything and everything they brought along.

We got off the plane and just enjoyed it. I said to the guys, 'Look, we won the series and nothing is going to change that, but I don't want you running out there and embarrassing us even if it is only an exhibition game.'

We were getting a bit of a towelling and at halftime I got up a few of them. I said, 'Now you are starting to make a joke of it, boys, and embarrassing your state.' We didn't win, but we turned it around a fair bit in the second half.

All the NSW clubs were demanding their players return immediately for weekend club matches. The Queenslanders? We were going to Vegas. The Canberra players and coach in the Queensland team had the club's blessing to stay on.

Tony Currie was a Maroon but playing club football for the Bulldogs and had suffered a bit of a cork in the game. I walked into the change room afterwards and there's Trevor Gillmeister and Vautin punching Currie hard as they could in the leg. I said, 'What are you doing that for, boys?'

They said, 'Tony doesn't want to go home but his injury isn't bad enough to rule him out for this weekend. But it will be when we finish with him.'

I said, 'Keep going, boys.'

I walked down the other end of the room and Peter 'Bullfrog' Moore, the Bulldogs boss who was also one of the New South Wales team managers, appeared. 'Why are you looking so sour, Grumpy?' he asked me.

I didn't know Bullfrog that well then, but he was cautious around me because I had a reputation for being cranky. 'How's Tony Currie?' he said. He'd obviously heard that Tony had hurt himself.

I said, 'I'll be very surprised, Peter, if he is available to play for you.'

'He's bunging it on, isn't he?'

I said, 'Peter, he's got a very sore leg, but you go down and find out for yourself.'

He did that, then walked back past me, 'You were right, he's no good, is he?'

Tony Currie loved Vegas. We all did. Three days later we headed home and, for the Raiders at least, the ride didn't stop until Manly-Warringah proved too good on grand final day.

I LEFT WITH A BANNER HEADLINE in an afternoon newspaper attributing to me the words: 'Sydney — you're not as good as you think you are!'

I've never been a rude person but I've spent my life in Queensland and the perception was that Queensland-based coaches struggle. My great friend and mentor Bob Bax coached Queensland in the early 1970s, long before the Origin concept was introduced, and I played in his sides when they were beaten by NSW teams full of Queenslanders playing in Sydney.

They were all bagging Baxxy for not being able to beat the Blues and I'll never forget him saying, 'If Frank Stanton was coaching Queensland and I was coaching New South Wales, I'd be the winning coach and he'd be the losing coach.'

He wasn't putting us down but his point was very true.

It was a great frustration in Queensland that our players had to go to Sydney to be recognised, to get all the accolades. If they were born in Queensland and played in Queensland the perception was they were inferior. But when they went to Sydney, players like Noel Kelly and Arthur Beetson suddenly became greats. I think Bob Bax is one of the really great coaches of our game — so was a guy named Duncan Thompson before him.

So it was a very big deal for me to come out of Queensland, get a coaching job in Canberra, in the Big League … and help guide the Raiders to the grand final. I had never played football in Sydney. I wasn't a *name*. I felt the frustration of all those before me, and was somehow echoing their sentiments when I made that comment.

Don Furner gave me an opportunity, and I will never forget it. He was always a great believer in me, and even when I decided to go home to the Broncos he told me I had to do the best thing for my family … I went with his blessing. He is a beautiful man and I hope he has had some joy in seeing me develop, knowing he was a big part of that development.

CHAPTER THREE

UNCLE EDDIE

He was my uncle, my mother's brother. He was a policeman. They'd been brought up on a farm at Greenmount near Toowoomba, a dairy farm, 11 of them in the family, and he didn't begin playing rugby league until he was about 20 or 21.

He went away with the 1948–49 Kangaroos, the last Australian touring side to go to England by boat.

I was born in 1950 so I never saw him play football. Obviously, there were no videos but he had these magnificent scrapbooks which became a source of inspiration for me. I first remember staying with him and his family when they lived at Moorooka in Brisbane and he was a policeman at Woolloongabba. I would have been six or seven. He had a son named Eddie junior who was a few months older than me. We became pretty good mates.

From that time on I remember spending time at Moorooka and then, when I was 11, he transferred to Warwick. My grandparents lived in Allora, a small country town outside of Warwick. We were living in Warwick then, and it was the beginning of a long and much closer relationship.

He had a huge influence on me, did Eddie Brosnan. He was a famous guy of sorts in the police force, and in rugby league circles.

He was regarded as one of the toughest men to play the game and I don't say that lightly. Everyone who ever saw him play or ever talked about him talked about his toughness. Just recently, I ran into an old guy whose name was Bishop. I can't think of his first name but he was at a Legends of League luncheon and he came up and said, 'You're Eddie Brosnan's nephew, aren't you?'

I said, 'Yeah I am.'

'He was the toughest guy I ever played against,' he said. 'I played for Wests, and in those days if the halfbacks got too close to the scrum the old front-rowers would rake them with the steel tags on their boots. Eddie raked our halfback in and I came out of the scrum just as the ref stopped the game, concerned about the health of the halfback. I said to Eddie, "Why don't you pick on someone your own size?" The next thing you know I'm picking myself up off the ground. He knocked me out with one punch.'

The President of the United States of America, Lyndon B. Johnson, came to Brisbane in October 1966. This was a time when there was plenty of opposition to Australia's involvement in the Vietnam War, so there were huge demonstrations and police from all over Queensland were summoned to the city to act as security for LBJ's street parade.

Anyway, during the parade this Secret Service agent was walking next to the President's car, and at the same time he was gesturing to the crowd, encouraging them to come closer. Eddie told him to stop it. He didn't. So Eddie knocked him out cold. Did what he had to do. The Americans feverishly tried to identify the Queensland policeman responsible for this 'assault', but though there were plenty of witnesses no one gave Eddie up. He really liked that.

All the stories, all the things people have told me show he was fearless. I didn't see all that. What I saw was a man in his later years whom everyone respected. He carried himself tremendously. His uniform would be absolutely spotless, his shoes so shiny you could see your face in them. I just hung around with him, never saying much. I wasn't game to say much around him. He was not a great talker himself, but the creed he lived by was if he gave his word, that was it.

He didn't trust a lot of people. Trusted himself more than anything. If you told him something in confidence, that's where it remained. He was extremely loyal. Never talked rubbish. Never big-noted himself. What he said he meant and people knew that. With him, there was just no going back. In the early 1960s, they formed the Police Credit Union in Queensland and there was an argument between a friend of Eddie's and another guy, and it became heated. So Eddie bought into it. The guy told Eddie, 'It's got nothing to do with you,' and Eddie said, 'Hey, if you want to pick on my friend, you pick on me. If you want to fight him, you first me first.' In his presence you always felt this extraordinary strength of character.

But he was a moody bugger and if he was in a bad mood he would scare the hell out of me. In a good mood, he was great company. I loved being around him. He had a magnificent work ethic — he was always doing something. Didn't matter whether it was gardening or whatever, he was OK so long as he was doing something.

I was observing all this. I'd watch when he left a group of people, and I saw how they responded, the comments they made about him. The things they saw in him. I was thinking, I want to have some of those qualities, I want to have some of the characteristics he displays.

WHEN I WAS 14, EDDIE junior came up to the house — I'd been away working for a while, in Brisbane with my father — and said, 'We've got a footy team and we're short of players. Will you come and play Under 18s for us?'

I said, 'Yeah, I'll do that.' So I went down and played Under 18s. That was the beginning of my junior footy career.

Eddie had been coaching the first grade in Warwick, but the following year he coached us in the Under 18s, and it was the best thing that ever happened to me. He coached us for two years and we won two premierships, and by this time I was spending a lot of time at their place.

Then I got sworn in. I had always wanted to be a policeman. I saw him and I wanted to be a policeman.

When I got sworn in he was stationed at Red Hill in Brisbane, just up the road from where the Broncos would live. Again, I spent a lot of time there. I was now in my 20s and still staying with him and his family. I loved his company and just loved being around him, even though we didn't talk a lot — that was one of the Bennett/Brosnan traits. Didn't have to.

In those days the police station had a house out the back where the sergeant lived. The front office was the station. There'd be three or four police out there. This day, he would have been 55 or 56 years old, I suppose, and, anyway, he just disappeared. He could disappear and he wouldn't tell you. That was just the way he operated. When he came back an hour and a half later he was absolutely white. He looked terrible, drained, and I said, 'Where have you been?'

He said the young guys had brought a suspect in for break and enter, but then the thief had jumped through a window on them and done a runner. He said, 'That's why they called me from out the back. We went looking for him, me and one of the young guys driving the car, and all of a sudden we saw him in the back streets. I got out and chased him.'

I said, 'How old was he?'

'Early 20s.'

I said, 'How did you catch him?'

He said, 'I wouldn't give in, Wayne.'

I said, 'But he would have been faster and you're not in shape.'

He said, 'Wayne, I wouldn't give in. I just kept running and running until I caught him.'

That's all he said, but it summed him up perfectly. That's what made him what he was. He just didn't know how to quit. That's the way he played his footy, and the way he lived his life.

He was a selector when I played for Brisbane Brothers and he just couldn't be intimidated. One night, coming home, I was following him because we lived in the same area. All of a sudden, he pulled up. He was driving the old red car he used to have — we reckoned it knew the way home by itself. I pulled up behind him and he walked straight towards me. But he didn't realise who I was, so I wound down my window. He said: 'Oh, it's you, Wayne.'

I said, 'Yeah. Who did you think it was?'

'I thought you were the coppers following me.'

'In that case, why did you pull up?'

'I was going to confront you,' he said. 'I wasn't going to let you pull me over — I was going to come back and confront you head on.' He was that type of person. Strong and forthright and honest.

EDDIE BROSNAN HAD A HUGE impact, as did Basil Phelan, the old farmer. They were the two biggest keys in my life. They gave me the foundations. I was seven or eight when we moved out to a railway siding called Berat (which is near Allora), where Basil had a farm, and I spent three or four years there, including lots of time at his home. His family made me very welcome. His wife's name was Betty. She was the tough one. She scared the hell out of me. She was a bit like Eddie.

So there was Eddie, with his physical aggression, his strong ways and manliness. Basil, on the other hand, handed me a different way of looking at life. There was a softness about him, as well as a firmness and great strength.

There was a great contrast between these men and because I experienced life with both of them I was able to pick, to choose … to disregard the things I didn't like about Uncle Eddie. To work out the things I wanted to be, and the things I didn't want to be.

CHAPTER FOUR

THE LITTLE THINGS

One of the great appeals of kicking off the Broncos was the fact that we weren't inheriting somebody else's problems. And we felt strongly about getting it right from the very beginning.

Chairman Paul Morgan had a couple of basic rules, or creeds. He said, 'Wayne, if you can't make them good footballers do the best you can to make them good people. I want them to be successful.' He wanted our players to be well dressed, well groomed and to represent the game in the correct manner.

'And if they don't make it as footballers, well, we'll still love them as much as we ever did and care about them ... we'll just accept the fact that they didn't make it as footballers but they are good people.'

The second thing he wanted was for Queenslanders to come to the football. 'I don't care whether you win or lose,' Porky said. I remember this clearly to this day. 'I want them to be able to bring their kids along to a place where there are no drunks and no one yelling abuse,' he said. 'Just play the game in the right manner, with a great spirit.' Porky wanted little kids going home and saying to their parents as they drove in the gate, 'Didn't we have a great time! Weren't those Broncos tremendous! They just never stop trying.'

THE FOUR ORIGINAL OWNERS of the Broncos genuinely loved rugby league, but at the same time they wanted to challenge the game because they believed it could be better, and that it didn't get the recognition it deserved. They wanted it to have a greater profile, and realised that the Broncos were their chance.

Gary Balkin played on the wing for Brisbane Souths as a young bloke. He was a school teacher who became a publican because he came from a family of publicans. He was also a very gracious person. I had got to know him through Brisbane Souths. He was their saviour. He was the guy who paid me when Souths had no money for a coach back in 1977. Every year he gave an award to the Brisbane competition's highest individual point scorer, so he was pretty much committed to the game.

Barry Maranta was a very successful businessman. He was in finance and land development, and had a high profile around town. He'd been a cricketer and a rugby league player and his son played cricket for Queensland.

Steve Williams was married to Barry's daughter Terri and worked in the advertising business. He played for Wests in Brisbane and for Redcliffe, and he also played for Queensland after coming from North Sydney. He was a five-eighth. He is the guy who got Porky involved. He knocked on Paul's door and simply said, 'You've got to be part of this franchise.' He said Porky just smiled and nodded.

What an extraordinary person Paul Morgan was. He represented Queensland in six sports. His 880-yard running record still stands at Brisbane State High. The only reason he gave away athletics was because he was nearly beaten once, and he figured if he couldn't kick clear in a district carnival he really shouldn't be running. The guy he narrowly beat went to Mexico the following year and won the Olympic gold medal. His name was Ralph Doubell.

Paul helped fund a movie after running into John Cornell and Paul Hogan and listening to them talk about the project they were working on — it was *Crocodile Dundee*. He was a stockbroker of note and a riverboat gambler by nature.

Porky rented us a little office on the 28th floor of his Riverside Centre in the heart of Brisbane and there, among the stockbrokers, merchant bankers and lawyers, we began building the business that became the Broncos. There was me, John Ribot (the general manager), Robyn Maranta (who ran the office and was an excellent asset) and Brian Canavan (a highly credentialled conditioner who'd worked at Valleys).

The first thing we had to find was a home base. Somewhere to sweat. There was dilemma and drama here because everything pointed to Valleys' home ground, which was called Neumann Oval; it has since been taken over by Queensland cricket. They had plans drawn for a leagues club and everything. But then Darcy Mitchell began working on Barry and Paul. Darcy was President of Wests Juniors, which had a little old club in Fulcher Road, Red Hill. All of a sudden the directors did a back flip — which I would learn they were prone to do — and we were going to Red Hill.

At the time the facility consisted of a canteen, a little clubhouse on one side (which the Juniors used), a bar and a change room at the other end with a couple of showers and very little hot water. There was a weights room which the adjoining TAFE college had built with besser blocks and, of course, the oval, which was pretty run down.

No lockers or anything. But, I have to say, nobody worried about that. I don't remember the guys ever complaining. Most of us came from Brisbane clubs and didn't know much better. If there weren't enough showers and there was no hot water they'd put the hose on themselves, that type of stuff. Everyone was happy. We just got into it.

They had won the licence in May 1987 and had started recruiting immediately, so I wasn't involved in the signing of Chris Johns and Billy Noke from St George or Terry Matterson from the Roosters. Brothers had won the Brisbane premiership in 1987 and they had some fine players: Mark Coyne, Clinton Mohr, Trevor Bailey and Peter Gill, but Ross Strudwick had applied for the Broncos' coaching job and when he didn't get it I think he influenced the gun players from Brothers to instead go to his old club, St George.

The key for us was getting Wally Lewis across the line — Wally, Gene Miles and Gary Dowling — because Gold Coast had been granted a licence at the same time and, of course, they wanted the same blokes. Existing clubs south of the border were also keen to get them.

Porky got so frustrated with Gene Miles. Geno was renowned as a procrastinator and Porky threatened to throw him out of his 30th floor office at the Riverside Centre. He was quite serious too. 'The difference between us and Sydney,' Porky told him through gritted teeth, 'is when you're burnt out in Sydney you'll end up hanging off the back of a garbage truck.' Gene just didn't want to make a decision. He kept putting it off and putting it off. Porky showed him the window and he signed, finally.

Wally's signing was a great moment for us. Because, well, he was The King ... The Emperor. He was probably at the latter end of his playing career but this was Queensland and he was still Wally Lewis — the number one guy. I'd coached him at Origin and we had no problems.

MY YEAR AT CANBERRA had been a blessing because it taught me — it underlined to me — the sheer importance of the discipline and attention to detail required to compete successfully in the Big League.

If it was simply about ability, the new Broncos could have matched any team. But it was never going to be that easy. It was about discipline and attention to detail, and if we didn't do the fundamentals well we were going to pay a huge price, because talent alone wasn't going to win for us.

The players had to change their attitude to training. They had to train harder and they had to train smarter. In the Brisbane comp you might have three or four hard games and then three or four weeks of not so tough competition. We had an ageing team. Wally, Geno and Greg Dowling, for example, weren't 21-year-olds. My focus was on getting them to recognise that, but I knew they wouldn't appreciate it until they were playing week after week in the 'Sydney premiership'.

Some things you can't teach people; they have to learn by experience.

The four directors, hardly fashion experts, got the consultants in to design a club jersey. They came up with a predominantly blue one that seemed hellishly wonderful until the advertising guru John Singleton set eyes on it at a club function. Singo looked at them and said, 'You guys are crazy. You are Queensland. You are maroon with a bit of gold or yellow. Why wouldn't you go down that path?'

So they cancelled all the orders. It created havoc. Singo was great mates with Porky and he was right — we needed that Queensland flavour.

Tony Spencer, Kenny Ragh and Graham Pryor came in as assistants, strapping the players and that type of thing. We had Dr Peter Myers as our orthopaedic specialist and Dr Peter Friis as our GP from the beginning and Holly Frail was the dietitian. Having a dietitian was a huge change for the guys. All six stayed 21 years.

In keeping with Porky's insistence on always looking the part, John Ribot took delivery of a new BMW. That was fine, but I couldn't do that. I got a Falcon because that's what I felt most comfortable in. Porky, by the way, drove a big black Merc and everywhere he drove it looked like the President had come to town.

Ribes took me out to Murgon in his BMW to sign Steve Renouf. Twenty-something years ago there weren't a lot of BMWs around the Queensland backwaters — you should have seen the good folk of Murgon when we drove in.

I learned very quickly working for a board was a whole different ballgame from working for a committee. Paul would say to me, 'Wayne, if we don't get this right, it's my house. It's Barry's house, Steve's business and there is no one behind us giving us money. We have no leagues club. We either make this work or we'll go belly up.' They were never ruthless, but they were certainly conscious and focused. And they were always confident about the game. What they were never confident about was the other clubs around them, who were run by committees and never thought about the bigger picture.

Knowing the huge downside for them if it didn't work made me a different coach: more than ever before, I realised it was my responsibility to not just win, but to do it right. It was the right time for me. I'd done nine years coaching senior football and graduated under Don Furner. I had always wanted to hone my skills under a great coach. For eight years in Brisbane I'd been on my Pat Malone. Having that year with Don allowed me to work out which things worked and which didn't.

Making sure the players were having fun was not a priority for me at first. Their mental toughness had to be developed through training, and it had to be developed as soon as possible. I wasn't confident we could hold that together for a long period.

WHEN WE WON OUR FIRST six games straight everybody thought we were premiers. We played Manly in the first game — they had beaten Canberra in the grand final the year before. Broncos 44,

Manly 10. Then we beat Penrith, Wests, Norths, Parramatta and Newcastle. But winning early games is not always a good gauge. Everyone was running around thinking it was only a matter of us turning up on grand final day. Everybody except me. I was the only one talking gloom and doom. I wasn't talking it because I was a scaremonger, but I knew we were living in a false economy and getting through on talent alone. It was the little things we weren't paying attention to, and the little things count for so much in an elite competition.

It's like a swimmer at the Olympic Games. He or she can swim as fast as anybody down the pool, but if you don't get your turns right it can mean a fraction of a second every lap, and over a certain number of laps all of a sudden you are second or third. That's the little things. Football is no different. We were good at the big things, but our turns would haunt us.

On 16 April, 18,434 fans came to Lang Park to see the unbeaten Brisbane Broncos take on Warren Ryan's Balmain Tigers. Ryan always coached tough footy teams and they absolutely muscled up on us. Steve Roach and Benny Elias gave us nothing all day. They were a quality team and we were far behind them in the first half: they led off with two tries in the first two minutes. I know what the scoreboard said — 14–0 first half and 26–18 full-time — but I also know what they did to us psychologically. The players began to understand that we had a long, long way to go.

I had a bust-up with Warren Ryan after that game. He questioned Allan Langer's tackling technique and said the Broncos were weak in the forwards. He boasted how Elias had drawn the short straw by being seated next to him on the plane to Brisbane, and how he'd told Elias how to beat the Broncos by targeting certain areas of our forward play.

Part of it was true. When we were under the pump we weren't used to grinding it out. We looked for the soft option. We looked for the big play. We looked for the big pass. I knew where we were vulnerable and Balmain exposed it.

But Ryan was wrong about Alf. Allan Langer epitomised all that is good in rugby league. Such skills and a brilliantly refreshing attitude. To find fault with a tackling technique that had already been cleared by the league was small-minded and petty. The NSWRL's Dennis Braybrook had no problem with Alf's style, having said three weeks earlier: 'If a player grabs hold of an opponent he can then use his leg to effect a tackle. If he uses his leg first it is illegal.'

The following week we lost to Cronulla, 38–8 at Endeavour, and suddenly we were third on the ladder. Things weren't looking great on the representative scene either — Wally Lewis was out injured for the first time in State of Origin history.

NO ONE GAVE US A chance in Origin I. The King was missing and the critics thought our selection of Martin Bella in the front row was doomed to failure. They reckoned Smokin' Joe Kilroy had come down to make up the numbers, and we'd picked Peter Jackson at five-eighth.

I never thought he'd be a great five-eighth, Jacko. He was a hell of a centre but I wasn't sure he had the temperament to be a five-eighth. But I also knew he loved the occasion, and he was replacing The King as a one-off, so maybe he would get it right. And he did.

The Blues had a hot side on paper: Docking, Ettingshausen, O'Connor, McGaw, Johnston, Lyons, Sterling, Pearce, Folkes, Cleal, Roach, Simmons and Les Davidson. Terry Lamb and David Trewhella were on the bench.

Right through the Queensland team there was a selflessness, a desire to succeed for each other. Jacko was a prime example. He might have sacrificed his chance of being selected in the centres for

Australia in the upcoming Tests against Great Britain when we used him at five-eighth, but he didn't care. More importantly, he didn't care where he played as long as it was best for the team. When I was asked when I had earmarked Jacko as Wally's successor at five-eighth I said, 'Five minutes after Wally got hurt in last weekend's match against the Gold Coast.'

Jacko and Alf were the stars. Queensland 26, NSW 18.

I'll never forget Ken Arthurson walking in before Origin II two weeks later. It was pretty tough, Game 1, and there had been a few blues, and there had been a few fights in the 1987 series. Nothing major, but Kenny, in his role as Chairman of the Australian Rugby League, came and addressed us in camp two days before the second game of 1988 and told us the ARL would not tolerate any foul play. Gave us quite a lecture about it.

When he left I said to them all, 'I don't necessarily believe what he has told us. New South Wales are 1–nil down. They will do everything they possibly can to upset us and to beat us. I'll tell you what we'll do: we will keep our hands in our pockets, but if they start anything I expect you to back each other up and if it means there is a bust up, well, there's a bust up. But we won't be starting anything.'

Tosser Turner had been involved in every Origin game since the concept began, and he said Origin II, 1988, was the toughest ever. Wally had recovered, Lang Park was packed, and no more than six minutes in, Bob Lindner had the ball and he was tackled by Blocker Roach. Bob got up and played the ball. After the ball was long gone, Blocker just went bang ... smacked Bob straight in the eye. This was after the Ken Arthurson talk, right? Bob Lindner had no recollection of the incident and still can't recall the match. For the next five days I waged a public and private battle to get Blocker cited. Wherever I went, from the QRL to the ARL and back to the QRL, nobody would listen to me. And nothing ever happened. I was never more disappointed in my life. We'd got this lecture from the Chairman of the ARL about playing in the right spirit and I'd told my guys there were to play in the right spirit. We had every intention of doing that.

Halfway through the second half the game erupted into an all-in brawl after a tackle by Blues prop Phil Daley on Queensland hooker Greg Conescu. I'd been banging on about Daley before the game, because he'd been head-highing guys everywhere and they'd taken no action against him. It was obvious why he was in the side. Greg Conescu's team-mates took exception to what Daley allegedly did and raced to his assistance. (I'm sounding like a policeman, aren't I?) Those team-mates included captain Wally Lewis, who knocked Daley to the ground. A vicious fight erupted that included several nasty one-on-one duels.

Referee Mick Stone sent Daley and Conescu to the sin bin for 10 minutes, and then he waved Lewis off for five for being the third man into the fight, sparking the brawl. The Lang Park crowd went bananas, pelting hundreds of beer cans onto the field — some hit newspaper photographers on the sideline. The police went to work as the crowd chanted 'send Stone off' for a few minutes before the play finally recaptured their attention.

I remember the cans, and I remember Wally standing up for everybody. That turned the game for us. Wally got the crowd behind us. He put the passion back into everyone. Wally was great at that. He could judge … he could sense the moment when we needed help, and this time it was the crowd we needed help from. Daley's head-high was a chance for The King to get everybody emotional. Leading into the game the NSW team manager, Peter Moore, had had a shot at me about accusing Daley of foul play in club matches. 'It's a cheap shot from Bennett,' he said, 'and lacks logic.' But I knew they'd picked a team that was coming to Brisbane to try to dismantle us with bullying tactics.

From that game on, I never took a great deal of notice any time an official ever talked to me about playing within the rules of the game. The headline the next day read: ARKO SAYS — BAN THE BOOZE FROM LANG PARK.

Queensland 16, NSW 6.

They tried to con us, and we got 'em. I was so proud of the Queenslanders, how they wouldn't be intimidated and wouldn't back off. I have this picture of Martin Bella with his eye badly cut and bleeding. He'd staged a private war with Daley all night, proving me wrong in the process. In all my time coaching Queensland, Marty is the only guy I asked selectors to drop from a winning side. That was in 1987. He was just different to deal with, and I was a young coach, and I didn't handle him as well as I should have.

For 1988, Test second-rower Bryan Niebling was out injured and Greg Dowling had retired from rep football, so I needed a couple of props. I had coached Sam Backo at the Raiders and he was beginning to emerge as a player of some ability and talent. I had a lot of confidence in him and knew I could help him. I had thought a lot about how I could get the best out of Martin, and asked for him to be reinstated. We had been without our top props for a few years — Dowling was out injured for the second and third games in 1986 and we missed him terribly, and though he came back in 1987 he wasn't quite the dominant player he'd been earlier in the 1980s. We were trying our hearts out but being outmuscled. Alf and Wally couldn't do what they do without big front rowers doing what they are supposed to do. New South Wales had a whole stack of big tough guys: Roach and Davidson and Tunks and Kelly for starters.

In 1988 Sam won two of the three man-of-the-match awards and Martin was very close in one. They were the catalyst. I remember saying to Martin, 'You're too smart to be a front rower.' He had a degree from Sydney University in physiotherapy, but I told him he had to take his brains out because he wasn't going to need them out there on Tuesday night. That was at our first team meeting. And then I turned to Sam and said, 'You are either going to be a footnote or a headline on Wednesday morning.' If he was a footnote, he'd never play for Queensland again. The pair of them were magnificent in that series.

WHEN I WENT BACK TO the Broncos I put a media ban on myself. I thought, I'm a coach not a politician, and I have a job to do as coach of the Brisbane Broncos. I felt there had been far too much Wayne Bennett in the media and was beginning to feel pressure I didn't need.

We then lost to Canberra, before beating Illawarra in Wollongong and St George at Lang Park. Then it was South Sydney at the Sydney Football Stadium. On the Tuesday before there was Origin III. Queensland won 38–22. It was the first time since 1924 that the Maroons had completed a series clean sweep.

Souths were down the bottom of the comp and we were hopeless. We played terribly. I'd never seen Porky crankier than he was that night; the rest of the Board weren't smiling either. But I knew what the problem was — our minds were still on Origin, and our bodies were back there too, all over the place.

When we got back to Brisbane the directors called a crisis meeting. By this time, I was over crisis meetings — we seemed to have one every time we lost. I thought I had to take a stand. From the beginning I knew they were an emotional lot, particularly about their footy. I knew Paul from our young days as players and I knew there was no way he could keep emotion out of anything. He was emotional about everything. That's what made him. So when I took the job, part of the commitment was that I had the last say on who would come to the Broncos and who would be leaving the Broncos. And they had no say in team selections. They all signed off on that. I was pretty confident within myself that I would be the rational one. It was the best thing I ever asked for, because over the years, believe me, they did try to buy in to those decisions — but never nastily. Often they couldn't understand why I was letting one player go or seeking another, but in the end it worked out fine.

After the Souths game the directors were on about this and that and finding fault with everything. I reminded the four of them they'd all been footballers and — in the politest way — that they'd all failed at different stages. They hadn't always played perfect games themselves, and they were too quick to find fault and too quick to criticise.

When I finished I said, 'I don't want to come to any more crisis meetings. I won't be coming to another one. If you're not happy, you have to tell me and I'll move on.' We never had another crisis meeting in all my time there with them. I had a few with the players over the years, but never with the directors. It worked great. Obviously, I kept them up to date but they stopped over-reacting every time we lost a game.

The following week we lost 25–10 to the Bulldogs, who went on to win the premiership. They were a good football team. With 20 minutes to go we had them, but stupid errors — the little things — beat us again. We got sloppy and handed them the opportunity to win. Two weeks before, we'd been third in the competition. Now we were seventh out of 16.

July was a good month for the Broncos. We won four straight, against Manly, Penrith, Wests and Norths; the Penrith game was a ripper. The score was only 8–6, but it wasn't about the score. Australia had played a Test the night before, so we had Lewis, Miles and Conescu on the sideline and Greg Dowling was nothing more than a passenger. The Panthers were back-slapping one another and carrying on like Russian weightlifters in a vodka bar. Big Mark Geyer was on fire as usual, setting out to intimidate our pack. That's when little-known prop Andrew Tessmann stood up. He stood up to MG and he stood up to the rest of them. He was the difference.

WE FINISHED ONE WIN short of making the play-offs, beaten 20–10 by Balmain in the final round. Balmain ended up playing Canterbury in the grand final. After the Tigers game a newsman gave me an opportunity to bag referee Graham Annesley over two controversial calls which had cost us 12 points, but I hadn't commented on referees all year. If I thought those decisions might have affected the result maybe I would have said something, but I didn't think that.

What we do, it's forever a process. If you understand that it helps you get through. I realised before the season began what we had to do. So you spend the season trying to get that right. Some days you do and some days you don't. But that's the thing you do. You are looking at that process, realising that it's going to take time. You are also continually looking at the players to see if they are the guys you want there and if they are not, you are making decisions about who you are going to get to take their place. How's it going to work? Where are those new players going to come from?

Sure, I was disappointed after that Balmain match. Put simply, we weren't doing enough things right on enough occasions. Straight after the match someone asked when I would begin planning for 1989. 'About five minutes ago,' I said. And that was probably the truth. Up until then I wasn't thinking about the next season because we might have been playing next weekend.

The fans were great. There was always this feeling that we were supposed to win the comp. With the Broncos the expectations have always been high. I taught myself early that when I make a decision I move on and do the best I can. If I make a decision about a player, or anything else, I have belief and confidence in that. I try to make it work. So I knew what I'd got myself into. I knew it was going to take time. I wasn't expecting miracles.

We wanted to build the club properly. If we'd been looking for quick fixes maybe we could have made the play-offs, but there were no quick fixes for me. I made hard-nosed decisions — with the backing of the Board on most occasions — about what was in our long-term interest and how we were going to get there. Of course, there was pain in what we did but I accepted the pain because I realised the rewards were going to be much, much greater when they came.

You don't like not making the play-offs. You don't like losing football games. I personally don't like making hard decisions on people. You don't like the criticism, but it all goes with the territory. You're not always walking around with a smile on your face — not that I do that anyway. What I can't accept is if I'm not doing the job right, if I'm not putting in. If I was letting them down by not being as committed as I should have been, and having rules for me and different rules for them, it would have been different ... but if the right things are in place, the rest you just accept. You keep the things that worked, that were good, and you don't keep the things that didn't work and you move on.

Our win–loss record was 14–8 from 22 games and we were not good enough to make the play-offs. The previous year Canberra finished third in the competition proper with 15 wins and nine losses from 24 games. We lost one more game than the top five did. We had to improve.

CHAPTER FIVE

IT WASN'T A DREAM

In my youth I had this ability — this gift — to live on both sides of the street. On one side of the street I saw money wasted, sadness and domestic disputes ... unsavoury arguments and straight-out fights, all because of money and alcohol.

But when I went to other people's homes I kind of adapted to whatever was there. I saw homes where there was no wasting of money or abuse. I saw people who felt good about having a new car. I saw people having success and not being embarrassed about it.

All my life has been lived around football and its people. From the time I was four, maybe five years of age, I was on the team bus with the senior players travelling to matches in surrounding districts. To places like Stanthorpe and Millmerran, Texas and Tenterfield, Pittsworth and Warwick. I soon became an observer of behaviour. There was a definite mixture of men on these team buses. There was the successful group and there was another group who chose another way of life, men who wasted their money, who drank heavily and missed out on so many opportunities.

When sober, these men were all good guys, and I suppose this is where my crusade began. I was proud to be a rugby league person, proud that I'd been brought up in this environment — it gave me the strength to become the person I am and to believe in the things I do. Because I always knew that the wonderful people on the team bus outweighed the others. I knew that from an early age.

Years later I would blow up and make unwanted headlines when Ray Price, the great lock forward, wrote an article criticising Bob Lindner for arriving for training at Parramatta in a new BMW. Price wrote that flash cars didn't suit the image of the Parramatta Eels. I couldn't get over it and still can't. Unfortunately, that's how some of us see ourselves; more unfortunately, the article came in an era when a majority of people saw us like that. As the battlers, living on the wrong side of the street, in poverty.

That's how the broader community once viewed rugby league. That was the game's image. Not among those of us who played it and were part of it, whose families were involved in it and loved it, but in the broader community: we weren't exactly the top end of town and we definitely weren't supposed to be driving BMWs.

I was a rugby league person and I was proud of it, immensely proud of it. I have always wanted to project a positive image of the game and the people in it: those people have great character and sense of community, and are worthy of success and of being applauded.

It was in the early '90s when I first noticed that our footballers were no longer embarrassed to say, 'Hey, I've just bought a new house. And a new car.' I wanted to work with people who wanted to be successful. When I heard a bloke say he had bought a house I wanted everyone in the club to hear it so they would work their butts off to get one too.

They started turning up to training in new cars. Then the next bloke would want one, and realise that if he worked hard he could have one. It wasn't a dream. I wanted them striving not only for the best but to be the best they could be. The critics in the game, the ones pulling them back, had just about gone, particularly at this level of the game — they were getting left behind.

Through State of Origin their public profiles were quickly growing bigger. There were endorsements and sponsorships and public functions where they had to speak. And behave. And impress. Suddenly they were shaking hands with investment portfolios and politicians, and their accountants didn't have to look at their files to know their names.

This is where fine people like Shane Webcke and Mick Cronin come in — these are people I admire greatly. So many footballers from the 'modern era' have developed into outstanding people. Not just outstanding football players but truly outstanding people. Today, you watch them on the sports shows, a whole host of them, and you can see that they conduct themselves with decorum and confidence. There is another large group doing extremely well in business.

Every time I see them I feel immensely proud because I know they are rugby league people and that the public perception of them and what they do has changed very much for the better.

There have always been rugby league men who have also been successful outside football, but there's more of them now and the key difference is that more players today expect to be successful and they have the confidence and belief to achieve things away from the game. When I look at an ex-player I'm always interested in what he's been doing since he retired, and I feel a real sense of pride if he's been successful. Football for most was a gift that they built on with hard work. To be a success after football is all hard work.

CHAPTER SIX

SAME OLD, SAME OLD

The twins Kevin and Kerrod Walters and Allan Langer, who was a year older, were the most exciting kids I'd seen play football. I think it was an Under-16s game, around 1983 or 1984, and they were playing for Ipswich. Love is a strong word, but I loved the way they played. They ran, they threw the ball — they did anything they wanted to do.

They threw it over the back of their head, around their body, most times without even looking. They didn't tackle too well but that didn't worry them because they didn't have to. They just got the ball and mesmerised the opposition. They'd run 40 or 50 metres, score, and then they'd do it all over again. They were pretty special kids. I'd spoken to Kevin about coming to Brisbane Souths and I was also talking to Alf ... actually, I didn't think Alf was going to make it. I told him he might make the Under 21s, or something.

Anyway, the Canberra job had come up in 1987 and I only took Kevin, because watching those kids play I thought the best thing for them and their future was to break them up. That way they would have to rely more on other players, and they would become better team players for it.

Greg Conescu, the Broncos' first hooker, was also the state and Test hooker, and he bought us the time to develop Kerrod, who came across from the Ipswich Jets in 1988. Kerrod just wasn't ready for the grind of Sydney football. He needed a bit more time, and he got that playing mostly reserve grade in our first season. In 1989, he started in the top grade and by July was in the Australian team. That was one of the important things in the Broncos' first couple of years: those older players gave us the time to develop the others.

Kerrod always thought he was a black man in a white man's body. That was his favourite saying. He was highly skilled and could read a game really well. He was a pretty good decision-maker too, but most of all he loved to play the game with flair. His older brother Steve was also a hooker — arguably the finest in the game, definitely the toughest — but they were very different. Kerrod dressed the way he played and liked flashy cars. Steve was just your hardworking truck. Get this — he even nicknamed himself 'The Tractor'.

Kerrod, Alf and Kevin — together at their best — were absolutely dynamic. They created havoc, the three of them, and they were to do that for the Broncos for a number of seasons.

But Kerrod worried more than I did about results, particularly about poor results. He used to get very upset and hated the feeling that he had let the team down, because he was first and foremost about the team. Publicly he came across well, as a wonderful trainer with a positive attitude about everything, but there was another side — not many people realised he'd ring me, upset about a loss. He was a worrier, Kerrod. Kevin and Alf would react differently to a loss, preferring to go for a drink and take the mickey out of their team-mates. If you had dropped a ball they would mimic your butterfingers all night and make fun of it. That's how they released their post-match tensions and disappointments.

The one thing those three boys had in common was that they were winners right through … and they were competitive buggers. Kevin and Alf would publicly laugh in the face of defeat, but Kerrod was more conservative and serious and needed to talk it through with someone equally serious, usually me.

THE 1989 SEASON ALSO SAW Sam Backo and Peter Jackson arrive at the Broncos.

In terms of mobility, Sam was probably the best big guy I've been involved with. He was a hell of an athlete, Sam. He could run long distances, even though he was carrying 110kg — he could still be up with the fastest guys on a 10km run. He was explosive, had a wonderful side-step. He was just a bloody monster of a guy. Very talented.

Don Furner had picked him out of North Queensland and brought him down to the Raiders. He had done three or four years there amid a huge number of adjustments. Things like training didn't come easy to Sam; nor did the discipline required to be a football player. He was a work in progress, I suppose, but I saw this huge upside to the guy — and everybody loved his company.

He was a big out-there type of bloke, a redneck monster, always fun. There was always something happening with Sam, and he was a good ball player too.

I've kept stats on players all my coaching career, and Sam Backo missed about one tackle a month — that's how good he was on his feet, at timing the tackle. He played the game with a minimum of mistakes. At times he got himself into a bit of trouble and he could get a bit lazy, but in terms of athleticism he was right up there with anybody I ever coached.

He had a bit of a falling out with Tim Sheens, the new Canberra coach, so I think he was happy to be coming to the Broncos. He couldn't always get himself to training on time, Sam. One time, he turned up three-quarters of an hour late. His wife had gone away for the weekend and with no one to wake him up, Sam just kept on sleeping. After that, I rang him all the time if his wife wasn't there, just to get him going.

Peter Jackson had befriended him in Origin camps. They always roomed together.

Jacko liked telling the story of how they'd had a pretty heavy night early in an Origin camp and some guy rang up from a radio station the next morning. Jacko slept through the ringing but was soon awoken by Sam yelling to the reporter to speak up, he could barely hear him. Jacko looked across and Sam, fairly well hungover, had the phone the wrong way around, with the mouthpiece at his ear.

Big Sam was fun to be around.

We had a dunce-of-the-week award which we brought from Canberra to Brisbane and Sam collected them the way other people collect baseball caps or stamps. It was a fun thing, awarded to someone for having done something silly away from football and training.

Jacko would ask me how I was going for the dunce award, and if I said I was struggling he'd say: 'Hang on, I'll just go and have a yarn to Sam for you.'

I COULD NEVER WORK OUT why Jacko decided to join the police force. That's where I'd met him, at the Academy. He just wasn't cut out to be a policeman, but he did the course and got himself sworn in. He didn't stay long after that, though. I asked him what had made him resign from the force. He said, recalling a couple of his nights off, 'When the coppers started chasing me, I thought it was time to get out.'

Jacko was a total extrovert who loved to party. He fell in love with quite a remarkable lady, Siobhan, who would become his wife. I said to him one day, 'Jacko, you are pretty keen on Siobhan, aren't you?'

He said, 'Yeah, I am.'

I said, 'Why's that?

He said, 'Because she can party longer and harder than I can.' He was very impressed.

We got him back to Brisbane because I felt we had an issue: we hadn't lifted our level of training sufficiently and the older players in the group were holding the young guys back. I felt that when the young guys tried to step up and lead a bit, the old guys would get together as a group and intimidate them and hold them back. I'd seen this happen in a couple of places during my playing career and it had a detrimental influence on the culture of a place. I needed someone to break the clique developing at the Broncos and that someone was Jacko.

I wanted him to set a standard for training. He was a great trainer. It wouldn't matter how much he'd hammered himself, how late he got home, how hungover he was, he would train his heart out the next day. He'd be vomiting on the run but he'd still be doing it. He would be leading the way and nobody could stand over him. The older guys would either be embarrassed and pick up their act or fade out of the game altogether. More importantly, the young guys would realise what the benchmark was and go with him. It happened exactly that way. The young guys wouldn't be held back any longer because when the threat of intimidation came, Jacko would tell the old blokes to get nicked and keep running.

One of the older guys who greatly benefited was Gene Miles, whose attitude to training changed enormously. No one trained harder than Geno towards the end of his career.

So Action Jackson had arrived and conquered. That's what he called himself, Action. He wasn't a complex guy, just full of life and roguery. He always had the BIG PLAY in him, but a lot of times the big play is the wrong thing to do, the last thing we need as a team. I'd see it happen in games and one day I remember asking him, 'What was going on in your head? Peter, just explain to me why you had to put that play on when you knew it was never going to work and could cost us the game?'

He said, 'Coach, when the guy I'm playing against does something big, I think to myself, I can do better than that ... I can do a *bigger* play than he's just done ... I'm looking for attention, coach.'

I said, 'Well, you keep doing it and you are going to get plenty from me.'

He loved that sense of occasion. It didn't matter where it was — on field, off field — he lived for the occasion.

Alf was never the greatest trainer, but he was a good trainer and he grew when Jacko came in, picking up his level of commitment. Queensland's different. It can be easy to be laid back here, and we all hailed from the type of footballing background where we enjoyed our footy but training was not always a priority. We had to change.

In June 1989 the Broncos won their first ever trophy — the Panasonic Cup mid-week knockout competition. On the way, we beat Canberra (18–13), Parramatta (42–6), Souths (24–4) and finally Illawarra (22–20, after leading 16–0). In terms of guts and commitment and all the things that count in football, it was a very good effort. There was a little bit of hunger and desperation. The change had begun.

IN THAT PANASONIC SERIES Terry Matterson was man of the match in the first round, in the quarter-final and again in the final. He'd been a junior at Eastern Suburbs in Sydney and I'd first noticed him when Peter Corcoran, a respected senior coaching figure at the ARL, asked me to do some work with the Australian Under-18 team at the Institute of Sport in Canberra. I couldn't get over his talents. In my last competition proper game with Canberra we played Easts at Henson Park and he starred for the Roosters. I called Paul Morgan about him but it was a waste of 40 cents — Porky had already signed him for the Broncos.

Matto played No. 13 for us for a lot of years, until he left for the London Broncos at the end of the 1995 season. You don't see a lot of locks like him any more. He was clever with the football and always setting up plays for Alf and Kevvie Walters.

In 1989, he and Chris Johns became the first ever Broncos to play Origin for New South Wales. John Ribot had signed Johnsy from St George. Chris's dad was buying a pub in Queensland and he wanted to come up too. He was one of the best guys I coached, Chris Johns.

No fanfare or fuss. There was no mug with him. If it was tough and gritty at training and we were having a bad day or it was pouring rain he was always doing his best. He wouldn't whinge; he didn't know how to complain. Always upbeat. He just loved being with his mates, his football mates. And he was always looking for ways to improve the club and improve the team and for things we could do to enjoy ourselves more. In terms of pure talent he was the least blessed of the backline players of that era, but he was a hell of an athlete. He could certainly run. He was a desire guy. A good defensive player whose game grew when he was playing in the centres outside Kevvie at five-eighth. There was no one I was more pleased to see playing for Australia.

I was in the car with him the day Johnsy rang Rupert Murdoch in 1995. I'm getting ahead of myself here because we're talking about the Super League war, which didn't erupt until the mid-1990s, but I'm going to tell you anyway because of the insight it gives into a player who would help build the Broncos.

Rupert was on holidays in the Bahamas or somewhere on his yacht. We were going to the airport. It was the middle of the war and the media was generating a rumour that Rupert was going to walk away from the deal ... and we were signed up. Years later, I was told the amount of money individual players got at that time, when the two sides were bidding against each other, and Chris Johns was one of the poorest paid players even though nobody fought harder. Nobody fought harder for players' rights than him.

So we were on the way to the airport and he was ringing Rupert Murdoch. I couldn't believe it. Chris Johns was ringing ... 'Rupert, it's Chris Johns here, from the Brisbane Broncos. I want you to answer something for me: are you going to walk away from us? Because the rumours are strong here. I want to know, because if you are, we need to know now. We've got to save some face ...'

'I need to hear it from you,' said Johnsy. 'I don't want to hear it from anybody else.'

Rupert said, 'Chris I can assure you I will not walk away from any contract we've agreed to and we are not walking away from Super League.'

'That will do me,' Chris said. There was a bit more chatter, and Johnsy hung up.

Chris Johns stood up for every player, even though he knew he himself wasn't getting paid a lot of money. That was Chris. He didn't care. He believed Super League was right, that it was right for the game. And once he was committed to a cause, as he was to the Broncos, no one would be more committed. He believed footballers deserved a better place, a better position in life. Our critics would have done well to spend more time with people like Chris Johns.

THE OLDER PLAYERS, WE HAVE to talk about them. Greg Dowling had been the premier prop in Queensland rugby league for much of the 1980s and it was important we got him to the Broncos even though he was closer to the end of his career than the others. He'd played a lot of tough games of footy.

Greg was the first guy to put his hand up and withdraw from Origin football because he realised he could no longer do both his club and his state justice, and his priority was the club. He was very committed, but playing in the Big League was a big adjustment for him. It wasn't that he couldn't play at that level; the difficult part was that he had to do it every week, come hell or high water, and there were no easy games.

Some said it would have been nice to keep the likes of Greg Dowling and maybe even Wally Lewis in cotton wool just for Origin and the five play-off matches.

How to play week in week out against the best is a learnt thing. These guys knew how to play footy better than anyone, but they took a while to realise what a tough competition this premiership was. Even back then it was a tough comp and teams were up every week and we were the Broncos so that made it even harder. It wasn't like when Canberra came into the competition, or Illawarra or Newcastle. They weren't expected to win from day one. The Broncos were. It went with the territory.

I liked Greg Dowling's honesty. He committed himself to the club. But he wasn't always on top of his game. I knew that and he knew that, but again he was giving us the time we needed to get the other props through some tough competition and preparation so that we could become the team we wanted to be.

Gene Miles was one of our first real success stories at the Broncos. He was magnificently built and a great athlete. All of them are athletes, but some have qualities that set them apart: his were his giant side-step and wonderful hands. He was one of the first guys to carry the ball with one hand and put it over the top or around the back of opponents. He was such a handful. There were some other great centres — Steve Rogers and Mal Meninga and Brett Kenny — and Geno was definitely up there with those players, but I doubt he ever quite got the recognition he deserved. I'm not saying he didn't get any recognition. What I am saying is he was very, very good.

Geno was a really laidback guy, not keen on responsibility or on having a real lot of pressure in his life. I changed both of those things for him, and when that happened, he grabbed the changes and grew with them. He was a great success story away from football too. If anyone back then had said Gene Miles was going to run a successful business, you'd have killed yourself with laughter. You'd have thought he had no chance, this guy, but he did run a very successful business. It was a great credit to him, just as being the first guy in the older group to change his attitude to training had been. In 1989 he realised he had to change and make a greater commitment and he did.

He lost a lot of weight, set a terrific example. Unfortunately, what he didn't lose was his uncanny and highly frustrating ability to give away the same penalty once or twice every game. He'd go into marker defence, once or twice every game, lean over and illegally grab somebody. In the Brisbane comp he'd got away with it, but in the Sydney comp the refs are on you more and it was difficult for him to get it into his head that he couldn't do it any more. Alf would drive him mad all week, mimicking him leaning over the play the ball and grabbing somebody. Drove Geno mad, he did.

AND THEN THERE WAS The Emperor. Wally Lewis had broken his arm in the 1988 World Cup final and then missed the Broncos' first Panasonic Cup game against Canberra in Parkes on 1 March of the following year. But he returned in a trial at Lang Park 10 days later, six days before the start of the premiership. He played 18 premiership games in 1989 and led the Broncos to the Panasonic Cup and Queensland to an Origin clean sweep.

In Townsville, for a Panasonic Cup game against Parramatta on 17 May, we celebrated a special occasion for Wally and the team. There Wally did his first ever double in a game. I'd been keeping stats on all the players over a long period of time, and it was the first time in a year and a half that Wally had made two tackles in a row. It was a great occasion for everyone and the celebration continues in our minds to this day. For all his reputation and standing, you could still have great fun with Wally.

His stats were always 18 to 20 tackles a game. Most guys fluctuate at least a little, but not Wally. I figured he might have been doing his own stats or influencing someone else who was, but it really didn't matter — it wasn't as if anyone was running through him. No one ran through Wally Lewis.

He and Darren Lockyer are the greatest on-field thinkers I've coached.

He was idolised in Queensland and hated in New South Wales. Being forever the headline act embarrassed him. And being around him with the Broncos was my first real introduction to the army that is the media. He hated being called The King, and the only time I ever saw him flare up with team-mates was when they called him by the title everyone else did. He wouldn't cop 'The King' from his mates.

Wally never asked for anything special and never put himself above anybody in any way, but his life had to be different because he couldn't move without waves of adulation.

Peter Jackson once said — and he was right — that when you walked into a stadium before an Origin game you'd be nervous and apprehensive, full of butterflies and not knowing what to expect — until you set eyes on Wally. As soon as a Queenslander walked into the dressing room and saw Wally, he knew he was going to be OK.

But at the Broncos Wally was pacing himself. He had to. He was playing midweek matches and Origins, Test matches for Australia and club football, and this was in the latter part of his career. I think our relationship was okay and I remember how, after the 1986 Origin series, he came over and said I'd done a good job. In the years since, every time I did something, achieved something, Wally has always brought it up the next time I've seen him.

People said he was aloof, but I reckon Wally was more introverted than anything. The two people he really trusted in football were Gene Miles, his best mate, and Tosser Turner, the legendary Queensland manager. It's not easy sometimes, to know who you can trust and who you can't.

His ability to captain the team was without question, but at the same time I could see this distance growing between him and the young people we had to bring through, and I knew it wasn't the chemistry we needed. But again, we were not going to make a decision without a lot of thought.

I let things ride, continuing to observe how others responded to him.

IT WAS A STRANGE SEASON, 1989, a season of change. At the beginning of the year I told all the players to burn their scrapbooks and stop living in the past. To be fair, if Wally had kept scrapbooks the forest would still be burning today. Kerrod Walters, replacing Greg Conescu, toured New Zealand with the Australian side, along with fellow Broncos Wally Lewis, Peter Jackson, Tony Currie, Michael Hancock and Sam Backo. Allan Langer and Gene Miles both suffered serious injuries in the Origin series. Greg Dowling was suspended for eight weeks on a kneeing charge. Alfie didn't come back until the last 17 minutes of the final round game against North Sydney at Lang Park. After we beat the Bears 30–0, the worst-case scenario for us was a midweek play-off to make the final five, depending on results later that weekend.

About a month earlier I'd watched Canberra play Canterbury over in Perth, and the Raiders had looked like shot ducks. If they lost that game, they missed the play-offs. I remember Ivan Henjak coming on late and swinging the game for the Raiders. It's such a fine line sometimes in football. People just don't realise — you can finish up with a great season or you can finish up with the middle of a donut. We had led the competition at various stages that year, and we had been no worse than third coming out of Origin, yet here we were late in the season battling to find form and a finals berth.

Gary Balkin, one of the four Bronco directors, decided to put on a barbecue for the players on the Sunday so we could be together to hear the results of games involving the other finals contenders. Gary owned a heritage-listed place in South Brisbane, a magnificent place for a barbecue. We took our wives and families along on a lovely spring afternoon.

The game down south began and Canberra won. That meant, to make the finals, we had to play Cronulla–Sutherland midweek. I sensed the mood straight away: it had changed. I was pretty sure we weren't going to win.

From the time I was small I've always thought I had a pretty good sense of people's reactions to things. I didn't think I would be wrong on this occasion, but I so wanted to be wrong.

With an airline crisis and pilots' strike crippling the nation we had to charter a plane to fly to Sydney for the Tuesday-night game against the Sharks. I knew the mood was not great. We were in this small plane and it took two and a half hours to get there. Alf had played only those 17 minutes of football in the last couple of months so he had to start on the bench. It was now up to the individuals to lift just a little bit if we were going to finish the season properly, and if the Broncos were going to rally around anybody, it would be Wally Lewis.

We needed players' actions, not coach's words.

We were beaten comprehensively, 38–14, and most of our stars didn't have a great night. It was a disaster. Back in the change room everyone was extremely disappointed, none more so than the director with the highest of hopes. Porky always led with his chin and had made some big statements before the season, and again halfway through. Now here he was, caged in a losers' room with nowhere to go.

Wally had called an impromptu meeting and wanted the directors in the room. All the players and staff. He apologised to everyone for our performance, for letting everyone down. I was watching the body language of everyone, as I had been doing for a long time, and felt no one was listening. I felt, Here we go — same old, same old — but the damage had been done.

I made the decision that night.

Our reserve grade had made the finals and were staying on in Sydney. Because we hadn't known when we would be going home — it had depended on the Cronulla result — there was no plane booking. So for the rest of us, it was onto a bus back to Brisbane … perhaps the worst 24 hours you could spend in sport.

I sat up the back with Sam Backo. Sam got drunk and went to sleep like a big bear. Every three hours, the bus driver would stop for another feed we didn't need. We were sitting in a roadside restaurant on the north coast of New South Wales when the bus began to move. And the bus driver was sitting with us. Sure enough, it was Jacko behind the wheel breaking the law and laughing, the way he always did. It brought the house down.

I HAVEN'T BEEN ON A long bus trip since, but on that slow journey home I had a lot of time to think about a lot of things, and I'm dangerous in that situation.

The decision had been made the night before, but I had told no one. It was now a case of getting the board behind me, plus John Ribot, plus the players' group. Within a week I had started the process.

You have to understand this was huge. And it was also the last thing I wanted from a personal point of view. But this club had made a statement from day one that it was going to be different, that it was going to be the best. Professional. No short cuts. We were working for a board of directors, not a committee. They didn't necessarily want quick results. We had agreed: if we have to make a hard-nosed decision, we will make it.

It took me so far out of my comfort zone it was unbelievable: I had never had to make a decision of this magnitude, and I'd never had to implement anything like it either. I'd been a coach, but never in a situation like this.

I had a great sense of duty to the Broncos' directors. They employed me to do what I believed was right by the club, and therefore right by them. So I was left with nowhere to go. I knew we had to have a change of captain. I couldn't gloss over it. I couldn't lie to myself and I knew I had to deliver. If I didn't have the board's support on it, I obviously wouldn't have gone on with it. I may have left the club, I don't know. I don't know what I would have done. It never got to that point.

Then I went to the players, the ones who mattered, explained the situation and asked them to consider it in the light of day. This was going to be big, and good judgments are best made in the light of day.

It would have been uncharitable to Wally for him to hear whispers before the facts, so I grabbed him within the next 12 hours. It had to go smoothly. When I say smoothly, I mean that from our end, as a club, we had to be as one, because once the news was delivered I would have no control. We would have to live with the consequences.

We met at the club house, just me and Wally. Nobody else. I wish someone else could have done it but nobody else could. Of course, I was nervous. Did I like it? No, I hated it. Was there any moment of satisfaction? No. There was no joy. But I knew what had to be done so I did it, as nicely as I possibly could.

In the meeting Wally was bitterly disappointed, but he held himself with class. I've always appreciated that. The genie was out of the bottle. I had just grown up a huge amount as both a man and a manager.

I walked out and didn't feel great, so I went straight home. I said very little to anybody, and to this day that's how I've remained.

Gene Miles agreed to become the new captain. I saw things in Gene he hadn't seen in himself at that stage, things that gave me great confidence. Importantly, he knew he had to grow into the job and that this could be the challenge he needed, the making of him near the end of his playing career.

As a coach your focus is on being as competitive as possible while planning for the future. At the Broncos we knew where we were going, so if it didn't come today it was still going to come. We were going to get it right so it would come. That is how 1989 ended.

We signed Kevin Walters from Canberra. Wally was in his last years and I knew we had to get another five-eighth. St George offered Kevin $70,000, I think. We offered him $25,000 to come home and he did come. After he made that decision, he was entitled to ask me where I was going to play Wally.

Wally was great about it. I said to him, 'Look, I want to play you lock next year.'

He said, 'If that's what you want me to do, I'll play lock.' This was after the captaincy, remember. It was very classy.

Well into the new year there were plenty of headlines about the captaincy furore and Wally, people stirring the pot. The first thing I'd be asked at public functions was: Why did you sack Wally? I'd say, 'Look, I love you — you're a great audience and I'd love to tell you all — but I've told no one and I'm not going to make an exception for you today.'

Early the next January I remember walking back into our Red Hill offices and finding the whole conversation still centred on Wally and the captaincy. I grabbed Ribes and got the staff together and said: 'Listen, it's over.' We couldn't control what others talked about, but we did have control over ourselves. And honest to God, we never mentioned it again.

Not the staff, anyway. I did go back to my mate Ged Nolan's Warwick dairy farm not long after and we were quietly milking away when his three-year-old daughter Rebecca came in and whispered: 'Why did you sack Wally Lewis as captain?'

I looked at her and said: 'Ged, where's this coming from?'

He laughed. At least someone could see the funny side.

CHAPTER SEVEN

ON THE RIGHT TRACK

In many ways 1990 was the beginning of the Broncos. The hard decision regarding Wally Lewis had been made. The other major change was the introduction of Kelvin Giles.

I had worked a bit with Kelvin at Canberra, mainly sprint work, and although I'd been very impressed by him, he wasn't someone I ever got close to because he seemed aloof.

People have often said that I'm 'military without the medals', and Kelvin was definitely a Brigadier without the medals. He was more military than the military, but also an eccentric in many ways. A man who smoked a pipe and burnt to excel. He had a tremendous presence, an air of authority, and was a guy who clearly knew what he was talking about, the kind of guy you rarely questioned.

Kelvin is a Pom. He began in the British Army and trained the English Olympic athletics team. He was working at the Australian Institute of Sport in Canberra when we first met, and with the Australian Olympic team. I remember bringing him up from Canberra for a one-off address to my coaching staff at the Broncos and he was outstanding. I walked out of the room and straight into

John Ribot's office. I said, 'Ribes we've got to employ this guy, and we've got to employ him now. He is what we need.'

To Ribot's credit, he went hard to get our man. I knew he would have difficulty, because Kelvin was happy working and living in Canberra. Kelvin went to see Tim Sheens, the Canberra coach, and told him he had an offer but was prepared to stay. He was up front, as usual. Tim said, 'Oh no, we are OK.' So we were lucky. I'll tell you something: I wouldn't have let him go.

Kelvin Giles changed the way everyone in rugby league trained. He was the first guy to bring in regular weights training throughout the season. Most clubs did weights in the off-season — Canterbury were right into it — but Kelvin's routines hadn't been seen in the game before. The repetitions and discipline were new; that and doing them in-season.

He had a great thirst for knowledge and was very, very knowledgeable. He could sit and talk to you about any subject, and he could entertain you too. But there was also a toughness about him that was unique. He wouldn't compromise, and that made it difficult for him when he first came, because not all footy players are dream athletes.

They love playing footy but they hate training. That's the difference between them and Olympians. If they could physically play football every day that's what they would do; they would never train. They would play touch and play football, that's all. And they'd say, 'What am I doing this for? I just want to play football.'

So Kelvin had some huge battles in those early years, but he ended up winning them because he just wouldn't compromise. Straight away you could see a difference, but it took the guys 12 months or so to get used to the toughness of the training regime. Gene Miles didn't even know what a weights room was and there was Kelvin talking to us about joining the '300 Club'. We didn't have a clue what he was talking about then, but we soon did. (The 300 Club is benchpressing 300 pounds: that was kind of the benchmark of strength in that era.)

I can still see Chris Johns doing weights. He'd get two 15 kg dumbbells, put them over his head and say, 'There you go — I've done me weights.' Johnsy was a hell of a player, one of my favourites. This is what Kelvin walked into.

We had to take this giant step up in fitness. The players never trained so hard in their lives. And they actually enjoyed it. They always feel so much better about themselves when they know they haven't cheated or taken shortcuts. Kelvin began bringing in boxing trainers — everything and anything he could do to toughen them up. When you know you are doing everything you can to win you are so much more confident.

Kerrod Walters excelled, and Kevin had always been a great trainer. I can still see Willie Carne burning out 400-metre runs. He was a tremendous athlete, Willie. Andrew Gee would come last but no one tried harder than he did. Alf was in cruise control. Mick Hancock — he trained well too, Mick. Mick couldn't train with Alf because Alf would be geeing people up all the time. Alf would be trying to get through that training session any way he could, without thinking of what he was doing. Mick Hancock would get as far away from Alf as he could because Mick had to be serious.

JUST BEFORE THE BEGINNING OF the season we went to the Sir Donald Longford Correctional Centre to visit Joe Kilroy. Working with Smokin' Joe was one of the great joys of my coaching life. He was just entertainment plus. One off-season he asked if I could look after his motorbike for him, find it a safe place to hide. Legend goes that he switched from Brisbane Norths to Brothers because Brothers bought him a Harley. This was back in the 1980s.

So, anyway, I said, 'Mate, what do you want me to do with the Harley?' He said the coppers were chasing him and trying to repossess everything he had and they could have everything except for his beloved motorbike.

'I don't want to lose my Harley,' he said. So we parked it at the back of the training shed for about four months.

When he was at the Broncos we went down to Newcastle for a club game and the night before the game we went to dinner and Joe ran into some people he knew. He asked if he could stay out a bit longer than normal. I said, 'That's OK, Joe.'

Next day rolled around and late in the game Joe hit the deck — for no obvious reason, but he acted as if it was a very, very serious injury. I was a bit indifferent — it didn't look too serious to me — but he convinced the doctors and everyone else and they stretchered him off the field and straight to hospital. We all flew back to Brisbane and left him with the doctor in the hospital.

The next morning I rang him to make sure everything was OK. 'Oh yeah, I feel much better today, coach.' he said. 'They are probably going to let me out.' So we organised him a flight home. Even went to the airport to pick him up. But no Joe.

About Thursday or Friday I got a phone call, and it was Smokin' Joe. I said, 'Where are you, mate, we can't find you. What's going on?'

He said, 'I'm at Tamworth.'

I said, 'What are you doing in Tamworth?'

He said, 'I ran into a few biker mates — those guys I ran into on Saturday night — and we are just riding our way home to Brisbane.'

I said, 'Good on you, Joe. Take your time, because you won't be playing first grade this weekend.'

He rolled home about Saturday or Sunday, with his mates on their bikes. He always had a great time, Joe.

Did I have some rules for some and different rules for others? Yeah, I did. That's right, I did. I always realised that. Some things and some players you can't compromise with, but there are others where you can give a little bit, and Joe was one of those guys.

Joe Kilroy ended up being jailed for three years and people asked me, as his coach, whether or not I thought I'd failed him. I didn't. You just accept that all you can do on your watch with them is the best you can. Set a personal standard. You aren't going to tolerate anything that compromises the team. There can be no place for things like drugs in a team environment, but what the players do individually and privately you have no control over. What you do have control over is what they do within the team and the standards you set. If they breach those standards, obviously there is a price they must pay. That's how it works.

The thing I regret most of all is when I see the wonderful qualities in them and they can't see them in themselves. If they could just see it ... For too many guys the glass is half empty all the time. I truly feel for those guys. But then another guy's glass is half full and he can see all the positives. Too many see what they don't have. I don't know how you change that. I don't know how you make a negative person into a positive one.

EARLY IN 1990, WE BEAT Canterbury in a trial match and I was elated with my blokes' new attitude. The making of this football team would be when it became a family. Until we thought and played that way we were always going to be putting ourselves under enormous pressure. The signs were there that night against Canterbury. Our guys were beginning to feel for each other. The individualism was out the door.

But we were under the pump early in the season — draw, win, loss, win, loss. And then it happened. In round 6 we turned up in Newcastle to play the Knights in front of more than 23,000 of their fans. Greg Dowling pulled out late and Wally had done his hamstring.

It was the day we introduced Willie Carne and Paul Hauff to first grade. Tony Currie, Peter Jackson, Michael Hancock and Steve Renouf were all out.

I remember going to Gene Miles' room at the hotel on match eve. He was stressed because of the captaincy, taking over from Wally — the whole club was under pressure. The media were all over us. I went to him and said, 'Look, Gene, I don't care what happens here tomorrow or the week after. You are the captain and we are going to make it work. I know it's worrying the hell out of you. I'm just telling you now, Gene, that the best thing you can do is be the player you are. I'll handle all the off-field stuff. You just get on the field and make sure you lead them. Lead from the front. Not by your words, but by your deeds. The rest will fall into place.'

He was really struggling with the expectations, all the other things that come with the captaincy, and with taking over from Wally. It had not been an easy time. We were down on numbers and troops and everything else. In Brisbane, there was a groundswell of opinion wanting Wally back as captain and I was quoted in the *Sunday Sun* saying that Wally had been relieved of the captaincy almost six months ago and nothing had changed. Nothing would change. The issue was finalised. I knew what I had to do as a coach — if I started listening to the fans I'd end up sitting next to them in the park. That's what I said in the paper but you don't want to know what I said when Greg Dowling pulled out on the Saturday night.

We put Mark Hohn into the front row. Just before they ran on, Geno went to Chris Johns and said, 'I want you to get in there and help me today.' (Johnsy told me this later on.)

Johnsy said, 'Listen, Geno, you lead from the front, mate, and we'll all follow you. But if you don't have a dig, don't look for the rest of us to follow.' That's Johnsy. He could have captained any team but he didn't need to be captain because he would give his best anyway. Being captain wasn't an issue for him.

So we went out. Some things stick in your mind more than others. It was about the third tackle, and Gene got the ball and charged straight into the ruck, sending Newcastle players left, right and centre. He came through the other side 15 metres down the paddock and we were a transformed football club from that moment. He led all day from the front. Hauffy was outstanding. Willie Carne was bloody sensational. The kids came through magnificently. Mark Hohn did a hell of a job for us that day. He led with Gene and everybody chipped in. The scoreboard read 28–4 but that was not the half of it.

We went on a winning streak — 11 games straight — not only turning our year around but also turning the club itself around.

WE'D BEEN UNDER ENORMOUS PRESSURE. A television phone poll asked: Should Wayne Bennett be replaced as Broncos coach? At the same time there was a politician under pressure and the same television station was having a poll about whether or not he should be axed. Apparently, something like 450 calls were received saying he should stay on. Some smart journo checked this politician's telephone records and of the 450 calls that were made in favour of keeping him, 442 came from his own phones. I'm proud to say no Bennetts called to say I should stay.

At the time of the poll, Paul Morgan called me into John Ribot's office. He said. 'The board has decided we want to offer you a lifetime contract.'

I said, 'Well, Porky, to be honest I don't think I can put up with you for that long, but I really appreciate what you're doing. We don't need a contract and all that type of stuff. We'll just do it the way we've always done it.'

In those days we had a media conference at Red Hill every Monday at lunchtime. We'd have a lunch together. This Monday, Paul walked in, gathered them all around and said: 'Guys, you can run your polls, you can do what you like — but the coach ain't leaving. He's staying as long as he wants.'

The scars remained, though. We were a new club and had done a lot of things right. I'm not everybody's cup of tea, I understand that, but the point was, this was all because of what happened with the captaincy. It was another of the cuts I picked up along the way that deepened the wound. I got a little bit more resentful, a little less co-operative.

I cut the lunches. Bugger having lunch together. I was just giving the media access to too much information. In the end they were just doing a job on the Broncos.

It reached a fairly negative stage before Porky stepped in. At training one night I remember our reserve-grade coach asking, 'Do you think they'll get rid of you, Wayne?' Steve Calder was a good friend and a good coach.

I said to him, 'I have no control over that. All I know is I'm doing the best job I can. I also know we are on the right track here. We are getting the right people in the club, and we are getting the right work ethic. We've got the players, and now it's just a matter of time. If they tell me to go tomorrow, mate, I've got no regrets about what I've done and how I've done it. They've just got to be patient now.' That's how I felt about it then and 21 years on that's still how I feel about it.

HALFWAY THROUGH THE RUN OF 11 straight wins, Jacko came out and said his move to the Broncos was probably the worst he'd ever made. Well, he'd been dropped. The day I told Peter Jackson he wasn't playing first grade was one of the worst days of my life. But Peter was struggling with off-field problems by this stage.

This was also the time when drug testing was just beginning. In my era, the 1970s, we understood about alcohol and guys getting blind drunk but we didn't understand anything about drugs. We thought it was happening in America and other parts of the world, then suddenly at the Broncos we had two of our players test positive to marijuana. I remember being silly enough at the time to suggest it was acceptable. I just didn't know enough about it.

Now, I've seen what it can do and how it changes people and what the ramifications are. As I say to everybody I talk to about it today, to every player I coach and every kid: you've only got one option with drugs — you just say no. It's something you can't negotiate. If you try to negotiate it you are going to fail. You just have to have a strong conviction that you will not take drugs and they will not be part of your life.

Drugs were beginning to become an issue in Peter Jackson's life. Things were falling down around him. He had a job at a radio station in Brisbane and he completely buggered that up, and in the end I knew I had to drop him. His form was indifferent, but still I hated doing what I did that day.

I had a policy that I would always tell the players if they weren't in first grade ... I'd tell them before training, and I'd also tell them why. I'd done that from the time I'd begun coaching, to make me more honest — it's not easy to tell somebody they are not in first grade, particularly someone you respect and like.

As a young player, I'd seen too many coaches avoid that issue. They'd say, 'You should know why you're dropped.' And maybe that's true, but I figured you still have an obligation to tell them. This way wouldn't allow me to play favourites or blame others. I had a policy with myself that before five o'clock on the Tuesday — that's when we trained in those days — I would tell whichever players weren't in first grade.

I remember the day I told Jacko, I felt bloody terrible all day and let the clock run down to about three minutes to five. I can still remember where he was: he was standing beside the goalposts kicking a ball around and I walked out to tell him. If I could have given someone else that job, I would have. But I knew what I had to do, and I knew I didn't have an alternative.

Jacko was terribly disappointed. Often, after players get dropped, they get dirty on you — generally, filthy. They want to blame someone, and they always take it out on the coach. That's fair enough and I live with that. I understand it and don't have a problem with it. The honest ones will accept it but the ones living in a bit of a fool's paradise will want to blame anybody they can, and it's always the coach.

I liked Jacko so much. He was such a great guy. Afterwards, we'd come to training and he would avoid eye contact with me and he would avoid conversation with me, but I made sure I went over and spoke to him. I made sure I didn't walk away from him. I made sure I made eye contact with him, because I have to deliver on the things I believe in ... that's part of being a man.

At times you get a setback in life. I didn't want to have a long conversation with him about it. I didn't want to take him on about it because I knew he was hurting and I knew he wanted to blame someone and I was the guy he was blaming. I just had to let him find his own way out of it.

When Jacko made that comment about coming to the Broncos being the worst move he ever made, it was all about resentment. He was playing second grade then, and when we did get around to talking and sorting it out I said, 'Mate, you were so indifferent to me.'

He said, 'You were indifferent to me. You didn't try to communicate with me.' I'd actually made sure I did everything I could to communicate with him, but I knew he wasn't interested then, so I didn't push the issue.

It was important to me in my own mind and conscience that I didn't walk away just because I dropped him. He was still Peter Jackson. He was still a decent person, a guy I had great admiration for. It all settled down later on. Our friendship resumed and we were great mates until the end. He was a great communicator and people just gravitated towards him. You couldn't help but like Jacko, he was such a fun guy. I always thought the world of him, you know. The end came too early for him.

In 1997, we caught up in Brisbane. By then he was on radio in Sydney. He'd done really well for himself. He'd gone from the Broncos to North Sydney, and after he retired in 1993 he was on television and calling games. He came up and interviewed me, and later we got talking and I asked him how things were going. I knew he was missing his mates, missing football. He was such a bloke's bloke.

They all miss it. Nothing can compensate. All of a sudden you are out there in the world by yourself; you are not training with your mates any more. Instead, you're waking up in the morning wondering what's next.

'Wayne,' he said, 'you've got no idea — I've seen the big picture and it scares the hell out of me. You've got no idea how hard it is, mate.'

I said, 'Peter, you've got to take small steps ... it's getting back into a bit of shape and getting back into a routine of life. Doing certain things at certain times of the day. Doing some exercise.'

He said he knew what he had to do, and that he wanted to do it. 'But it just seems such a dark place for me,' he said. A little bit later he was dead.

We led the comp in 1990 until round 19, and in round 20 we played Penrith at Penrith. That's the day I knew we couldn't win it. We'd come a long way but they put us to the sword. A young Brad Fittler had a good game for the Panthers and they were a good team. The Broncos had had a long winning streak, but losses to Manly the week before (18–4) and then to Penrith (18–2) showed the many Achilles heels I knew still existed within us. When the going got really tough we were still walking away from the contest just a little bit, looking for a soft place. Still wanting to rely on our flair and skill levels rather than our toughness.

In that game against Penrith, Kevin Walters made a speech behind our tryline that was destined to become part of Broncos folklore. Kevvie was one of the most passionate players I ever coached. It was a really windy day and there was no grass on that ground — it was just one of those terrible days. He got them all behind the tryline. Penrith had scored and Kevvie just lost it. He said, 'You are playing against a mob of imposters and you are letting them do this to us!' Then all of a sudden he turned, screaming: 'No, we are the imposters! It's not them, it's us!'

That was the day we knew we couldn't win it.

A MONTH LATER WE FINISHED the competition proper in second place but then lost to Penrith 26–16 in the major preliminary final. Then it was sudden death against Manly in the minor semi-final. I remember talking to John Ribot before this game against the Sea Eagles — he'd played in Sydney and I'd coached Canberra — and we both agreed that to finish second on the ladder only to be gone completely after two finals games would create a real hangover for us. The media would crucify the Broncos every time we made a play-off in future. I had resented the way my team was treated by some of the media after the Penrith loss. A lot of teams didn't get as far as we did, but I didn't see them getting the scathing comments we were getting.

We lost Dale Shearer and Greg Dowling before kick-off and Wally was out because of a broken arm he'd suffered against St George. Gene Miles led from the front. Langer and the Walters boys, Terry Matterson and James Donnelly were all inspirational. Jacko, back in first grade, was outstanding too. James Donnelly hadn't played a lot of footy, but was a guy with a huge amount of talent, most of which he didn't recognise. He was outstanding this day … the day the Broncos' never-say-die attitude was hatched. Against all odds we won. We played through a lot of adversity for that win and the standard of football the Broncos' produced didn't get any better. 'Let history record this as our finest hour,' I told the media.

The following week, against Canberra in the preliminary final, we lost 32–4 but I was happy with what we'd done. I could see we were beginning to realise our potential. We had survived the season. I had survived as coach. And Geno as captain.

AFTERWARDS THE BIG ISSUE WAS whether or not Wally Lewis would make the Kangaroo tour. Dr Peter Myers, our club specialist and a wonderful orthopaedic guy, had cleared Wally to play, and he came off the bench in the final against Canberra wearing number 36. A few days earlier, he had intimated to me that he would be leaving the Broncos for the Gold Coast because we could no longer offer him the money he'd been making. They picked the Kangaroos a week later, and there was no Wally — believe me, there was an outcry.

He had those injuries during the season and maybe the Australian management thought they'd be better served by a better player. I knew this much — he was keen to go and I was keen to give him every opportunity to put the pressure on the Australian selectors. In the end he wasn't chosen, because the team doctors ruled him out.

There was another decision made in 1990 that would have a huge bearing on our club. Allan Langer's form was very indifferent that year. He had the broken leg in 1989 and those things create their own demons. He had missed half that season, and when he came back in 1990 his form was up and down like a yo-yo. There were at least three occasions when I wanted to drop him. He didn't know that … and he won't until he reads this.

With my grandson Will at Broncos training, 2003

Left: My uncle, Eddie Brosnan, a Kangaroo in 1948–49 and a huge influence on the way I live my life.

Below: Warwick Collegians 'Junior Minor' team in 1966, pictured with the trophies we won during the season. Uncle Eddie, our coach, is far left in the front row. His son, Eddie junior (No. 6), was our captain. I'm sitting to the skipper's immediate right, wearing the No. 1 jumper.

Bottom: Basil Phelan, a wonderful and wise man who I think of as the 'old farmer', pictured on his farm at Berat in Queensland.

Above: The Brothers fullback makes a break during a club game at Lang Park in 1974.

Right: The Souths coach with his three children — (from left) Justin, Katherine and Elizabeth — at Lang Park in 1984.

The scene on the field immediately after Souths won the 1985 Brisbane Grand Final over Wynnum-Manly. The two players with their backs to the camera are prop Mark Meskell (left) and fullback Gary Belcher. At far right is team manager Dave Elder.

With Don Furner (centre), co-coach of the Canberra Raiders in 1987, during that season's finals series.

Above: With my wife Trish at the Broncos' presentation night in 1992.

Top right: More than anyone else, it was my mother who taught me the value and importance of family.

Right: With Mum and her twin sister Noela (right) at a 'Queensland Greats' awards ceremony in 2002.

Bottom: My mother-in-law Jean Veivers (right) and her sister Nola Gray, two women whose advice I value.

Above left: With my daughters, Kath (left) and Beth, at the Broncos' season launch in 2006. Above right: With Beth on the team bus after the 2000 Grand Final. My brother Bob is to my left, with future Broncos CEO Bruno Cullen sitting behind him.

In the tunnel at the Sydney Football Stadium after the 1998 Grand Final. From left: Kath (in front), Beth, me, Trish and Gorden Tallis.

Above: Ben Ikin — Queensland five-eighth and my son-in-law — and I survey the crowd at Suncorp Stadium after Origin III, 2003. Queensland won 36–6.

Left: In the early '90s, my son Justin and I owned (almost) matching Australian jumpers.

Below: With Justin on our farm at Warwick, about 130 kilometres south-west of Brisbane.

World Expo '88 chairman Sir Llew Edwards (far right) waits to be presented with a jersey at the Broncos' 1988 season launch. Also in the photo are Broncos directors Paul Morgan (far left) and Steve Williams (third from right) and NSWRL chairman Ken Arthurson (to Steve's right).

With Justin and the retiring Tonie Carroll (far left) after the Broncos' final regular-season game at Suncorp Stadium in 2008.

Each time I held my nerve because I realised it wasn't in the Broncos' long-term interest to drop him. Jacko was different. Alf is a fierce, fierce competitor, and I believe that from 1991 until he retired he was the best player in the NRL. Week in and week out, no one played better than he did. No one was more inspirational than he was. Until Darren Lockyer came along, he was the greatest player I'd ever seen at leading a team to come from behind and win. If you were behind on the scoreboard and Allan Langer was running you, he would get you home nine times out of 10. If you had a fire in your belly he would get you home.

Dropping Alf was never going to improve Alf so I rode it out, and I have never regretted doing that. Again, at times a coach has to take a bit of stick and a hit around the head — and you can't always explain why you do things. But I knew our long-term benefits were with him and I also knew it was in our best interests to keep him happy, to keep him onside rather than letting him get resentful and start second-guessing himself. He'd had to battle for recognition and acceptance from the very beginning and I'm sure he was looking over his shoulder in those early years. I didn't want him to lose confidence in either himself or me. That was the bottom line. If I had dropped him he would have begun to doubt me, and himself, and I knew that wasn't going to make him the player he could become.

Two of our key players in 1990 were Kevin Walters, in his first year at the club, and Michael Hancock, who'd been with us since the start and had made his Test debut in 1989. Kevvie had already played in a grand final for Canberra. I'd heard about Hancock when he was a teenager playing for Stanthorpe, and I'd been going to take him to Canberra until the Brisbane job came along. Until 2008, when Darren Lockyer went past him, he was the Broncos' highest capped player, with 297 games. I asked him one day, 'Mick, how come you didn't play 300?' He said, 'Because of you, coach.' Like Kevin, he was a great team man, and one of the great wingers.

In the end he played second-row and did a hell of a job. He just loved running into people. He loved bumping them off and he'd do anything he was asked to do. History will not regard him as a high-scoring winger but he played outside Steve Renouf most of his career and Steve didn't need anyone to help him. Steve Renouf only needed help in one of every 10 tries.

Sam Backo had a bad knee and was just about gone. He played only three games all year. Tony Currie tore his Achilles. He played a total of six. Wally had the broken arm and torn hamstrings. He came back from one hamstring tear and Geno threw a pass at his ankles — which he was prone to do — and Wally tore it again. He was already dirty on Gene because of the captaincy and now he had another reason. But they are good mates again now, which is tremendous.

There was no great discussion when Wally left. Just a handshake. Sometimes you're better off saying nothing, because there's nowhere to go. The club had done everything it could to get him on that Kangaroo tour because no one wanted to rain on his parade. He was, after all, The King.

Six Broncos made the tour: Kevin and Kerrod Walters, Mick Hancock, Allan Langer, Chris Johns and Dale Shearer. Kerrod played the first Test in England ahead of Balmain and NSW hooker Benny Elias. He was in the team hotel counting down to the second Test when Elias' parents arrived. 'I realised then and there I was in a bit of trouble,' he said. I always liked the kid's dry sense of humour.

CHAPTER EIGHT

THE ONE YOU FEED

One evening an old Cherokee chief told his grandson about a battle that goes on inside people.

'My son,' he said, 'the battle is between two wolves inside us all. One is evil — it is anger, envy, jealousy, sorrow, regret, greed, arrogance, self-pity, guilt, resentment, inferiority, lies, false pride, superiority and ego.

'The other is good — it is joy, peace, love, hope, sincerity, humility, kindness, benevolence, empathy, generosity, truth, compassion and faith.'

The grandson thought for a moment and then asked the Chief: 'Which wolf wins?'

And the old Cherokee replied, simply, 'The one you feed.'

WHEN I SEE ANGER OR jealousy, arrogance, resentment, I know those traits are in all of us. But the key words are: 'The one you feed.' If you don't teach yourself to control your anger, if you don't teach yourself not to resent what others have, if you don't teach yourself that you're not better than someone else, then that's what you do — you feed that personality inside you.

That's what we are doing every day. Some of us are doing it consciously, some of us are doing it subconsciously, through laziness or maybe because we don't care enough. We are feeding one or the other, the evil or the good.

So when you come across a person — they might be 20 or 40, even 60 years old, whatever — and you see and feel these evil qualities, you realise they have spent a lifetime feeding the wrong beast.

And when you come across someone who is gracious and giving and humble, a person with empathy and generosity, you think, well done. Good on you.

It's not about being perfect. That's the fallacy of life. It would be nice to be perfect, but none of us are. We are all imperfect. That goes without question. But what we can do is make these deliberate choices: to not be jealous, to not feel sorrow every time something goes wrong … I don't want to live with sorrow all the time.

Is that to say we won't get jealous? Is it to say we won't have sorrow in our lives? Of course, it's not. We will have our pang of jealousy and we will have our moment of sorrow, but they don't have to be the dominant parts of our lives.

A lot of people are great at masking things. They come into an environment where they know some of this stuff is not going to be tolerated so they mask it. They control it for a while but they don't minimise it, and then they go into another environment where it's OK to let those things out and those things become the dominant parts of who they are.

I've coached some guys who never showed those traits while they were with us, and I've run into them years down the track and it's a whole different person I'm looking at and talking to. You think, where did all this come from?

It was always there; they just weren't feeding it in our team and work environment. They suppressed it.

I've had team members who thought I played favourites but I don't. I don't see colour in people, I don't see black and white. I don't see Asian and African, I just see people. When I form a relationship it is never at someone else's expense. I don't have to hurt someone to be kind to someone else. I do the same for the guy who thinks I don't like him.

I've coached lots of guys I'm not great mates with, but when it comes to the team environment they are all the same to me. I just do what's right. That's what being part of a team is about. After the game is over and the career is over and a player wants to go his own way … what he does then is his choice. It's down to the one he feeds.

CHAPTER NINE

WHATEVER IT TAKES

THE BRONCOS WOULD BECOME famous for great comeback wins, and for never giving up no matter the size of the challenge. At the start of 1991, we were in Broken Hill playing the Lotto Challenge pre-season final against a mighty Penrith Panthers outfit, 16 points down and looking shot.

And then it happened. The little big man, Trevor Gillmeister, put on a stink and from that point on we never looked back — we pulled off a miracle win.

John Ribot had walked into my office in late 1990 and said, 'Trevor Gillmeister just rang. He wants out of the Roosters. Would you be interested in having him?'

INTERESTED? I said, 'Get him back on the phone, I'd love to have him.' Ribes said he would be ringing again in half an hour and I should wait in his office.

We virtually did the deal on the phone. Trevor was keen to return to Brisbane and his price wasn't over the top. I can't tell you how much he brought to our team. He was most definitely one of the guys most instrumental in the club's turnaround. He instilled a really tough attitude.

The fact that he was little made him the player he was. He wanted to prove everybody wrong every time he went onto the footy field. His nickname was 'The Axe'. Gilly's motivation was simple: he realised he played football better than he did anything else, so he made himself succeed. He willed himself to do things and create things out there.

His tackling technique was nearly flawless, which it had to be, and he had great timing. Timing is not something you can really teach; timing is something born into you. He had timing, he had technique, and most of all he had great courage. Defensively, he was as good as anybody I ever coached and he was quite skilful with the ball. He had a good pass in him and while he didn't have great speed or size it was a real credit to him how he had learned the art of getting himself into the game.

And if you talk about mental toughness — I can't remember him missing a training session in three years at the club. He just refused to miss training. He didn't believe that's what footballers did. Even if he had an injury or a knock or a bump and you wanted to give him the day off, forget it.

Throughout life, people think big guys should be tough and rough and little guys should be meek and mild. Well, I've coached many little guys who played like lions and quite a number of big guys who weren't tough and rough. Size has nothing to do with it. The issue is your mental state and what you demand of yourself. That's what makes or breaks a player. I think lots of little guys feel they have something to prove and are prepared to do whatever it takes.

ALLAN LANGER WAS LITTLE TOO, but he had a different kind of courage from Trevor Gillmeister. Alf could never have done what

Gilly did. At his peak Gilly was probably 90kg; Alf's peak playing weight was 75kg.

I think backyard footy was the key to Alf: with his older brothers and mates all beating up on him, he had to learn evasion and decision-making just to survive. Many players are creatures of their upbringing, because they develop their skills and traits playing in backyards and in school grounds — places where there are no rules. The big 13 or 14-year-olds are playing against 8 and 9-year-olds, and everybody is into it.

In 1991, Alf took the Test halfback spot back from Ricky Stuart and was well and truly on his way to being a champion footballer. His next step would be to captain the club, but first we had to re-sign him. John Ribot had always promised Alf that he would become the Broncos' highest paid player as soon as Wally left. Well, in 1991 Wally had left. One day early in the year John called me in and said, 'Can you talk to Alf Langer for me?'

I said, 'What for?'

Ribes said, 'He is in the other office and he won't even talk to me. I'm trying to do a deal with him, and he won't even talk to me.'

Alf didn't like that environment. He was never comfortable negotiating his contracts. I said, 'What's going on?' Alf was always open with me. I've always had a great ability to communicate with him.

He said, 'Ribes promised me that when Wally retired I'd get the top money here, and what he's offering me isn't the top dollar here.'

So I went back and told Ribes and he fixed it all up. Alf talked to him after that.

I WILL ALWAYS LOOK back on 1991 as a season where we missed the finals, but had we got there, I believe we could have won the biggest prize.

We won our last five games, beating Canberra, Parramatta, Norths, Gold Coast and Wests, playing outstanding football. I knew the ingredients were all there, all coming together, but we missed a finals berth by one damn win.

It wasn't a year lost — it was just another year we had to wait. Another year where all our younger players advanced that bit further. Another year in the competition.

We did have a soft underbelly in those early years, I knew that, and we were toughening that underbelly up. The more games we played, the tougher we were becoming. Our players were finally beginning to realise that the things that might have won them the Brisbane competition weren't enough to get them home in the Big League.

AT SEASON'S END THERE WERE two significant changes for the club: the arrival of Glenn Lazarus would prove to be a defining moment in the club's history; Gene Miles' decision to join Wigan in England meant one of the club's original heroes was departing.

For the Broncos, Lazzo was the final piece of the jigsaw. And I didn't even know we were negotiating with him. We were certainly on the lookout for a front-rower but I couldn't believe it when Porky and Ribes told me we had Glenn Lazarus.

He'd played for Canberra in the 1991 Grand Final against Penrith. He'd been out injured before that, but he came back for that match, and I couldn't believe how well he played for a guy with so little match fitness. That's where he got the nickname 'The Brick'. He was the man.

Some people are just winners; you can see it in the way they carry themselves and what they do. I'm always looking for those players, those qualities. Tough players and tough people. The tough guys never ever talk about being tough. They never shape up to somebody without hitting them. They never talk trash. They don't talk at all; they just whack you. The ones who make out they're tough get around talking it up. They shadow box, then back away from the guy who wants to hit them ... and they are still talking trash.

Winners are the same. They don't walk in and say, 'Well, I'm a winner — get with me, boys.' They just bring an indefinable quality. In Lazzo's case it was a work ethic: every time he played, he did his best. He was Shane Webcke before Shane Webcke.

These people don't give you second best. Lazzo did the toughest job in the game — taking that ball up week after week. Never once did he get outside where he should have been. Never once did he want to be running in the centres or at five-eighth. He knew what his job was every week and he went out there and did it better than anybody in the game, throughout his career.

I had coached him at Canberra when he was only a kid and I put him in the grand final squad even though I hardly knew him. He was a serious human being, so Kevvie and Alf were great for him at the Broncos because they made him laugh. They could hang a fair bit of rubbish on him and get away with it. But no one else would have dared, I'll tell you that.

Glenn Lazarus was an extremely tough guy but he didn't throw any punches. He didn't have to, because everyone knew he was tough and everyone knew he wasn't someone who was going to back off.

Gene Miles was tough too, and his going to the UK was a hard decision. He'd done a great job for us in his two years as captain and he'd certainly changed his attitude and the club's attitude. He was as committed to the place as anybody, but there was a good opportunity for him to go and play in the UK. We probably convinced him he should go, and that's what he did. But it was a hard one. There were a whole bunch of young guys coming through.

It's always tough when you know your older players can still get the job done, but they are running out of time, and the longer they stay, the more you're in danger of losing your young guys. If you're not careful, you can lose both.

Gene Miles is an outstanding person. He carries himself extremely well. There has been so much self-improvement and development in him. He's still a laidback, casual kind of guy, but he's done a great job with the FOGS (Former Origin Greats) organisation. He was instrumental in its beginning with Tosser Turner. He knows his footy, and he cares about it too.

The thing that really impresses me is that Geno went into the dry-cleaning business, something he didn't know anything about, and he made a success of it. He was out of bed at five in the morning, going to work. Gene Miles the footballer never got out of bed before nine; he didn't have to.

I STILL HAD A LONG way to go as a coach and decision maker, but I'd come a long way too. I still don't understand when people say football is a business, that decisions are made for business reasons. What I do understand is you want your club to remain at the top of the game, at the cutting edge of your sport. You have to be continually vigilant about your playing roster. I don't see that as business. The great clubs I'd followed or watched always made the hard decisions when they had to, and did it with class. The clubs who used to be great and weren't great any more had stopped making those hard decisions. They stayed with players too long and for the wrong reasons. The demise of most clubs is self-inflicted. So we coined the phrase 'better to let them go a year too early than a year too late'.

CHAPTER 10

THE MAKING OF US

Go through life as if you are mute and be judged by your actions, not your words ... When you cross the white line give 100 per cent ... Let's have a season where we don't have to justify each other to the public ... If you don't do it, who will? ... If you don't do it now, when will you?

IN 1992, THE BRONCOS FINALLY realised the difference between playing with skill and poor discipline and playing with skill and good discipline. They waited for their chances and when they came they took the right options. Football is all about taking the right options, about not forcing the play and committing unforced errors.

The player attitude was great throughout the 1992 season. They pulled together, particularly during the representative program. When they were tired they continued to give 100 per cent. They accepted much more responsibility for their actions and took it upon themselves to ensure that they came ready to play. There was a tremendous spirit and our game plan worked well, particularly our ability to attack from anywhere on the field. That ability was certainly a strength, and I knew it concerned other coaches.

The public response to our grand final win was something I'd never experienced. It obviously meant a lot to a lot of people. I have often been asked what a grand final win means to me. I probably haven't answered, but here are my thoughts as written in my notes six weeks after the event:

> I think I will enjoy it more when I retire, because in the back of my mind I know the joy I feel now will be short-lived if we don't have a good season in 1993. I've got more enjoyment seeing what it has meant to the people around me. That has been where my real satisfaction came from — family, friends and fans. Even my players have been a bit like me … they know it's all on again soon.
>
> To sum it up, it gives you a nice warm feeling like wearing a dark suit and weeing yourself. You get a nice warm feeling but no one else notices. If it changes any of the players or the club, then to me it won't be worth it. I can live without winning the 1993 season as long as we do the best we can every time we play. If we do that, then we'll win in 1993. I must make sure I pick a team each week that is hungry and comes ready to play.

Allan Langer was now captain. One of the things I always wanted was that the captaincy of the Broncos carried weight. I'd been at other clubs and been a captain but never felt it carried enough authority or position, kudos even. Sometimes, clubs are too quick to change captains, and don't give them relevance or importance. I didn't want that at the Broncos.

Some clubs have co-captains. We don't, because we believe it belittles the position. At the Broncos we have a big photograph of all the captains together and I want young players walking into the club to aspire to one day be one of those captains, and knowing that if they get there, they've earned it. It is a special place and position.

Every time I've chosen a captain it has been very deliberate, because I'm very reluctant to change … one change wouldn't hurt, but chopping and changing every couple of years would undermine the whole thing about being a Broncos captain. When someone says he captained the Broncos I want him to feel proud about being the captain and a Bronco.

And I'm sure Allan Langer did. Of all the players in the team, Alf was the one who most needed to be challenged. He had more natural ability than many, and I knew that not making him captain would not challenge him. As a coach, I knew I had to get a little bit more out of him and I thought the responsibility of captaincy would draw that extra ounce of power and drive from within.

Alf was not a good communicator on the field but I wanted him to lead by example. That's the first criteria of a Broncos captain — to lead by example. I do the talking, I'm the coach, but I can't play. I need men out there who can lead from the front. Everybody loved playing with him and he was a great competitor.

The other two guys in contention were Kevin Walters and Chris Johns but they didn't need it. It wasn't going to change them. They did the same things every week and they were Alf's best mates. So they weren't going to be offended by me choosing him, or put off by it, and I structured the team to make sure they were doing most of the communicating.

Kevvie has a forceful personality, as does Chris. Terry Matterson at lock was good as well. I had all the right people around Alf.

One thing with Allan Langer, when he was angry with you, you knew it; he didn't need to tell you. He just had a manner about him, and it was a feeling you didn't want or like. He communicated without opening his mouth. That's where people are wrong: when they talk about communication, they think you have to be talking all the time. There are many forms of communication and talking is only one of them.

And then there was conditioner, Kelvin Giles. He had a relationship with the players that was similar to what they had with their dentists: they knew he was going to make things better but they would rather not go through the pain to get there. His work with the team was beginning to make them glisten.

AFTER ALF AND KELVIN, the next major happening of the season was the round-4 match against Penrith at Lang Park. It was a hot autumn day, really humid, and I remember it as if it was yesterday. Penrith, the defending premiers, were still the yardstick, and for the first 20 minutes we played tough with them. But it got too hard for us. The Broncos lost 24–10 but it was the making of us. If we had not lost that game we would not have won the grand final. Until that day we still had not learned how to play the tough brand of Sydney football every week … how to grind it out from our own line. We had to realise we couldn't just throw it out to the wingers and pray for the best.

For me, it was a reality check. From that day, I knew I had to be mentally stronger and I put a plan into action to help cultivate that attitude within the club. Why? Because we were still mentally soft. You don't like to admit that about your footy team, but it was true. We had battled with it and I thought we were getting better, but Penrith showed us up. Our soft underbelly was still hurting us in the big games.

Now I knew what I had to fix: mental toughness. So I did things with them, challenged them in different ways to toughen them up. We wouldn't have this happen to us again.

AROUND THE SAME TIME, Wally Lewis released a video and in it he said some players were not suited to my coaching style, citing himself, Peter Jackson and Dale Shearer.

Of course, it's only logical that you're not going to hit it off with everybody in life, but I took Peter Jackson out of the equation straight away because we had a wonderful relationship, even after the pain. I coached him at Souths in Brisbane, Canberra, the Broncos and in State of Origin. We'd won a premiership at Souths, gone to Canberra together before he came back to Brisbane. We were compatible, me and Jacko.

But it's life sometimes that it doesn't always gel. I am probably stubborn about a lot of things because I just can't compromise when I know there is no other way. I can bend a little but not to a point where it is going to impact on the rest of the team. For every one you might have a bit of a problem with, there are another 14 or 15 enjoying what you do.

TO A MAN, EVERYONE ENJOYED the round-6 victory against Newcastle. We've all watched a lot of games in our lives and this one rated in the top 10. Broncos 12, Knights 8. In those early days we played some sensational football against Newcastle in Newcastle, with them throwing everything at us. The two clubs came into the competition together, and for a long time they never beat us at their home ground. We won this one right on full-time.

Kelvin Giles proved to be a soothsayer, because he had said to me beforehand that the game would go down to the last five minutes — it would be that tough and tight. He told me to convince the guys we had to hang in right to the end. He was spot on, because it wasn't until three or four minutes from the end that Willie Carne, defending on our tryline, got the ball, split them and scored. We were all believers by then. Those games in Newcastle, they were absolute wars.

Come round 9 and we went in against South Sydney without 10 of our regular first-graders because of Origin. They were going pretty well, the Rabbitohs, and everybody was raving about them, but after what we did to them that day I knew they were not going much further. That was probably one of our first ever wins without our Origin players. We were maturing. Suddenly, we had people saying, 'Don't worry if you're out — I can take your place. I can be counted on. We can win without you, mate.'

A week earlier, we'd played St George in Adelaide. It was after the second State of Origin game and we were busted, gone. We played a big kid in the front row, Shaun Keating, and there was this belief that we could hang in there and win. It was a special victory: Broncos 20, St George 18.

By round 19 we were ready to be tested again by the yardstick team: Penrith. On the Friday I did the eulogy for Eddie Brosnan, and I caught the plane to Sydney for the game against the Panthers with great sadness in my heart. I'd realised that Uncle Eddie was getting sick when I was in Canberra in 1987; then he got Alzheimer's in 1988 or 1989, so he didn't really know what was happening in my years at the Broncos.

I did the eulogy, we went to Penrith and they were ready for us. It was a cold, blustery, windy, miserable night — the kind you get in Penrith — and the Panthers played as if their lives depended on it. They were disciplined and tough. Their coach, Phil Gould, could always make it difficult for the opposition because he'd draft a good game plan and they'd stick to it. Everything was against us — the crowd, travelling and playing on a Friday night, playing the premiers who were fired up because if they lost, they'd be out.

This was the game, the one that sealed it for us: Broncos 12, Penrith 6. Earlier in the year they had taught us a lesson and we had worked our butts off to turn things around. Yes, this was the making of us. I don't think any Broncos left that ground that night not knowing we could win the premiership. There is always a special moment, a special place. It happens and you just know. It had happened at Brisbane Souths in 1985. And now it was happening again.

Already, we'd won three games in a row. Penrith was the fourth, and in the six games left of 1992 we didn't lose again.

But I have to say we were never cocky. I have never coached teams that were cocky. We were simply confident of getting the job done.

WHEN WE HAD OUR game together there was just so much confidence and belief. The round-19 Penrith game ticked every box: all the things we'd been working on, all the things I'd been preaching to them, all the things I wanted them to do. This great team came out and applied the pressure and we responded by sticking it out and believing in what was going to work for us. The important thing is not going away from what you know will work.

We began slowly in the major semi-final against Illawarra, and that was because I'd pumped them up too much — this was a lesson I was still learning. But we overcame those early nerves to beat the Steelers 22–12, and then two weeks later we were at the Sydney Football Stadium along with 41,560 others — and St George — for the grand final. We love that stadium. It's a great place for the Brisbane Broncos.

· The Dragons had done remarkably well to get to the grand final. They were underdogs all year and had been beaten by Illawarra in the first week of the finals. They were battlers. The big guns with the big names, Canberra and Penrith, weren't there.

Penrith had failed to go back-to-back. It wasn't that they didn't have the talent — I can tell you they did — but, you know, faltering the following season can be a side effect of winning. Sometimes that's what happens.

St George were game and courageous but we never doubted we were going to win. Brisbane 28, St George 8. We were in a class of our own.

THE YEAR WAS NOT OVER. There was the small matter of the World Club Challenge against northern hemisphere club champions Wigan. We had eight players away for the World Cup in England and now the rest of us were on a plane too.

We arrived at Wembley on 24 October, in time for the World Cup final, Australia versus England … our players, their wives and girlfriends. Porky wanted everybody there. That's Porky.

Australia were under the pump, there wasn't much time on the clock and coach Bob Fulton got Kevin Walters off the bench. There were only seven or eight minutes to go and Kevvie threw the ball … it was a pretty special play. He hit Steve Renouf with an 'outball', putting Steve on the outside of his defender and in to score for an Australian win.

Seven days later, with all eight blokes who'd been in the World Cup squad in our line-up, we were playing Wigan in the World Club Challenge at Central Park. Or at least, we were supposed to be. The mood was not good. I knew we were struggling. For a start, half of them were on the drink. I told them to stay off it, but some of them didn't want to come down to London for the World Cup final so they stayed in Wigan and went to the pub. One of them let a firecracker off in the hotel and a curtain caught on fire. I was not happy.

When the Australian players and the girlfriends and wives and the rest of the players arrived in Wigan, it was bitterly cold, freezing. Probably the coldest weather I've experienced in my life. Alf was training with his hands in his pockets. He wouldn't take them out.

How can a halfback train with his hands in his pockets? He'd been in the Australian team and he'd had enough of football for the year and he reckoned it was too cold.

It was miserable out there so we all went back to the hotel but the mood was not right. I called a meeting. 'Guys,' I said, 'there is something going on here, and I need to know about it. Do you want to tell me what's happening? I'll leave you to yourselves for 10 or 15 minutes. I'll come back and you tell me what's going on, but we've got to play the World Club Challenge on Friday night and we are not going to embarrass ourselves.'

When I came back, I don't know who it was, maybe Lazzo or Kevvie, said the problem was that they had been away for a month and they wanted to go home. They didn't really want to play Wigan. We sat down and talked about it and realised that none of us could go home. We had to get the job done. And to their credit they all committed to each other.

When we got to Central Park, Wigan, they were scaringly frivolous. Mucking around, carrying on. I was thinking, we have no chance here tonight. This ain't a Broncos change room. Word was they'd all backed Julian O'Neill to score the first try, and they were big bets too. Johnsy was running the plunge, and Ribot was involved too. The reason they backed Julian was because they call him 'The Pope' — he wouldn't pass the pill — and they believed if he got the ball near the tryline he would definitely score.

So they go out to warm up and I'm absolutely beside myself. I realised we are so far off the pace it didn't matter. They go, they warm up, they come back in.

And I sensed a change. Something had happened. I can't work out what, but this was not the same group of men who went out to warm up. Anyway, they kicked off. I had said just one thing to them, something I'd never coached. I said, 'Listen, if they put it on you guys, don't cop it. Stand up to the bastards.'

Within five minutes, Andrew Gee had ignited three fights and they were all into it. They fought as one. And they went on to play some great football and won the game comprehensively — Broncos 22, Wigan 8.

When they came off the ground I asked Andrew Gee what had got them going. He said, 'The best thing that happened to us tonight was the warm-up. Kelvin took us over close to the crowd, and they bagged us unmercifully. They bagged the tripe out of us and I said, "Boys, we're not going to cop this crap. We'll get out there and get into them."' And that's exactly what they did. I owed that crowd. Without them I have no doubt we would not have won the World Club Challenge.

CHAPTER 11

TALK ABOUT TOUGH

IT WAS A TOUGH YEAR in many, many ways. First of all, there is no doubt the team was not as hungry for success in '93 as they had been in '92. I had to work a lot harder with them and challenge them on and off the field as much as possible. At the beginning of the season their attitude was very poor — they thought they only had to turn up to win. We lost to Canterbury and South Sydney at the World Sevens and Souths beat us in the first round of the pre-season Tooheys Challenge competition.

To the premiership proper and the high-rolling, over-confident defending champions turned up at Endeavour Field and really struggled against Cronulla in front of a thankfully small crowd. We scraped home but then lost the next two weeks to Canterbury and Parramatta. And we played badly. In the fourth round we played Canberra at home and began to turn things around.

The Broncos had moved base from Lang Park to ANZ Stadium, which had been built for the 1982 Commonwealth Games and was originally known as Queen Elizabeth II Sports Centre. For the 1993 season the Broncos would average a home crowd of 43,197, a record not approached in rugby league in Australia before or since.

Just over 46,000 Queenslanders came to see us beat the Raiders 12–8 and for the next three weeks we played well, beating Balmain, Penrith and St George at Kogarah. We really had it together by the round-7 St George game — a day Glenn Lazarus was outstanding. Lazzo had played rep football for City the night before and he came back to play for us on the Saturday afternoon. He was absolutely outstanding. I couldn't believe a big guy could back up in that fashion in such a short period of time.

But then State of Origin hit, taking 10 of our players and for the next seven weeks we were battling again. There were also three Tests against New Zealand where we lost six players. During the rep season Illawarra and Wests led us by 14 points or more before we came back to win, but we lost to Manly and North Sydney. Easts gave us a scare by coming back and almost winning on the hooter.

With your rep players away, what happens is you either begin games well and finish badly or you begin badly and finish strong. All through these games it was one or the other.

We had a great win against Newcastle after I challenged the players in the rooms. I'd sensed their attitude was poor. I got among them and told them they were ready to lose, and picked out Kevin Walters and Lazzo. They were outstanding in a 31–2 win but the following week Cronulla almost beat us with 12 men. We led the Sharks 38–12 and won 38–34. That left us fourth on the competition table with six rounds to go.

Everything went fairly well until the last round, when St George beat us at ANZ Stadium. There were nearly 60,000 people there, 58,593 to be precise, and we played badly for the first 30 minutes allowing St George to lead 14–0. We tried very hard for the next 50 minutes but couldn't quite get there, losing 16–10, which dropped us to fifth on the ladder, last team into the semi-finals. However, from that day on we were at our very best. I don't believe we ever played with more commitment and authority than we did in the last month of '93. The team was outstanding.

From a personal point of view, I don't ever remember coaching as well. All the years of experience came to my aid and allowed me to do the best coaching I've done.

For 24 hours after the game against Saints I was shattered. I woke on the Sunday, after we'd played on the Friday night, and just knew I had to follow my gut instincts. No team had ever finished fifth and won the grand final, but I knew if any team could do it — win three straight and then the grand final — this was the team. I rang at least 80 per cent of my players on that Sunday morning, reassuring them and asking them to come to training with a happy face and some real enthusiasm on the Monday. Johnsy told me we could do it and, what's more, he'd put his money where his mouth is and backed us to win the grand final. Backed us big.

On the Monday I had no video session on St George and no mention was made of them. Everything was about the following Sunday and Manly-Warringah. I changed our training to straight ball work and we dropped sessions right back in length. I made sure the week was enjoyable and that we all enjoyed each other's company. We did a big job on how to beat Manly with our defence doing certain things.

We did all that and gave Manly a real work over. After that, all the players had their confidence back, not only in themselves but in each other. Manly was the danger game and it gave us great confidence for the next three weeks. We went on to play Canberra without Renouf, Lazarus and Matterson, and then Canterbury with Lazarus still out and Matterson on the bench. Renouf had broken his jaw six weeks out from the play-offs. Matterson got hurt against Manly and so did Lazzo.

This made our performances even more significant.

Grand final day and seven players were carrying injuries and four received injections. We'd tired badly against Canterbury in the preliminary final, holding on to win 23–16, so the training in grand final week was completely different to anything I'd done before. We didn't train until the Thursday and that was for only one hour, and then we had a light session on the Saturday. We never discussed tactics or our opponents until the Thursday session.

For that finals series I had sayings for the players and we said them a lot:

- A champion is someone who is consistent and rises to the occasion.
- To be a team member you must help those around you play above themselves.

The players did those things and did them particularly well. The second premiership was harder than the first but that last month was as gratifying as anything I've ever done.

Since I'd changed our game plan in 1991, we had played a total of 56 matches for 46 wins. We won our last five in '91, 22 regular-season games each in '92 and '93, two finals in '92 and four in '93, plus the World Club Challenge game. The major change had been around the 40-metre zone in our own half — our backs were to go through their opponents and not around them in that area. That's in attack. They don't run around them, they run through them. To go around them becomes a lot easier once you begin going through them. I wrote in my coach's notes after the '93 Grand Final …

> The significance of the 40-metre position is that it has given the team direction in the dangerous part of the field. They all know what they are working for and the backs, by going through and not around them, have stopped calling the ball when they have nowhere to go. That's where they had been generally getting driven back and losing confidence in what they were doing. But no more.

Another strength is the ability to keep the same squad of players together, a squad of around 19 and very seldom do I pick other players. This allows harmony and team work to develop which in turn allows confidence to breed individually and collectively. All the things learnt in the '92 season stayed with us. We did not make many changes, just kept doing the things that made the team successful.

They can defend as good as any team when they want. They have the best defence in the finals series because they want to defend well. Technique and tactics wise they don't have any concerns. I learned this season when defending the premiership you must not let anything change. Things and people do change after success but the way the game is played doesn't. You must keep your life in order and this in turn keeps your attitude in order which allows you to play the game the same as you did when you won in '92. It took a while for that to sink in but when it did it allowed us to win in '93.

1994, what does it hold? I'm going to work hard and keep the same attitude to performance. Give 100 per cent. We must not change from what has made us a successful side.

OFTEN, I REFLECT ON THAT last month. Manly had finished the season winning eight or nine straight and they were going to be hard to beat. It was the danger game because they had a lot of confidence and we had been beaten the week before by St George. We had to win that Manly game to regain confidence and move on.

Canberra had finished the season poorly. Ricky Stuart, their great halfback, had broken his leg a month out and they never won another game. He was the only one they had injured but that's what he meant to them. Some 15 years on, nothing has changed when the key players are missing from certain sides.

We accounted for them, but then the Canterbury game was a hell of a tough one. Steve Renouf was back and the first time he touched the ball he scored, but we were locked up at 16-all in the second half. We kicked a field goal and I can still remember the Bulldogs restarting play. Alf had wonderful hands and hardly ever made a mistake but he dropped the ball from the kick-off. I can see Kevvie marshalling the troops and convincing everybody all we had to do was defend for six tackles. It was late in the game. We were tired. Part of our tiredness was we'd been on the road for three weeks in a row because in those days all finals were played in Sydney. The travelling was catching up with us. Anyway, we held on before setting up a late try, a typical Broncos try. Alan Cann came bursting through somewhere, beat a couple of guys with a sidestep and the game was ours.

THAT NIGHT, LEAVING SYDNEY, an acquaintance came up and handed me a sheet of paper. At that stage, clubs were giving their players tip sheets on opposition players and this was an old one compiled by St George, presumably by Saints coach Brian Smith and his staff, on us. We were down on our knees, tired and bruised, and we had a grand final to win. Going home, I'm looking at the sheet and I'm thinking and then I thought of my great friend Bob Bax. He was a great man and a great motivator. He could get people to lift beyond themselves; I'd seen him do it so many times as a coach. When I played for Queensland under him I'd seen him do it with us.

So I rang him up and said, 'We need a bit of help.' I want you to come over and doctor up a bit of a script for me, something he absolutely excelled in. My next dilemma with my very tired football team was when do I use the doctored tip sheets? How do I get the maximum benefit out of this?

St George had beaten us a month before and won the major semi-final to go straight into the grand final. They were good. They were confident. They were going to take some beating. Lazzo and

Terry Matterson were back. When I did the videos on St George I knew this much — I knew they wouldn't change their game plan. I knew they weren't capable of changing their game plan. So defensively I knew what we had to do and on the Thursday I drilled my blokes pretty extensively about what we had to defend, certain things they would do to us. I did this complete in the confidence that that was all they would throw at us. If that didn't work for them, they wouldn't have a Plan B.

I knew we didn't have a lot of points in us, that this was a game where we would just have to hang on and pick up our points when they came ... hang in there and play with a spirit I knew was in the team.

On the Sunday morning we were in Sydney waiting for the game. In those days we always stayed at the Novotel at Brighton le Sands and at about 10, 10.30, we went out to the tennis court to assemble and have a get-together. I produced the piece of paper then. I produced the document and read out to them what had been said about them, individually, and I made sure it wasn't pretty listening. I could see they were quite filthy and, of course, I elaborated a bit more on them all and added a bit more drama to it. Kerrod was no more than a speed bump. Kevvie was an over-rated little fat lair. Trevor Gillmeister wasn't as tough as he made out ...

We got to the game and it went to script. St George played the way I believed they would. When they went to their big plays we were there waiting for them, had every answer. And we were conservative with our energy, steering away from our normal up-tempo game. Picked up a couple of tries and got the job done.

My biggest mistake of the day was I forgot to tell the players after the game that I had doctored that document with the help of Bob Bax. In the euphoria of the moment it just completely escaped me. Later on, I received some feedback about the players being less than gracious on the radio, singing and chanting, 'St George can't play.' It wasn't a reaction we planned, it was just the guys getting too much into the spirit of the post-match celebrations. I should have told them what Bob and I had done straight after the game, and I regret that I didn't.

Brian Smith was filthy with me for a long period of time, and it's probably fair enough. I'm not complaining about it, I'm just telling the story and that's what happened. That's the way it went.

I can still remember Chris Johns' face. His wife Lisa had had a serious illness that year which few people knew about, and fewer knew about his grand final bet. He had $5000 on the Broncos at 4–1. After the loss to St George, Johnsy went back to the function room and someone was mouthing off about us being shot, gone … finished. Johnsy told him to put his money where his mouth was. And he did. $20,000. He asked a couple of the boys whether they wanted a share of the bet. Kevvie jumped. I think Alf might have. Johnsy's wasn't a false belief, it was a great belief. He kept quiet about Lisa because he didn't want it to impact on the team. That's the thing — to Chris Johns, the team meant everything.

I SAID IT WAS A tough year, but for me the hardest part wasn't our ordinary start to the season, or the finals. It was the process that culminated in a call we had to make in July. Talk about tough. He was tough, and the decision we made was even tougher. From the time he joined us he put his heart and soul into the place and he never let us down for one moment. Even now, he wasn't asking for a ridiculous amount of money.

Paul Morgan and John Ribot had come to me about the salary cap. Everyone was all over the Broncos about having all the star players even though we'd developed the majority of them from within. Porky and Ribes assured me we were under the cap but, I'm not trying to justify anything, it was obvious we had to make some hard decisions and lose some players.

That's what occupied my mind at different times during 1993 — a lot of painstaking thought about who would survive and who wouldn't. It would be the way we conducted business for the next 15 years.

We had a young back-rower named Peter Ryan and we knew he was entitled to a shot as a first-grade starting spot. Peter was 22 years of age. Trevor Gillmeister was nearing the end of his footy career. And we had to make a decision. Do we keep Peter Ryan for 1994 and let Trevor Gillmeister go at the end of the season, or do we keep Trevor and let Peter Ryan go?

I'd seen what had happened to Parramatta in the late eighties, early nineties. To their detriment they let all their good kids go to other clubs so they could keep their old heroes from the glory days. We just couldn't go down that path. So I went around to Trevor's place. I couldn't tell him at training. I can still remember walking in, feeling so bloody miserable. Just something I didn't want to do. Then I had to come back and confront the team, tell them what had been done and why it had been done. No one sat there clapping, saying, 'Good decision, coach.' No one wanted to see him go.

They all knew the player Peter Ryan would be. He was a hell of a tough hombre and a great hitter in the Gillmeister mould. We were losing an older warrior to bring a younger one along but that didn't make the one-on-one or the team meeting any more comfortable. At least the players knew we were under the pump with the salary cap and to their credit they all got on with it. Gilly signed with Penrith for the following season, and then was good for us during the last few competition rounds and tremendous in the finals.

I'm not looking for forgiveness. I'm just telling the story. If you want to be a competitive club and if you desire longevity then you have to pay the price, you have to make the hard decisions.

CHAPTER 12

CYRIL

PAUL MORGAN CAME TO ME one day in early 1990 and said, 'You've got to give my old friend Cyril Connell a job.'

I said, 'What are you talking about, Porky?'

He said, 'No one knows football better than this bloke.'

I said, 'Yeah, I know Cyril.'

He said, 'He is the best, mate.' He said Cyril was a great coach at Brisbane State High, where he had taught Porky important things like maths, sport and manhood. He had worked for Paul in the stockbroking business but was now retired.

'He just loves his football, Wayne,' he said, 'and wants to be part of the Broncos.'

I said, 'Is that right?'

At that stage no football club had recruitment officers. We found players by word of mouth. You got a phone call from a mate who'd seen someone or something, somewhere. And you took his word for it. It was pretty intimate stuff.

Then along came Cyril. I wasn't going to fight Porky because you couldn't have talked him out of this one. To Porky Morgan, Cyril Connell was Christmas-on-a-stick. 'Best buy we've ever made, Wayne.' He'd been second-in-charge of Secondary Education in

Queensland, an absolute icon in the school system. He'd been a wonderful footballer, playing for his state and country. Been around football all his life. Been a commentator. There was no finer man — or better person — to be our first and only recruitment officer at the Broncos. The best recruit the Broncos ever got was this gentle little man.

BESIDES THE CONSISTENCY THE Broncos have had in their football over the 21 years, the one thing that stands out for me about the club is the number of quality young players Cyril brought to the club and put into our system. He brought us some of the really wonderful players of the game. Eighteen years on, we would win a grand final with a side of 17 players of whom he alone had recruited 14.

He brought us all sorts: front-rowers such as Petero Civoniceva and Shane Webcke, who are now in their 30s and played with us for a decade and more, and Karmichael Hunt, who was a teenager when he was fullback in the 2006 premiership team. That was always our strength — Cyril's ability to continually find boys who would come to us and become men of the finest order. Recruiting is not something you can be taught — you need the eye for it. Everyone has an eye for something. Cyril's was for identifying talent, seeing something in someone others couldn't see. It's easy to pick a star who's always been a star; Cyril could see things in kids others missed.

Darren Lockyer is a good example.

Darren didn't make the Australian schoolboys' but all the other scouts still watched him play. They didn't make him offers. But Cyril did and Darren was playing first grade for us in 1995, when he was 18. Petero was the same. The list goes on and on. Cyril had this gift to identify the indefinable, the thing you and I can't see but he could. Don Furner could do that, and he and Cyril are great mates. They went right back to playing together in Toowoomba. I put Bob Fulton in that category as well. I worked with Bozo a few times at team selections and know he has the eye.

And Cyril is such a gentleman with it.

I remember working with the QRL back in 1985, and being in Atherton when Cyril came through to interview a teacher who'd been charged with misconduct. I said to this guy with him, whom I'd only just met, 'How's Cyril going to handle talking to a guy about misconduct?' Here's this wonderful, beautiful person who'd never knock anybody, never put anyone down, who's always constructive and positive, how's he going to give anyone a dressing down? He wouldn't be tough enough, would he?

He said, 'Wayne, Cyril's the best toe-cutter in the business. He'll do a job on you before you know it's being done.' I thought for a while, and figured that you don't make second-in-charge of Queensland secondary schools without having a tough, uncompromising side for when the times are, well, tough.

Tough is about what's inside, not outside. Is Cyril tough? In more recent years I've seen him getting around our facility with broken ribs after a fall and never complaining. He's a guy who played in an era where they took your head off, an era where there were no videos, no linesmen running in to protect you. He must have been one hell of a tough cookie. I've talked to other halfbacks from his era and they were either cheeky or rough and tumble, men who could give as good as they got. But I never saw that in Cyril. That makes him even more special in my mind.

NOT SO LONG AGO I attended a Queensland Academy of Sport gathering for 16-year-old footballers at Noosa, on the Sunshine Coast. Most of these talented kids already had contracts to go to various NRL clubs, so they were most definitely not all Broncos kids. I walked in and they all said, 'Hello Mr Bennett.' They were cordial enough.

Less than five minutes later, Cyril walked in. They all stood and clapped him. He made no announcements, no statements … he just walked in. I couldn't believe the impact he'd had on these kids. They were all going to different clubs, but at some stage they'd all been touched by him, whether it was a word of advice, of encouragement, or some help. They were all standing, spontaneously clapping. Cyril smiled and looked down, the way humble men do.

He is caring way beyond what I consider to be caring. He's done all these different things in his life — and Paul Morgan always made special mention about his gifts as a maths teacher — but genuine humility just drips off him. It's quite unbelievable. In the world we live in you need men like Cyril around because people can get so full of themselves.

I would describe his personality as beautiful and genuine. His ability to identify talent and then to encourage them to come and play was second to none — parents knew their boys were going to be looked after. However, I will always remember Peter 'Bullfrog' Moore upstaging him over one player who shall remain nameless (even though it was Brett Dallas, in Mackay). Bullfrog bought chocolates and flowers for Brett's mum, and the kid went to the Bulldogs. Cyril learned a lesson there.

But not too many guys have upstaged him.

Also, I've never seen so many women kiss a man. It doesn't matter where you go, somebody knows him, especially school teachers, and they all rush up and kiss him.

He knows every pie shop between Brisbane and Rockhampton and to the west. You name it and he'll tell you where the good pies are and the bad pies too. When they were last good and the last time they were bad. There's not one pit stop he doesn't know. He travels everywhere by car, or at least he used to. They won't let him drive any more, and I think it breaks his heart. He'd drive down to some far-flung spot in New South Wales and you'd say, 'Why are you going there, Cyril?'

'I need to see the boys and tell them we're still interested in what they're doing,' he'd say. Whatever it was, off he'd go for two or three days.

At times, he brought kids along who I knew weren't going to make it, but that was his compassion at work. He sensed they needed an opportunity, whether it be education or to get out of the environment they were in, and knew we could provide it. He'd say, 'Wayne, he's got a few rough edges but we might be able to do something with him.' So we'd put them in the system — and I've seen them coming back to thank him after finishing their apprenticeships in carpentry, refrigeration mechanics, whatever. A couple ended up in very high positions in their work but never got out of Under 21s. That was Cyril's charity work.

I'd continually ask him whether Petero Civoniceva was his love child. For a couple of years we didn't see a lot in Petero. It was like that with a number of them. Cyril'd say, 'Wayne, just hang in there.' I never let a kid go without talking to him. And invariably he'd be right.

He found Lote Tuqiri down at Woodridge, on the south-east outskirts of Brisbane, in the late '90s. No one knew about Lote except Cyril, and I was looking at the kid and wondering, Cyril, what are you thinking here? I watched him play and he'd miss tackles and he'd muck things up and he had an ordinary attitude to training … 'Cyril, what are you doing to me?'

'Wayne, he's got something. Just be a bit more patient.' Twelve months later, Lote was playing first grade and within two years, Origin.

Cyril brought Wendell Sailor down too. I'd seen Wendell play as a kid and said I didn't think he'd get the job done. He said, 'We'll give him a scholarship. He's got nowhere else to go. Just give him a go, will you?'

Next thing Kelvin Giles walks up and says, 'This Wendell guy is the best athlete I've ever coached. If he can't do anything else, he can run, this bugger.'

I said, 'Are you and Cyril partners?'

Cyril smiled. He's always had this beautiful smile. The kind that makes everybody feel good, the very way it is intended.

CYRIL DECIDED TO RETIRE at the end of the 2008 season. He always told Paul Morgan and me he would stay only as long as I wanted him or I stayed. With a tear in his eye, he came to me and said, 'Wayne, I always said I'd go when you go. It's time.'

He's 80 now. So soft and sincere. Lots of people claim to be Christians, and when they do I often think, I don't know if you really are a Christian, mate. Cyril never talks about being a Christian but he truly is. Does that make sense? To me, Cyril Connell epitomises what is wonderful about human nature and what kind and caring people can be and do.

CHAPTER 13

EVEN CHAMPIONS GET INTO RUTS

THERE WAS TROUBLE BREWING. At this stage, most of it was behind the scenes, ready to blow up in the not too distant future, but we all knew it was there. Whispers were about that the ARL was questioning just how legitimate some Broncos' players contracts were — in terms of the dollars we said we were paying them — and this would become a real issue at the start of 1995, when the League would publicly refuse to register the contracts of a large number of the Broncos' players. In March '94, John Ribot privately submitted his first draft of the Super League concept to News Limited CEO Ken Cowley.

The big issue as far as the contracts was concerned was the ARL's salary cap, which they'd introduced primarily so that poorly run clubs couldn't spend themselves into oblivion. For us, the issue came back to Wendell Sailor in particular. Wendell was now good enough to be playing for Australia, which he did at the end of 1994, going on the Kangaroo tour. We had him listed as being paid a certain amount of money but no one would believe it. It became a hell of a fight, that one.

The ARL was doing its best to enforce the salary cap, and the Broncos were very successful by this stage, having won the past two competitions. Everybody was having a whinge about us and I'm sure League chiefs John Quayle and Ken Arthurson were under great pressure. Word was out that the Broncos' monopoly was about to end.

We did have a wonderful football team, but our players had always signed for less to be at the Broncos. They all loved the environment and the lifestyle. They had always been prepared to take less to play here but it was not easy to convince other people of that — to outsiders, it's all about money. The only 'imports' we'd signed in the previous couple of years had been Glenn Lazarus, who we'd brought from Canberra, and Trevor Gillmeister, who'd come from the Roosters.

I'd never thought Paul Morgan and our board and John Quayle and Ken Arthurson were far apart in what they wanted for the game. A couple of times they tried to become friends but they couldn't make it work, the friendship thing. You have to remember that Porky, Barry Maranta, Steve Williams and Gary Balkin were all ex-players. They felt the game had been undervalued, that it was a better product than it was being given credit for. They felt the Broncos were already proving some points to do with better marketing, exposure, media attention and record home crowds — and those crowds have not been matched since. They wanted the whole game to be like that. They honestly believed that if the game was run just a little bit differently everyone could benefit.

And it was true: the game was healthy. I think Quayle and Arthurson had done an extremely good job. I'm certainly not a critic. But while the game was in good shape, I'm not so sure some of the clubs were.

IF PAUL MORGAN HAD A dream or belief, he wanted everyone else to dream and believe it. He was a great salesman. When you saw him turn up in his hard hat and foreman boots trying to sell you something, you knew it was because he believed in it with every fibre in his body. But there were people who found him too outspoken, who didn't want him telling them how to run *their* game.

I mention Porky more than the other three Broncos directors because he was such a dynamic individual. I sometimes wonder whether I'm being fair, but he was just such a dominant personality. The other directors were great and they certainly stood behind him — if they didn't at first, he grabbed them and pulled them along, and in the end they believed too. You can't talk about the Broncos without making Paul Morgan the centrepiece even when you know he wasn't always the centrepiece.

Super League was his idea. John Ribot would have put all the dressing around it, but Paul was the dreamer, and once he had a dream he was relentless about pursuing it. He would have had the board's backing because they all agreed about what was holding the game back, about why the game could be better ... should be better.

Pay TV was also a catalyst, and those contracts. It was all coming together. In the beginning, I tried to stay at arm's length but I understood that while a local club chairman or chief just didn't have the clout to walk into News Limited and tell Rupert Murdoch, 'Boy, have I got a deal for you,' Paul Morgan did.

BUT 1994 WAS ONLY the beginning. Super League remained behind the scenes for now — the football went on. The Broncos played the Tooheys Challenge pre-season final against Souths in Albury. We were staying at a water park hotel and I came out after lunch on game day and they were all on the slippery slide, having a hell of a good time. I got dirty with them, thinking this was not the way they should be preparing. And Souths played out of their socks.

That was the night Willie Carne took a swing at Les Davidson. He didn't realise who he was swinging at until it was too late. Souths coach George Piggins used to say you could put any man anywhere into a room for a fight with Les Davidson and he would back Les to walk out. And George knew about these things. Willie Carne didn't.

We lost by a point and were up and down all year. All of a sudden we were guilty of thinking we were better than we were. Alf was mouthing off in games, back-chatting referees. We'd never done that before. We were looking for easy options to the tryline, for soft plays, because we weren't prepared to pay the price any more.

For the first three rounds of competition we didn't win a game. Then we played Eastern Suburbs at the Sydney Football Stadium. There are times a coach goes to a game knowing that if he doesn't win that game he's in trouble. I went to the Easts game knowing I would probably survive a loss but that I'd most definitely be under the pump from the media and the fans. It begins with a significant defeat like that, and then it escalates.

It was April Fool's Day, right, April 1, and Easts had lost their first three games too. Mark Murray was their coach, but he wasn't to be that for much longer. We beat them 44–12 and won again the following week, at Penrith, to take some of the pressure off. But we wouldn't win more than two in a row until the middle of July, by which time we were running ninth and in grave danger of missing the finals. A sequence of four straight victories got us back in the five, and we managed to stay there — without ever really playing the sort of football we were capable of, the stuff that had won us comps in the previous two seasons.

IT WAS A BAD YEAR for coaches: Bill Gardner got the sack at the South Queensland Crushers even before they played a game in the premiership. Murray was dumped at Easts and Warren Ryan at Wests. Phil Gould resigned at Penrith before signing with Easts 12 hours later.

Of these, the one that had the biggest impact on me was Warren Ryan. He was a hell of a coach. Different from Jack Gibson. Jack had presence, persona. But in terms of a coach with a great football brain, great knowledge, Warren Ryan was your man. He introduced real structure to rugby league. As far back as Canberra in 1987 I'd heard all about Wokball, and marvelled at his nous. His players were the first to get instructions, game plans, to know that they had to get to certain points on the field and then do this play or that play. That's probably why he was at odds with champion halfback Steve Mortimer — Steve preferred to play off the top of his head.

I never had a relationship with Ryan. I stayed away from him because he looked crankier than me. I didn't know him at all, but I watched him and followed him and got information about him where I could. I asked players about him, and tried to work out what was going on with him. His teams always played tough. That was his catalyst: toughness.

IT WAS CERTAINLY TOUGH DROPPING Glenn Lazarus late in the season, but I'd kept him in the team as long as I could. It was a Kangaroo year and I didn't want to cost him his representative jersey — and I knew he just had to stand up to be picked for Australia.

I calculated that the Australian selectors wouldn't go away without Lazzo and I also calculated that he would be back in first grade by the end of the season. I also thought the change of scenery in the seconds would do him the world of good. So I dropped him and, oh, he was cranky big-time. The last time I saw him that day he was standing up against the fence and kicking the panels, waiting for the reserve grade to begin training. This guy had won five premierships.

But even the champions get into ruts. No one has ever had a perfect career and he was having a rough time. He might have had a bit of an injury, I'm not sure, but he'd played for New South Wales in their Origin clean sweep … which was nice for him, but not for Queensland.

He was only gone for a week, and came back to play well in our final-round 41–6 defeat of Balmain at ANZ, in front of the biggest premiership crowd of the season, and then in the finals, when we knocked out Manly but then lost to North Sydney. That was the end for the Broncos, though Lazzo would make the Kangaroos, along with Alf, Wendell, Mick Hancock, Steve Renouf and Kevin Walters. Norths led 15–14 late in the semi-final at the Sydney Football Stadium as Julian O'Neill lined up a penalty kick at goal to put us in front. It was certainly kickable by Julian's standards, but he missed it, and that summed up our season.

Much later in the night, when everything had settled down and I'd realised we couldn't have our time again, I said, 'Julian, how did you miss that kick? You never miss them from there.' Because he was a very good goal kicker.

He said, 'Coach, I'm on my run-up and I hear this guy in the crowd yell out, "You'll piss this one in, Julian!".' Of course that was the year he got into trouble for relieving himself in public at a casino.

We still had the best side, but we had been to the well and enjoyed too big a drink, niggling and back-chatting. We just didn't have the hunger.

Canberra won the grand final. We'd always dreamed of meeting them in the premiership decider there but it was never to be. The two greatest teams of the era were never to meet in a grand final.

CHAPTER 14

SUPER LEAGUE

KERRY PACKER SPOKE TO all the club chief executives the day they closed the door on Super League — 6 February 1995 — and after I heard how that meeting went I thought the new concept was gone forever. Mr Packer had explained to the club bosses that he held the TV rights, including the pay-TV rights, and that he wasn't going to hand them over to anyone else. Furthermore, he said, if anyone was planning to break that contract, he'd 'sue the pants off them'. After that, the ARL insisted the clubs all sign a 'Loyalty Agreement', binding them to the existing competition, and eventually they did. Later, those Agreements would be the subject of the infamous ARL–Super League court cases.

Over the next month or so, whenever anyone whispered anything about Super League I laughed and made comments like, 'Why waste our time talking about it. It's finished ... dead in the water.' But on the eve of our first competition game of the season we were in Auckland and John Ribot said he wanted to see me. I went to his hotel room and he began telling me what was going to happen with News Limited and Super League. I couldn't believe what I was hearing.

From this point on I kept notes, records, of all that happened with my involvement in Super League ...

Ribes said, 'We are going through the back door to sign players and coaches first and then get the clubs involved.' I thought, what a great move. Told me the type of money the top players would earn etc. It was pretty exciting stuff. He told me there would be a deal in it for me. I didn't ask much about myself but discussed my thoughts and how things should be handled. I left sworn to secrecy ...

We had a few more conversations in the following weeks, about issues and players, but each day I was seeing less of John. So I rang him and said, 'You're going to leave the Broncos, aren't you?'

He said, 'Yes' — and wondered how I knew ...

I said, 'Because I know you and I know you can't get away from the challenge of making this happen.' Ribes said, 'News Corp are deeply hurt by the way the League handled their request for a Super League and they won't give up this time. They are prepared for a long battle.'

On 26 March, we were playing Illawarra in Wollongong, and John wanted to see me. When I arrived, he said he was resigning the next day and they were moving to sign players. We talked about different things in regard to Super League. Again he spoke about me being contracted to them. But again I brushed it aside without any great discussion, confident I'd be looked after when the time came.

We beat the Steelers 34–20 and then John rang on the following Tuesday. He told me he wanted to talk to the players and sign them on the Wednesday. I said, 'No, I don't want any disruptions before the game on Friday night.' We were set to play the South Queensland Crushers, one of the clubs who'd joined the competition at the start of '95. Ribes rang again on Thursday and said he needed to sign some players fast.

I said, 'You know their numbers, just ring them, but only the ones you know will handle it and not worry about it. I'll organise the rest of the team for Saturday morning at 10.' It was my intention to tell them what was going on after the match. But then I went to the press conference after the Crushers game and was questioned about the fact that News Limited had released information about my signing.

As I had not signed — I had only had discussions, as already outlined — I was most upset.

I had already been appointed Queensland Origin coach for the 1995 series, which meant I couldn't sign anything that might be in conflict with that. And I hadn't agreed to join Super League, either, not formally. It was obvious I would be going, but there were issues for me.

So I was extremely disappointed, and when I went back to the team I never mentiond the proposed Saturday meeting. I thought if News Limited had misrepresented me, they would do the same to the players. I'd lost a fair bit of confidence in News Limited's ability to protect our best interests until the deals were done ...

> On Saturday morning John rang seeking the players. I told him what happened and that I would not at this stage enter into any agreement with News Ltd. He was not real happy. I explained my reasons, saying I may at a later stage talk to them (the players). I told him if he wanted he could talk to the players individually. I left and went to the farm for the weekend. (That sums me up.)
>
> I arrived back on Sunday night and Lazzo rang to say he'd had a phone call from the ARL wanting him to sign with them. It was then I realised that if the club was not to break up I had to make a move. I called a meeting for Monday at 10.15 at the club. There I informed the players of all I knew about Super League and my involvement etc. I told them what I believed their rights were and that their decision was exactly that — their decision. But under no circumstance were we to break up as a team.

So if we went to the ARL, we went. If we stayed with Super League, well, we stayed. We must all stay together through this. I gave them John's address and told them to go there and he would talk to them and negotiate a deal with them. They were under no obligation to sign, but I wanted everything finalised by Wednesday. If not, I'll consider leaving you out of the team.

I did not want this to affect the team. I did not want the ARL and Super League playing one player against the other. I went home, and when I arrived back at training they informed me they'd all signed with Super League except for Kerrod Walters. Kerrod will sign. Great relief.

Then the ARL flew to Brisbane in the Packer jet. James Packer and John Quayle met at the airport with a group of players that included Alf, Steve Renouf, Lazzo, Kerrod and Kevin, and offered them more than they'd been offered by Super League. But they all stayed strong, stayed at the Broncos. It was a defining moment for us.

JOHN RIBOT LATER SAID we had put the Super League coup behind time and were probably the reason they didn't end up with all the clubs. But that's not quite right. The North Queensland Cowboys, another of the new clubs, were the first hurdle. News Limited met with North Queensland straight after their game that weekend and their players and coach hung out on them. So that wasn't straightforward either. It seemed to me that News didn't have enough rugby league people on the ground. They had good business people, but not people who knew and understood rugby league.

I'd been sworn to secrecy. It was a pretty ugly time and I couldn't believe News Limited, who run the bloody papers, couldn't keep their mouths shut until the deals were done. My first loyalty is always with my players. It wasn't going to change that day or any other day. Like it or lump it.

I went back to see the QRL because I'd signed a three-year deal to coach Origin. The first thing they asked was whether I'd signed with Super League. I said I hadn't, which was true. I hadn't agreed to anything, but Super League had made me an offer by this stage. I asked QRL Chairman John McDonald and CEO Ross Livermore about the QRL's position on Origin players: would they select players who'd signed with Super League? They didn't believe they could or would.

That was fine. That was their position. Then they said that if I signed with Super League I certainly wouldn't be in a position to coach the Queensland team. It was on that day, at that moment in that office, that I realised I couldn't have a foot in both camps. I made the decision to resign as Queensland coach.

NONE OF US COULD believe the money we were being offered. Lazzo once said to me, and Kevvie said the same, that it wasn't a hard contract to sign: it meant doing the same job in the same town, living in the same house, and getting paid a truckload more money to do it. I could understand what Super League was trying to do. They were trying to upgrade everyone's contract because they believed that's what the game could generate.

At some stage John Ribot said, 'We regard you as one of the top coaches. You and another couple of guys.' And he offered me significantly more money than I was then earning. 'That's what we think you are worth and that's what we want to pay you,' he said.

But money doesn't interest me. It doesn't motivate me, and never has. I've always been able to do what I've wanted to do and only then have I worried about the money.

I know this attitude towards money has helped me enormously in life. Because it's never been a priority, I have been able to do things for the right reasons and the rewards have followed for the right reasons. It's easy after that, because you're already there, doing what you want to do. You're not there just because someone's come along and offered you a lucrative contract.

For me, it's a bit like selling your image for commercials or endorsements. Often people come to me and say, 'We'd like you to do this, Wayne, we'd like to use your profile. And there's going to be a fair bit of money in it for you.'

But I don't want to know about the money. I want to know what the promotion entails, what's my commitment, how they are going to use my image. Ten times out of 10 I feel uncomfortable with everything they're going to do, so I say no. Money distorts the picture and I don't want that. I want to know I'm comfortable doing whatever it is. I couldn't stand to see my face on a billboard and feel uncomfortable about that image — no matter how much money they were paying me, it wouldn't make that feeling go away.

Chris Johns was the same, and that's one of the many things I love about him. He might have been one of the worst paid people in Super League, yet no one fought one yard harder for their team-mates. No one gave up more and no one was more committed to Super League than Chris Johns, because he believed the other guys were entitled to it. Whatever he was given he was happy with. His selflessness and commitment to his mates and the concept itself were a great lesson to all of us.

I DON'T THINK EVERYBODY believed in the dream, because we were constantly being checked on. There was no trust in us, and the whole thing was on the brink a couple of times. Strangers kept coming to meetings of players and coaches that had been organised to discuss the latest developments, politicians and businessmen, and I was thinking, what have these people got to do with us? Then I found out they were there to make sure our meetings went to script, to plan. But they didn't have to worry about us.

English rugby league chief Maurice Lindsay turned up from the UK. He was the White Knight. Everyone kept talking about the White Knight. He arrived and was pretty involved in giving us direction, telling us what we should do and shouldn't do. He's a great guy, I love him, very charismatic — but it was obvious he had agendas to run.

I didn't like the fact they wouldn't trust us. I didn't feel comfortable about that. We were all in this together. We'd made the decision to go with them and a lot of us went for the right reasons and believed in the concept. And if you were a Bronco you believed in the concept because Porky and Ribes were involved and you just wouldn't let them down. Johnsy was in there fighting like hell for everybody. We were never going to let them down.

When you coach you can't preach one thing and do another. You have to keep a focus and one of my strengths is that I'm very focused. I won't let stuff that doesn't matter get to me. I won't let it distract me and I don't want to know about things that don't really concern the team — in this instance, the court cases and the innuendo. During the birth of Super League I did seek information but I didn't waste time sussing out what other people were doing. I was involved, but never to the detriment of the team. There were certainly plenty of headlines, and each day seemed to bring a different crisis.

One of the biggest headlines came when Canberra's Laurie Daley, Brett Mullins, Ricky Stuart and Bradley Clyde launched legal action over their non-selection in the ARL representative teams. I told Paul Morgan the case was a waste of time, that selection is a matter of opinion. I said, 'It's just somebody's opinion and you won't get the ARL on that.' News Limited stuck up for the players but it was never going to work. Like I said, News Limited really needed more rugby league people on the ground.

I also told John Ribot the ARL clubs wouldn't go down: 'They will play to the end. They'll lose all their money, they'll lose everything, but they will fight to the end. This isn't about business, it's different.' I told Porky the same: this is football, and football runs on emotion and passion.

I don't know about a lot of things in life but I know rugby league people. I've been one of them all my life and it's been embedded in me since childhood. I know their psyche and I know what they fight for. I know what their passion is.

I believe Super League was right at the time. My greatest disappointment is that we never got it right. I learned a great lesson from it — if you're going to do something this big, you've got to get the planning 100 per cent right. In the end, the battle itself became bigger than what we were fighting for. But that's just my lesson. You've got to get on with life.

SOMETIMES IT SEEMED like we'd all forgotten, but there was also a competition being played in 1995. At the end of the season, when I wrote my coach's notes that looked back on the year, I began by writing, 'When we were knocked out by Canterbury in the second week of the finals I commented to my close friends that we got what we deserved. Canterbury went on to win the premiership ...'

I continued ...

> After winning the pre-season and going undefeated for the first eight rounds of the competition we lost only five games out of 22. But the wheels fell off.
>
> One of our major weaknesses was that discipline off the field has been ordinary. I have a number of players who socialise too much. They find training an inconvenience to their social life. They are getting paid more and doing less. Football is not their Number One priority any more.
>
> The end result is a football team with a number of weaknesses. And those teams always get exposed at finals time.

I have addressed these problems by putting bandaids on them instead of making some hard decisions. I have been getting short-term results from the last two seasons but long-term failure. Example: losing in the play-offs so early. Short-term has been making the play-offs.

We had a tremendous amount of injury this year. There has not been one game where we could put our best team — our best backline — on the field. When the finals arrived we had injuries. Six of our top players. I'm not using this as an excuse. They are facts. The reasons above are why we failed.

Technically we are pretty solid and can go at other teams. Our weaknesses are locking the ball up in defence, not being aggressive enough in defence, the forwards not backing up and offloading ball.

I'm aware of the problems and I am working on them.

One thing I've learned is that if everything is not in order before you go into the finals you will not proceed very far and that was the reasoning with us. I have to address the problems I have mentioned and I'm prepared to be quite ruthless about it. I have to, otherwise the Broncos will be a team with no future.

I will record this just for the memory: I was offered a coaching position at another club by their chief executive. While it had a lot of appeal to me I turned it down for the following reasons: 1, I have never walked away from anything when it began to get tough. And right now it's tough at the Broncos but I'm not walking. They need me more than ever; 2, my family. The kids aren't keen. We came home from Canberra for them. I can hardly take them back; 3, the Broncos administration has been great to me and I could not let them down; 4, the players. They would feel I have betrayed them. I would never do that, so I cannot leave them.

CHAPTER 15

FOUR GOOD MEN

IN MANY WAYS, THE 1995 season came to be dominated by Super League and inevitably it's the first thing I go to if you ask me to recall the year. But it's not the only thing — there are also some people I quickly think about, football people, not because they were necessarily involved in the controversy, just because they had an impact on me that year, in one way or another ...

First, I think of Kerry Packer, who was involved in the drama from the day he realised his TV deals with the ARL were under threat. I only met him once and it was one of the greatest days of my life. He'd just had a heart bypass operation, and there he was at the Gabba in Brisbane for the one-day cricket match, Australia versus the West Indies, in the Fourex corporate box. It was quite a day. He was opinionated about everything and I loved his opinions. He told it how it was and he didn't miss anyone.

Some Channel Nine people he employed were in the next corporate box, and at one stage he went in there and told them in no uncertain manner they should be all at work and to stop wasting his money. I remember him saying to Bernie Power that he had great admiration for him. Bernie, of course, ran Power's Brewing, the Bronco's first jersey sponsor. Kerry said: 'Any man who uses his family name in his company has to have a great amount of courage. You've made a great product. You've done a great job.'

I knew Kerry was great mates with Bob Fulton, because he told me all about the Australian team — and about a couple of players he didn't like (who shall remain nameless). You know, I'd heard Bob talk about the same players the very same way. In fact, he'd dropped them by then.

But Mr Packer was an engaging person. My great regret is I only got to spend five hours with him.

THEN THERE IS LOCKY. Cyril Connell and I had watched this kid play in the Queensland Under-17 championships in 1994 and I just liked him. In the frenetic game that is schoolboy football he was somehow calm. I said, 'We've got to get that kid, Cyril.'

And Cyril said, 'Don't worry, we've got him.'

Then he came into the Under-18s in 1995 and he was playing there for half the season before he came to us. Again, I watched him play and again he just had this calmness about him. He was playing five-eighth and a few other positions.

Anyway, we got a few injuries. And we got to the Parramatta game in round 13 and it was between this kid and a young Ben Walker as to who came in. I talked to the reserve-grade coach Steve Calder and he had a huge wrap on this kid, on Darren Lockyer.

Ben Walker was a year or two older and certainly had a big future too. He'd been a schoolboy superstar, but I just liked the way Darren never seemed to get flustered. He always seemed calm and in control, even at 18 years of age.

So I gave him the benefit of the doubt and he came off the interchange bench against Parramatta and was quite sensational. At the time we had Kevin Walters at five-eighth and he was in the prime of his career and we had Alf at halfback, so that wasn't going to change. But we still had to find a place for this kid. I noticed him at training catching a few high balls. As usual, he looked very, very comfortable. We made him into a fullback.

He was a lovely boy, well brought up. You can't help but like him. Darren is introverted by nature, and a lot of his challenges have come out of that. He's not perfect and he knows that, admits it himself, so I'm not trying to make him out to be perfect, but he is one of those guys who took his football seriously while never taking himself too seriously. That's the key to this business. So when he failed he would laugh at himself a bit, not beat himself up about it. That allowed him to come back the next week and play a greater game than we might have seen him play because he wanted to get the taste out of his mouth.

We'd see a great example of that in New Zealand in 1998 when he played his first Test match. He had an absolute shocker in the Test on the Friday, dropping balls and missing tackles, after there'd been a huge debate over whether he or Newcastle's Robbie O'Davis should have been picked at fullback for Australia.

Darren came home and two days later was outstanding for the Broncos. They pressured him with every kick and every ball because of his performance on the Friday night. They figured he'd be fragile. Instead, he was calm and devastating at the same time and we won by 60.

IN 1995, GORDEN TALLIS was a Queenslander playing for St George. The ARL had spoken to the Dragons, but Phil Gould, who was working with the ARL during the Super League battle, annoyed Gordie when he said, 'He is an interchange player, that's all he is.' Gould didn't rate him.

So Gorden said, 'Let's go to Super League and see what they want to do.' Ribes is a pretty astute guy and he wanted Gorden, but he wanted him to go to North Queensland and the Cowboys. That's where Gordie is originally from — he was born in Townsville and played his early footy there.

But Gordie refused to go to Townsville. He wanted to play for the Broncos. And because Super League regarded him so highly, as too valuable to lose, Gorden Tallis turned up at our place. I was struck by his passion, the firmness of his convictions. He wouldn't play for us until 1997, but it was 1995 that I first came into contact with him.

Or was it? I'd actually met him once before, years before. The Broncos were in Townsville to play a testimonial game for Gene Miles and Greg Dowling, and this big, brash kid appeared through the darkness.

'You Wayne Bennett?' he said.

I said, 'Yeah, I am.' I didn't know who he was but it was obvious he had a ton of front.

He said, 'I'm Gorden Tallis.'

I said, 'Are you?'

He said, 'My brother Wally is playing for the Broncos.'

I said, 'He is.'

'Well,' he said, 'you've got the wrong one. I'm the one who can play.'

I just thought, holy smoke!

FRED DALY WOULD NEVER have been so brash, but he was from a different time, different place. Fred was a long-standing politician of great wit and I first met him when I went to coach in Canberra. I went around to his house three or four times after he kindly offered to help me with public speaking. Because he was a great orator, I hung on his every word and even today I still use this great line he gave me to begin public addresses. I probably do it as much to honour his memory as anything else.

You know when they introduce you and they say all these wonderful things about you, waxing lyrical? I get up, pause, and everybody is not expecting me, of all people, to have a sense of humour. I just get up and say, 'Well, after that introduction I can't wait to hear myself speak.'

Works every time. Loosens you up. He told me a couple of others I still use occasionally.

Fred Daly loved Newtown. The Bluebags. The battlers of the League. He'd say, 'Every time we won the toss, we'd do a victory lap' … New coach says, 'OK boys, take up your normal positions', and they all went and congregated under the goalposts. I know it's an oldie, but Fred could always make you laugh.

He said you should always use a dais when you talked, and that you should give the same effort whether you were talking to one, 101 or 1001. He told me if you don't strike oil in five minutes, stop boring.

I went to his funeral in 1995. Fred Daly was just one of those guys, a bit like Kerry Packer, who you'd like to see every day of the week — and you'd be a better person for it.

CHAPTER 16

WHO ARE THE BRONCOS?

I'm going through a period of depression. It's 15 September 1996 — 24 hours after our exit from the play-offs. For the past three seasons, from 1994, we've been beaten in the second match of the finals series and these moments of depression have been coming and going all day. And they will continue up until the grand final.

It's the disappointment of not playing our best football when it matters most. I've been through it before so I know how to cope with it — but it's still not nice.

In 1994 we were never going to win, and in 1995 we were not good enough to beat Manly, Canterbury or Canberra.

But in 1996 I thought we were good enough to at least make the grand final. Manly was the only team I thought could beat us. I believed everything was in place, but the two finals matches proved me wrong.

The major issue that hurt us most of all was our lack of ball control … our inability to do the little things right: catching high balls, being desperate enough and picking up loose balls on the ground. We'd make an error and then compound it straight away. Make another error. Drop the ball … give away a penalty … miss a tackle.

I thought we had it all under control but in the pressure of finals football we went back to our old habits. Our ball control was dismal compared to our opponents, and in both games we had to come back from at least 12–0 down. Both times we came back by scoring three tries but it wasn't enough.

Glenn Lazarus and Darren Smith took no part in the finals series because of injuries. Andrew Gee broke his hand and missed the first final. Steve Renouf, Kevin Walters, Peter Ryan, Alfie Langer — they had only one good game out of the two. Alf just tried too hard in the Cronulla game, got frustrated with officials and in the end had a poor game. Michael Hancock was not at his best in either game. Andrew Gee was outstanding in his only game. Of our senior players, Kevin Walters was our best. It was our senior players who created most of our poor handling.

We had a team goal of completing 75 per cent of our sets of six tackles in each half.

In our 21 competition matches we completed this goal in the first half on seven occasions. In the second half we completed it on eight occasions. We completed the average of 75 per cent in both halves on only two occasions. These were our two best performances of the year as well — against Canberra (50–16 in round 8) and Auckland (38–6 in round 22).

In the first finals match against Norths we completed 11 out of 20 sets in the first half and 10 out of 20 in the second half. Norths, as an example, completed 20 sets out of 26 for 75 per cent in the first half and 18 out of 19 in the second half, which is 94 per cent.

It was a huge difference.

At the Broncos we turned a lot of things around in 1996. Players drank a lot less alcohol. They trained better than they had ever trained. They took a lot more responsibility. They scored more tries than any other Broncos team. They had the fewest tries ever scored against the Broncos.

I repeat, we did a lot of things right. I'm not going to throw out the baby with the bath water. I know what I have to do and this involves making some very hard decisions with players and I intend to do it in a very determined and committed manner.

Regarding our on-field performances, I need to do the following:
- Reteach them not to beat themselves. How? Ball control. Penalties that can be avoided. Taking better options in opposition half. Not doubling up our mistakes.
- Defence. Better marker defence. Off the line quicker.
- Improved taking and courage of catching the high ball.

THESE COACH'S NOTES I WROTE at the end of the '96 season don't make for very happy reading. At the beginning of the year, I'd got all the players together and told them straight: 'The great majority of you have been playing first grade for a number of years and if you're in that group I feel like I'm wasting too much time on you.' We had a lot of young guys coming through and they needed more of my time. The older, more experienced players had to take more responsibility for their own performances.

I could no longer spend long periods of time drilling them on the things I'd already done with them. If their attitudes didn't change and we didn't turn things around, I'd be forced into a position where I'd have to let players go at the end of the year.

I wasn't trying to threaten them; I was simply telling them exactly how it was. Some coaches, even parents, like threatening people. I don't, because they can't be thinking it's a bit of a con or just hot wind. I also try not to do that because I really want to be accountable and, more importantly, I want them to be accountable.

I've had players come to the Broncos from other clubs, and I've had to tell them they weren't playing well. They've looked at me and said: 'You're just trying to gee me up, aren't you?'

I've said, 'No, I'm not trying to gee you up — the facts are you aren't playing well.'

They've said, 'Well, where I come from the coach might have said that but he didn't really mean it.'

And I've said, 'Well, you know I'm not going to tell you something I don't mean.'

So in that meeting at the beginning of the year I told the whole group that if they didn't take responsibility I'd make the hard calls. I had gone as far as I was going to go with them and it was now time for them to deliver.

Our first competition game was supposed to be against Auckland but we had to forfeit: the players were on a semi-strike, the Super League officials were in court and no one was really sure what the hell was happening. Justice James Burchett of the Federal Court had ruled against Super League, but an appeal was lodged. There were the ARL players on one side and the Super League guys on the other.

GORDEN TALLIS HAD SIGNED WITH us from ARL-aligned St George but the Dragons wouldn't release him. So he made a very strong, firm decision which showed great courage — he decided to sit out the 1996 season. Gordie spent the year doing a little bit of training, but not too much, because he wasn't keen on training if he didn't have to do it. The club looked after him really well. In fact, he won the Broncos club man of the year award, working hard as our leading 'promo boy'.

He is good at talking, Gordie, loves talking. And he is generous with his time. He can talk it up in any company and match it with just about anybody with his quickness of mind and mouth. And he has the physical attributes to back up anything he says. When he played, every so often, those crazy eyes would start rolling like cash registers. He could be be very intimidating, and he could end any argument with a punch ... that's not the way he operates, but you knew he could resolve things in that manner if it was.

Of all the players I have coached, he was the one I had to be most careful with; I couldn't get him too excited before a game. He was just dangerous. No way could you tell him to go out there and do a job on someone. That would have been like giving a gangster a machine gun and telling him not to kill anybody. He had that flash in him, that scary spark that only the really aggressive ones have. They have to learn how to control it and it is a battle for them all their lives.

They love the confrontation. Gordie loved it. He lived for that moment, and as a coach I had to recognise that and manage it, because without management his reputation could be shot in a blur of madness.

They'll never be saints. You have to live with their indiscretions, but at the same time you have to support them and understand the responsibility you have: to make sure you're not the reason that moment has occurred. They know it will always live within them, just under the surface, forever ready to explode. It doesn't have to be an overly aggressive game or a complex situation that starts it — it can just happen from nowhere. Snap.

This intimidating factor is also one of the reasons they are so good. No one talks about it, but the opposition knows it's there. And no one wants to stir it up if they can avoid it, unless they are a little crazy too.

People like Gorden Tallis won't back off you. Doesn't matter if you have an axe in your hand, they're going to keep coming at you.

Once we were doing a leadership training course at Canungra, just outside Brisbane, and I sat in on the briefing with Gorden. The officer in charge gave him a grid reference, a location, and told Gorden he wanted him to set up observation posts around the village to observe the enemy. He said the enemy had been going into the village. 'They've been intimidating the local people,' he added, 'sexually molesting the inhabitants … making an absolute nuisance of themselves.' He told Gorden to get his men to stay in their concealed position. 'Make note of their movements and report back to us in two hours' time,' he said.

Gorden had been selected as a leader of his group, about six or eight guys, and I could see him talking to them. It was killing me not knowing what he had said, so about 10 minutes later, just before they moved out, I grabbed Ben Walker, who was also in the group. I said, 'What were Gorden's instructions to you?'

'We have to go to this grid reference on our maps,' said Ben. 'We find that, and Gordie said then we find this mob of bastards. They've been coming in, bashing up the old people, looting the place and forcing themselves on everybody. He said soon as we see them we have to go in there and bash the crap out of them.'

That's one of the reasons why, in 2001, I made Gorden Tallis captain of the Broncos.

I knew he might not always follow orders, but I also knew he would most definitely seize the moment and take whatever action he deemed necessary. Gorden always had a high sense of righteousness. He couldn't sit there and watch the wrong thing being done by anybody — he'd buy into it.

WE WON OUR FIRST EIGHT matches straight in 1996 and played some good footy, but the team meeting we had at the beginning of the year would eventually ring loudest for Willie Carne, who went to rugby union at the end of the season, Kerrod Walters and Alan Cann, who both went to the Adelaide Rams, Chris Johns and Michael Hancock.

Kerrod was a great loss. He was a wonderful guy but he probably needed a change. His heart was always in the right place. Alan Cann needed a change too. He had come to us as a kid and made his first-grade debut in 1990, but by '96 he'd got into a comfort zone. That happens. It's no one's fault, it just happens. Chris Johns retired — he'd probably stayed a year too long, distracted by Super League. He also had a busted arm and too many birthdays.

Mick Hancock had a pretty disappointing year in a lot of areas and needed to make some changes for '97 if he wanted to keep playing for us. I have to say that, to his credit, I guaranteed him nothing and he still backed himself to stay. He accepted the challenge, changed some of his habits and went on to play another four years for the Broncos.

Loyalty is a huge issue for us all. I think most of us regard ourselves as pretty loyal but, as Kelvin Giles always said, you have to be loyal to performance. Kelvin's advice has helped me enormously with regard to the hard decisions. He showed me that loyalty relates not just to the effort put in on the field; it has to be across the whole gamut of what you do.

You expect people to have hard times and a bit of bad luck, and that's where your loyalty comes in — you stick with them and do what you can to get it right. That's what I was doing at the beginning of the year in that team meeting. They were going to make the choices themselves.

Players like Willie and Kerrod and Alan had all been tremendously loyal to the Broncos and I'm sure they felt the pain, questioning themselves and questioning me. I thought back to the Gillmeister time, to Wally Lewis. Always, the one over-riding thing for me was my loyalty to the Broncos. I used to ask myself, 'Who are the Broncos?' The Broncos are not me, they are not the board, they are not the players — they are the fans who pay their money every week to come and see their footy team play. The fans can't run the club so they entrust that job to us. We have to do that, and guard the brand that is the Broncos.

At the end of the previous season I remember one of my coaching staff saying, 'You've stuck with some of these guys for too long. You need to make some really hard decisions.' Deep in my heart I knew he was right, and that I'd been trying to ignore and avoid it. It's not my nature to be ruthless. It's not who I am. I became defensive in that conversation because I knew he didn't have to make the decisions and because he was telling me what I already knew. Still, I had to hear it. I showed my loyalty to those players by giving them the opportunity to prove me wrong or right.

AND ALF LANGER WON THE Dally M Player of the Year award. The only time Alf ever played badly was when he was nervous. Not nervous, really — he was always nervous — but when he thought too much about the outcome. I'll never forget the day we played Cronulla in the finals in 1996. He asked to see me. He had never before asked to see me leading into a game, and he never did again, and I coached him in over 200 matches.

The fans loved Alf, because he didn't play for himself: he played for his parents, his team-mates and the fans — he didn't want to fail his parents and his team-mates and he hated failing all those fans who idolised him. It was a real driving force for him. Our greatest moments were when he'd come to me after a game and say: 'We let no one down today, coach.'

And I'd say, 'No mate, we didn't.' I knew he was happy inside because he knew he hadn't failed anybody.

This day before the Cronulla game he started asking me, 'What happens if we lose today against Cronulla? What will people say? How many people will we let down?'

I soon realised what was going on. I said, 'Mate, you've got to get all that stuff out of your head. You're not going to play well if you keep thinking like this.'

'I'll be right,' he said. 'I'm pumped up today. Keen to play.'

I knew then that we were in trouble.

Anyway, he ran out and played accordingly: trying hard but totally ineffective. Maybe a week or so later, I said to him, 'What happened in that last game? How come you played the way you did?'

'I was running out the tunnel,' he said, 'and I just didn't want to be there. I'd played the game so many times in my head that I was mentally and physically worn out.' This is what sent him into retirement two and a half years later — the weight of expectation. He fought it all his career but this was the day it caught up with him. It's a real burden, expectation, if you don't learn to manage it. This day the expectation overtook his performances.

IN MAY OF '96 THE BRONCOS announced the signing of Anthony Mundine for the following season. It was a traumatic time. I didn't want Anthony Mundine. I said it publicly at the time, I said it privately, I said it everywhere.

The Gorden Tallis signing had created a lot of dissension within the Super League ranks because it had left some people looking at Brisbane as the powerhouse … and now it was becoming even more powerful. No one was in a harder position than John Ribot, because he'd been the Broncos' chief executive and was now the Super League chief executive. He was trying to convince people he wasn't playing favourites. Gorden was a major coup and he was the right fit for Super League, but he was meant to go to Townsville. However, Gorden said that if he didn't play for the Broncos he was going back to St George. Sure, I knew what a talent he was and was excited about getting him, but it soured everybody else.

That had just settled down when all of a sudden Anthony Mundine was signed by Super League. He went to a Canterbury training session. He didn't like it one bit and he rang me up. Chris Anderson, the Canterbury coach, to this day, I'm sure, doesn't believe it happened this way, but it did. Mundine rang me and I rang Chris Anderson. I said, 'Chris, I don't want to take Anthony Mundine. I'm trying to talk him into staying down there but he is adamant about coming here.'

Anthony was great mates with Gorden. They played at St George together.

I did everything I possibly could to talk him out of coming. But again, he was a huge talent and no one didn't want him playing Super League. First Gorden, then Anthony Mundine — and we had a pretty hot footy team anyway. There was so much animosity towards us at this stage from the other clubs, particularly from the coaches.

The other great mistake we made — and we still feel terrible about it to this day — was parading him in a Broncos jersey in the middle of the '96 season when he was still under a contract and playing for St George. It was bad taste. We got it totally wrong that day.

ANTHONY WASN'T PLAYING FOR us until the following season, but there was no waiting for young Shane Webcke. I'd watched him play junior football in Toowoomba and we'd brought him along slowly. That's one thing we've always done well at the Broncos: bring the young guys along slowly, without too much pressure.

From the very beginning Webby just played flat out. He didn't play with any brains at all. Pretty smart guy, but didn't play that way. If he had a breath of oxygen in his body he would run as hard as he could and if he had none he wouldn't do anything. Once the oxygen returned he would take off again. If he had the ball he would run as hard as he could into as many guys as he could find. If he didn't have the ball he would hit you as hard as he could. I loved him. I had never seen a guy play like him. He was either full on or full off.

The first year he came down he played for Brothers. I went to watch him play the Under-19s grand final against Redcliffe, who had a strong forward pack. He took the whole lot of them on. I really felt sorry for him by the end of that afternoon. He got a bit of a hiding.

I knew we had something special. It was just a matter of teaching him discipline and how to play more consistently, without going in bursts. The process began.

He turned up at The Gap, where the Broncos do their pre-season training. It's pretty tough at The Gap and Webby couldn't run the hills. He was working at the Commonwealth Bank at the time and he couldn't get to training until after everyone else had left, but he still came, night after night, and he kept coming until he was able to reach the top. That epitomises who he is.

There was never a problem with Shane Webcke. He was always good, always punctual. Did the right thing. The skeleton of who he was to become was there: he was always very perceptive, always learning from different people. I knew he could play but I didn't realise what he would become, not initially. He had to always give his best. That's who he is. He's the only player I've coached who always trained the same way he played. He'd bash you at training. If you were carrying the ball, he'd put a hit on you. He'd want to hit at training because that was his psyche.

I remember taking the team to England, and it was so cold. We'd pull up in the bus and he'd be sitting at the front. He'd have his shorts and T-shirt on, and he'd jump out of the bus and start running straight away. Not sitting around talking, not complaining about the weather — just straight out and running. I took him on two Kangaroo tours and World Club Challenges and he was always straight out of the bus. Willing himself, steeling himself: 'This is what I've got to do. I'm going to do it properly. I'm not going to make any excuse. I'm not going to whinge about it.'

We did a thing in Western Australia when he was 20, maybe 21. We hired this guy from the SAS. We were over there playing a game in the pre-season, and we stayed for a few days to do a training camp. I wanted to piss them off … there was a bit of moaning around the place and I wanted it to end. It had to be 1996, because I remember Johnsy being there.

So we got these three rubber dinghies and they had to paddle them. They were like big tractor tyres, big circular things. They were hard to handle and it required great teamwork to get them anywhere. It took them hours to work it out. They had to paddle 100 metres offshore, but they couldn't do it until they worked out how to work together. They were bitching and carrying on. In the end the penny dropped but they were really filthy with me. Had to be angry with somebody.

We came back to the bus and I thought, I'll finish these blokes off here. I said to the bus driver, 'There's a restaurant and bar, showers even, a few kilometres up the road — let's head there.'

They all got on the bus, making snide remarks at me, carrying on. I didn't care. Off we drove, for about 20 minutes. They all thought they were going to have a shower, freshen up and have lunch. As we pulled up I said, 'OK guys, get the dinghies off the back, we're going back out and we're going to get this right.' Well, you should have heard them. 'We're not doing this …'

I said, 'Guys, I'm telling you, we are doing it.'

All of a sudden Webcke stood up. He was pissed off too. I could see that. He said, 'Guys, if we have to do it, let's do it and get it over with.' That was the bottom line. He got up, stormed off the bus and started getting the dinghies off the back. That was always his attitude. If it's got to be done, let's just get the thing done and then we can get on with our lives.

By the time they all got off the bus I told them they could go and have a shower and have a few beers as well. They were cuddling me and kissing me and yahooing. That was Webcke's strength — everyone else was whingeing, but he just stood up and said, 'Hey, if we've got to do this, let's go and get it done.'

ON 4 OCTOBER 1996, THREE Federal Court judges overturned Justice Burchett's original ruling in favour of the ARL, opening the door for a 10-team Super League competition the following year. We were excited to finally have a competition, but didn't know where we would end up. As John Ribot was prone to say at the time: 'Maybe with only the middle of a donut, mate.'

CHAPTER 17

JUSTIN

I SPEND A LOT OF TIME with my son Justin and I love him as much as I love my life.

The thing you can't help but love about him is his spirit. Big Jus has had so many bad days with seizures and goodness knows what, but he doesn't whinge. He doesn't feel sorry for himself. Every day, he does the best he can. Every day. And in that sense he makes things a lot easier for us.

In other ways, he is a bloody handful. He is 24-hour care. You've always got to know where he is, and what's going on. When he was a little boy, he had behavioural problems because of his disability and Trish and I made a conscious decision that we didn't want to be going to people's places, as a family, and them cheering when we left — everybody thanking God the Bennetts are going … and hoping they won't come back in a hurry.

So we worked extremely hard over a long, long period, right up until today, to have Justin well mannered, and it is one of our proudest achievements. He is wonderfully mannered. He is so good now that he dobs in the other kids — he has got into so much trouble over time and he thinks now it is their turn. He gets great pleasure out of it.

If they don't say 'thank you' or 'please', he says, 'Hey Wayne' — he calls me Wayne most of the time — 'Hey Wayne, Joe didn't say thank you or ta.' Before Joe and Will, my grandkids, could talk Justin would be dobbing them in for bad manners. It's one of his kicks in life, dobbing people in.

Justin loves his football jerseys. As soon as a logo changes he picks it up straight away. You can't convince him that it's not the case; his old jersey has been superseded. He knows the number of every player. If he says he wants to wear a certain club jersey with a certain number on it, well, he means it. You can search the house looking for the Sharks No. 6 ... he's like a woman trying to get dressed to go out, saying 'I've got nothing to wear. What am I going to wear?' ... It doesn't matter if you are in a hurry, running late. There'll be no change until he finds the Sharks No. 6. You can say, 'Justin, you haven't got a number 6.' I've tried that; it doesn't work. You keep looking, and sure enough, there it is.

On match days, he will dress depending on the team he is barracking for, which is usually the one playing against the Broncos. One year we'd lost seven games in a row and just scraped into the play-offs. We hadn't won a game since beating Melbourne in July and suddenly it was the middle of September, two months later, and we were playing Penrith, who'd finished first. We had a hell of a dig down in Sydney that day. We were down 12–4 in the penalty count and running into a gale force wind. When we were running into the wind the referee found fault with everything we did but when they were running into the wind ... I don't normally go on about refs, but I did that day.

Anyway, we couldn't have given any more. The season was over and we were devastated. Plus we'd lost eight games in a row. So we flew home to Brisbane that same night. It was pretty late, probably about 11pm. I pulled into the carport and he must have heard the car coming and the door go up. He was on the landing as I pulled the car up and he had a Penrith jersey on. I was really peeved off. There was a whole lot of crap being thrown at us. I was walking towards him and he walked down and threw his arms around me and gave me a big cuddle. He said, 'My team won. Your team lost.' Well, I felt like knocking him out, but at the same time he just put it all into perspective for me. I suppose that's one of the great things he's been in my life. He does put things into perspective for me.

He has taught me to be much calmer and not get uptight about a whole lot of issues that you can get uptight about, but at the end of the day mean nothing at all. The game was over. The season was over. It was all over: 'Get on with your life, Wayne, because I'm getting on with mine. I'm going for Penrith and we've just won and tough luck, Dad.'

He's highly coordinated. It's quite amazing considering the amount of medication he's on. One day, my wife Trish took one of his tablets by accident. He takes four of these a day. She was a bit off colour and grabbed what she thought was a cold tablet for herself at the same time she was giving him his afternoon medication. She was distracted and put the wrong tablet in her mouth. It was about 3.30 in the afternoon. About an hour and a half later, Trish said she felt a little bit sleepy, so she put her head on a pillow and when she got up she couldn't walk straight. She was bouncing off the walls. She went to bed that night and slept for 14 hours straight, and still reckons it's the best night's sleep she'd ever had. Justin takes four of those tablets a day and lives life to the fullest.

He can play cricket. He can pass a footy, he can catch a footy. He's a good pool player. He has an eye on him like a dead fish. His coordination skills are very, very high for his disability. He's taller than me, and he's a bit like royalty. Gets everything done for him and likes playing on it. You can say to him, 'Justin, can you please give me a lift with this?' and he'll say, 'Oh, I've got a sore shoulder, Wayne. I've got a sore leg.' He always wants to go to the hospital. Loves hospitals. He's always got a bad back. As soon as he gets a scratch he has to go to the hospital and there's a bag packed ready to go. It has about 20 football jerseys in it, one pair of underpants and nothing else. If he gets a bruise on his face, if he's had a seizure and hit his head, people say to him, 'What happened to you, Justin?' He says, 'Wendell Sailor hit me.' He's always blaming Wendell for everything.

He brings a lot of joy to a lot of family and friends. No one minds having Justin around.

Opposition clubs are great with him. We take him to the footy but he doesn't like sitting in the stands with Trish (though he's getting better). When we played at ANZ Stadium against Canberra one year, he started on the Broncos bench but in the second half he ended up on the Raiders' bench, besides their coach, Tim Sheens. In 2008, when we played Wests Tigers, he told me Tim Sheens (now with the Tigers) was his coach and he was going for the Tigers and he wanted to sit on their bench. Afterwards, he went into their dressing room and the players were great with him. Benji Marshall, I understand, was excellent. I can't stop him going into the rooms; he just gets dirty and digs in. He's very, very stubborn. Got a bit of his dad in him. Once he digs in, nothing is going to change his mind. Nothing.

His best ever was a night Parramatta beat us and he disappeared with Eels coach Brian Smith. Justin went in there, and finished up wearing one of their jumpers and singing the team song with them. That was the end for me. I said, 'Trish, he is not going to the football any more. I can't have him singing the other team's song.'

At times I look at him and can't help but wonder what might have been. Justin is the same age as Darren Lockyer and Ben Ikin, my son-in-law. It's when their birthdays come around ... it's something I've tried not to dwell on too much because it just breaks your heart. Takes you nowhere. But I can see traits in him, you know. He has a real sense of righteousness and fairness. You can see that. I say to myself that he probably would have been a policeman or something like that. He knows what he wants. And he doesn't like people getting rough: he realises straight away when it's not fun and gets a bit uptight about it.

Once, when we were playing cricket, I bowled to him underarm and he blew up a treat. He has a wonderful eye and wants no favours. At Christmas we go to the park to play cricket with the kids and there he is, this big guy, taller than me, gangly, and I'm holding his hand to get him across the road and helping him down the stairs — he looks terribly uncoordinated. Then he faces up and they bowl to him and he goes whack. Hits them straight back over their heads, and they look at me as if to say, where did that come from? This big grin stretches across his face.

Then he starts the Dennis Lillee run-up and comes in to bowl. He has a pretty good bowling action. Again the kids think, what's he going to do? He bowls straight all the time and the kids' wickets are rattling and they look at me and say, 'How did he do that?' You throw him the ball and everything looks so uncoordinated, but somehow the ball sticks for him. Quite remarkable.

Once, at Broncos training, I remember getting frustrated with first-grade players not being able to catch high balls. I said, 'Justin, come and show them how to catch the high ball, will you?' So I put up a high ball and he took it beautifully. Everybody looked. All the boys were standing and clapping and cheering.

He loves all that.

He's my mate. I think it's more than a father-and-son relationship. We're both busy doing the best we can.

CHAPTER 18

COACHING TOUGH

STEVE RENOUF WAS A shot bird until we played Halifax midyear in the World Club Challenge.

The Pearl needed a kill — he was playing with no confidence. He'd been out for a long period of time with injury and he was playing tentatively, with no real zip in him, as if he didn't want to be there.

The game against Halifax was our third of three in England. It was part of a Super League competition involving Australian and European clubs that was played on top of the Super League premiership, and I was hoping we wouldn't have a tough game. Halifax weren't going too well in the English comp that year and we got our wish, and Steve made some breaks and scored a couple of magical tries. I think he scored four that night, actually, as only Steve can do. I knew then that he would be right.

The previous year, we'd arrived in America on an end-of-season trip and took the players to a Denver Broncos game — we had a longstanding relationship with the like-named American football club. Only the night before Evander Holyfield had fought Mike

Tyson in Las Vegas and he'd beaten Tyson. At the time Tyson was considered just about invincible. No one could believe it.

Anyway, at the Denver game I was introduced to a guy named Jerry Glanville. He'd coached the Houston Oilers and Atlanta Falcons in the NFL. I'd read a book on him — loved him. He was quite a character. Before big games he'd leave tickets for Elvis at the box office because, one, he couldn't believe he'd died, and two, he couldn't believe that he'd miss such a big game even if he had.

This night in Denver, Jerry was working as a commentator for one of the US cable networks and we got talking about Australia and sport in general. Some of our Broncos had met him on an earlier trip to Atlanta — I wasn't on that trip — and given him a Drizabone as a gift and, you wouldn't credit it, he was wearing it this night. He just loved it, he said.

Jerry Glanville knew Holyfield really well because the great fighter was from Atlanta. He said that about three months out from meeting Tyson, Holyfield had lost all his confidence. He wanted to call the fight off. Even his sparring partners were beating him up. Holyfield was going really bad.

Jerry said: 'I had a yarn to a couple of his handlers, trainers, and suggested they employ a couple of bum sparring partners who couldn't fight, just to let him have some victories and rebuild his confidence.' And that's exactly what happened. He began to beat up on the guys who couldn't fight — the bums, as Jerry called them — and rediscovered his confidence.

The Halifax game did the same for Steve Renouf: it was the turning point. All of a sudden the breaks were going his way again. It wasn't against a top-quality team, but I still gave him huge wraps because I didn't care who the hell he was running past as long as he was running past someone again. He got his footwork going and his confidence followed. That's all he had to do. He turned everything around and played great all the way to the grand final.

STEVE RENOUF IS ONE of those players I wish had never retired. I just loved watching him play. He was the most casual of guys. He didn't have a great interest in rugby league away from playing and he didn't have a lot of interest when he was training, either. He just managed to do what he had to do. He was non-competitive at training.

Alf and those guys would be killing themselves to beat each other in the training drills and Steve would be down the back somewhere, twirling his hair in his hands, standing around. I'd say, 'Pearl, are you going to have a bit of a dig here, or what?'

He'd say, 'I'll save it for Sunday, coach.' That was pretty much his attitude. He was always saving it till Sunday.

A lot of centres and three-quarters from that era became good dummy-half runners. Steve was very capable of doing that but hardly ever did. I said to him one day, 'Are you all right to have a run from dummy-half, mate?' I wasn't pushing him about it.

He said, 'Oh no, I'm a strike centre! I don't want to use my gas up. When I get the ball I want to be as fresh as I can be so I can run and use my legs as best I can.' It's a pretty good point, actually. That's what he was, an absolute strike weapon ... a premium centre with very few peers. As I've said before, Michael Hancock should have scored a lot more tries in his great career, but Pearl didn't need to pass to him because he was mostly going to score anyway.

Kevin Walters was a wonderful five-eighth, the right man at the right time for the Broncos. Just about the entire backline was playing for Australia, and he was the conductor. He provided great delivery, lots of options and with very few exceptions the blokes outside him always got the ball at the right time. Kevvie did get Johnsy a couple of times, but never Steve — the Pearl knew that it wasn't on and just didn't turn up for him.

IN 1997, STEVE RENOUF scored three blistering tries in the grand final win over Cronulla. Another highlight was a tackle by Peter Ryan on the Sharks' David Peachey.

He was a tough dude, Peter Ryan; plain, tough and mad. A great guy to coach. No fanfare, no fuss. I'd only have to say, 'Pete, this is how it is, that's how I want it.' He could really handle himself on and off the footy field. He was capable of memorable moments because he was always so full of passion when he played. He was about 92kg, and a magnificent hitter. He also had great timing. When he boxed and when he played it was all in the timing.

We were playing Wests one night and he wanted to fight me. He kept dropping the ball — he had a history of that — and I got into him at halftime. He stood up as if he was about to hit me and a couple of the boys jumped to their feet, worried we were going to have a dust-up. I was filthy bigtime with him, and he was filthy bigtime with me. He could fire up pretty easily.

I'll never forget this one: we were playing the Gold Coast and our goal-line dropout sailed 50 metres through the air. This guy's catching it and, bang, Pete hits him. Colossal hit. Best one-on-one tackle you would ever see. Hit him magnificently after running 40-odd metres flat out to the target. Then he jumped up, cocked his elbow and dropped it onto the guy's head. That was Peter Ryan: pure adrenalin. He copped two or three weeks for that.

So we had him coming through to bolster our forward pack, along with Gorden Tallis, Shane Webcke, Andrew Gee and Brad Thorn. But Alf had a groin problem in '97 and could only play every second week, and Lazzo broke his leg — it was a horrendous break. He did it against Wigan and Andrew Gee came off the interchange bench to take over. Andrew really stood up for us. He wasn't Lazzo; he was Andrew Gee.

THREE MONTHS AFTER HE suffered that bad injury at Wigan, it was announced that Glenn Lazarus had signed with Melbourne Storm, who were set to make their premiership debut. It was a really good offer and he felt that it was time to go. No one disagreed. We had a lot of players coming through, pushing from underneath, and the salary cap remained a big issue. This was a really good opportunity for him to go down there and do something special towards the end of his career. He immediately gave the new club the leadership and direction they needed.

Lazzo is a member of that minority who bring something indefinably special to a football club. He was part of five grand final-winning teams, and that's not counting 1997, when he missed the premiership decider because of injury. He won premierships at three different clubs — Canberra, Brisbane and Melbourne. Says a lot about him.

Whenever I've recruited older players — the young ones you can teach — I've looked at their records, naturally, but more at the environments they've been part of and the impact they've had on those places. Were they part of premierships or not part of premierships? Some guys bring positives with them, while others bring negatives wherever they go, and no matter how hard you try they will never be part of something successful.

It's a package, I suppose, a presence. You look at them and you think, you might not be the most popular guy in the club sometimes, but you still stand out. Chris Phelan had it. Mal Meninga and Kevin Walters. Glenn Lazarus. Alfie Langer certainly had that quality. Shane Webcke. Darren Lockyer has it. Look at their records: some of them never left the Broncos, true, but Mal went to Canberra after he'd played a lot of grand finals in the Brisbane competition. And Chris Phelan, I think, played in 12 out of 13 grand finals in his footy career in first grade.

Sometimes I think it's a pedigree thing too: they've always been winners. Are they the best trainers? Do they make great statements? No. They just have this indefinable thing others respond to. Look at Alf: he'd lead by example and everyone could easily appreciate the impact. Others, like Lazzo, were just out there going about their work, doing their job. He'd be doing it better than anybody and he'd be doing it every week, but not everyone noticed. He'd get angry with other players around him not doing their job, and he'd let them know, but without ever being over the top.

I think their presence and the way these players keep putting in an effort makes others feel guilty if they let them down. I think that's half the battle. There was an American footballer called Joe Greene, who played for the Pittsburgh Steelers in the 1970s, when they won four Superbowls. 'Many days I didn't want to pay the price,' he said. 'But, there was no price I wouldn't pay for my team-mates.'

And their team-mates know that person, the one who says, 'I don't feel like playing well today. I don't feel like going over there and making that run, making those hard tackles and plays. But that's the price I'm going to pay because that's what I do and everybody knows that.' These players are the ones who won't ever let the team down.

History likes these individuals.

'BY THE END OF IT,' I wrote in my coach's notes for 1997, 'this was our best season since 1992. This was a very committed team, a team that stood up time and again. Some of the major things they had to overcome were the length of the season — it began in February and finished in late October — and major injuries to Lazzo, Alf, Steve Renouf and Anthony Mundine.' I continued ...

At our first meeting in late January I told the players, 'Premierships are hard to win and you have to be doing a lot of things right.'

We did a lot of things right and the young men given opportunities were great: Johnny Driscoll, Shane Webcke, Darren Lockyer, Tonie Carroll, Michael De Vere. The club was a lot better. They did not drink as much but still had a lot of fun. I enjoyed coaching them because of their attitude.

I formed a senior players group of Kevin, Alf and Lazzo. This worked really well. We would meet once a week and discuss everything. Their input was great and they backed it up on the field.

The Cronulla game was the turning point for us. We lost 32–4. I identified at the beginning of the season that for us to win in the play-offs in 1997 we had to do certain things: ball control, defence across the whole line, across the whole team and better attacking options inside the opposition's 40-metre zone. I gave them ownership of these.

At training I coached tough on these things. I coached as tough on these as I've ever coached. Players had to come back for training on days off if they hadn't performed the drills to my satisfaction, and when we played games at training there were penalties for errors …

The players were down in the 48 hours after the Cronulla loss. The media bagged us and said our season was over. I was disappointed, but also mildly pleased — they had scored five tries on us but only one came from a team effort. We had made too many unforced errors: 15 handling errors, 13 of which were by the backs. I knew we had only failed because we did not stick to the game plan when we'd been put under extreme pressure. The issue was to handle the pressure better and to apply pressure back on our opponents.

My views were reinforced after I watched the match on video. The key now was to re-convince them and get them back to executing the game plan better. I conducted a series of extremely productive team meetings and video sessions, and got them thinking right again. I used the video to back up my statements: we had tried hard but poor handling let us down; we played with no brains so we could not compete; when we got to the fifth tackle our finishing was poor; we would kick short when we should have kicked long. I told them we had seven matches to go and each one would be a mini-exam, with the finals series our final examination.

We began practising our weekend game plans against ourselves at training ... and we lived it all week ... and went on to win 13 games straight to complete the premiership/World Club Championship double. The closest any team got to us at any time in these matches was six points. The players got more confident as each week passed ...

> Our finest wins were against Canberra in Canberra, Wigan at Wigan, Cronulla in Townsville and Auckland in Brisbane. That was the World Club Challenge, the Auckland one. And Wigan.
>
> Canberra (round 15, 19–4) was the win of all wins. I knew after that that I just had to keep their minds on the job. And that was easy because they were committed and knew they could win.
>
> After the home-and-away games we played Cronulla in the major semi-final in Townsville, and the first half was as good as any half we have ever played. We had them down 30 points. In the second half we kept them try-less. 34–2. We just blew them apart and they never recovered.
>
> To back up after the grand final and win the World Club Challenge was a magnificent effort, particularly considering the way Auckland played in Brisbane and how we had to fight to beat them in the semi-final. The final, against Hunter Mariners in Auckland, was over at halftime. We had them down 30–4 ...
>
> It was a wonderful season overall, and because of the players' attitude I enjoyed it as much as any other season I have coached. The

lessons of the last couple of seasons had been learned and put well behind us. The great thing about this season was that we didn't have to justify anything or make excuses to anyone. That's what made it so enjoyable.

THERE WAS ONE DEFINITE change to rugby league history in 1997: Brisbane, not Sydney, hosted the grand final. I believe rugby league grand finals were born out of Sydney and that is where they should be played. Without doubt, Sydney is the grand final's spiritual home. But having this one played at ANZ Stadium meant a lot to Queenslanders.

At times you let a bit of history go because it's not relevant any more, but you have to be careful. We'd won a few grand finals in Sydney, though, so playing one in Brisbane in front of 60,000 fans was extremely nice. The best aspect was the access for Queenslanders. A lot of people simply can't afford to go to Sydney, and having them as part of such a wonderful experience and moment was more than memorable.

We had a ball all week. The Super League did a great job with a street parade, a black-tie ball. That's what grand final week should be about — a week of celebration.

The World Club Challenge was too young to boast much of a history. I was called to Sydney early in 1997 when the concept was thrown up and Ken Cowley, the boss of News Limited, was there. I thought it was a great concept. I still do. Perhaps there should have been a modified version, but the games we played against Wigan, both in Brisbane and over in England, were among the toughest we played all year.

It also broke up the season. We spent three weeks in the UK on one of the most enjoyable trips I've done in my life. The WCC had its share of critics, but I wasn't one of them.

IT DIDN'T MATTER WHAT we did, there were knockers everywhere. Even about the speed of the play-the-ball. The play-the-ball was too quick in Super League, said the knockers, and too slow in the ARL. I'm over this play-the-ball rubbish. I was over it then and I'm over it now. I was brought up in a game where no one ever talked about anything but getting off the tackled player and allowing him to play the ball. I still don't understand why that's changed. Nobody goes to the football, whether it's Super League or any other league, to watch people lying on the ground pulling guys all over the place and doing everything they possibly can to break the continuity of the game.

Even at the grand final, where we had 60,000 fans cheering us, the knockers kept reminding us we were only winning half a competition. I had convinced our guys long before that we had no control over the competition other than to win it. So we didn't feel any less champions, but when the game came back together we knew what 1998 would be about — whacking it right up everybody in the only possible way.

The breakaway had been a huge issue in our lives, something we all lived every day of the week. We just tried to eliminate it from our minds and do our jobs, take control over the things we could control. Then on grand final day the *Sunday Telegraph* reported that News Limited was poised to agree to a merged 20-team competition for 1998, and on 19 December a peace deal between the ARL and Super League was agreed. The Perth Reds folded. The Hunter Mariners were gone. Gold Coast too.

It was certainly the right decision to get back together. I supported it and wanted to see happen. We'd hurt ourselves enough. They simply didn't get the coup right. If you are going to attempt a coup you have to get it right, otherwise there is a hell of a lot of blood. I don't think anyone anticipated the damage that would be done; if they had, I'm sure they wouldn't have gone ahead with it.

For me, sport is about idealism and the things I have believed in all my life but, you know, business people do deals. They play under the rules of business and we play under the rules of sport. Kerry Packer, who backed the ARL, and Rupert Murdoch, who supported Super League, were both obviously hurt and neither had an advantage, so they did a deal. You either accept these things and get on with it or you become bitter and twisted and finish up isolated — and no one cares in 12 months' time anyway because the caravan has moved on.

The fans are only interested in their players and their footy team. Their colours. All week at work and even at home all they get is arguments and politicians on the television. They don't want that in their footy because that's their relaxation. That's their enjoyment. It's about the players and the game.

Between 1995 and 1997, I believed what I was saying when I got up on my soapbox, preaching the Super League gospel. Then someone got up there and preached the ARL gospel. I began to realise we were turning everyone off — they weren't interested. They just wanted to know who their team was playing this week. Who's playing well, who's not, and why not?

Go the Tigers.

Go the Dragons.

Let's go, Broncos.

CHAPTER 19

RIBES

John Ribot was a great guy to work for because he just let you do your job, didn't interfere.

One day, not long after the Broncos were born, he came into work with a briefcase. I'd never before seen him with a briefcase. I said, 'Hey Ribes, what have you got in there?'

He said, 'Not much.' I opened it up and he had an apple and an orange.

He just thought that's what CEOs did — carry a briefcase. Back then he wasn't the type of boss who'd have a briefcase full of papers. He was an ex-footballer who was in the right place at the right time, and I'm glad he was because we were an excellent combination.

He was an extremely good communicator and facilitator, and at the Broncos he was pretty astute at getting good people around him. He got the right people in the office, all dedicated to the place, and that meant his only problem was keeping the board happy, which was important because they could fly off the handle. The original board was pretty easy on the business side of things but had plenty of opinions on the footy side, and Ribes would spend half his day justifying a selection decision I had made or something I had done with the team. 'What's the bloody coach up to now, Ribes?' they'd ask. Or if we lost two games in a row …

That was the understanding I had with him — he'd handle the board and I'd handle the footy team. It worked great.

I suppose I was a bit surprised when he took on the Super League job because, on paper, it was way out of his league. Or at least it was a league he had never been in before. But he was smart. He'd watched Porky, and Porky was wonderfully generous in that he would pass on everything he knew if that's what you asked for. Ribes spent a lot of time with Porky. They did a lot of deals together setting up the Broncos and Ribes learnt things he wouldn't have known would help him so much in the not too distant future.

I always felt for him as the Super League CEO because it was a very, very tough gig. I had my biggest ever blue with him in that period. We'd never had an argument until then and we haven't had one since. I went in there one day and was just so over some things that had happened. I went to Sydney to see him and we were pretty animated with one another. It's not either of our styles to be like that.

In the end I was nasty. I said, 'If I knew this was going to happen, John, I would never have allowed the Broncos to be part of Super League.'

He said, 'You don't mean that.'

I said, 'I bloody well do, mate.'

EVENTUALLY WE SORTED IT OUT, but the trouble for Ribes in this gig was that this was only one of many difficult arguments and tough situations for him.

With Super League, I don't think he had enough good people around him. I'm always on about having good people around you. Whether it's a footy team or running a business, and whether it's five people or 10 or 1000, the good people around you make it that much easier. The poor ones make poor decisions. They do things that upset your clients. They do things that upset your customers. They don't have the work ethic. Then it all falls back on the few with the work ethic. It has a snowballing effect.

I always hated losing good players. I hated when they had to retire. The ones who got the job done every week and knew what to do, the ones you never had to worry about and wouldn't let the team down … you wished they could have played on as long as you could coach. Maybe no one is irreplaceable but no one should underestimate the work and training and sweat it takes to replace the great ones. The ones who get the job done with a minimum of fuss week after week.

RIBES AND I ARE NEVER going to live in each other's pockets, but if I ring him up and ask for a favour tomorrow I know he'd do it for me, and vice versa. We enjoy seeing each other but he lives in another world to what I live in now. One day soon, though, I'm going to walk into his office, straight past him, reach down and open up his briefcase. Chances are the apple and orange have long been replaced by papers.

I still coach; he lives in that corporate world. The world Porky introduced him to is a world I still try to avoid.

KIM

She was a beautiful person, Kim Walters, she really was. So very brave.

About the time Kim was diagnosed with breast cancer, her husband Kevin had convinced himself he was going to the Cowboys. I went around to see Kim privately and we agreed that it wasn't the time for them to be moving to Townsville.

I didn't want to lose him but more importantly I realised and Kim realised they needed his and Kim's families around them like they had never needed them before. I then went back and at some time in the next day or two I told him he wasn't going anywhere and to get it out of his head. It was a tough conversation. I never told him that I'd been to see Kim.

They were such a young family, Kevvie, Kim and the kids. And his parents — KG and Sandy — are wonderful people who gave lots of support, as did Kim's family.

We'd had Peter Jackson pass away in 1997 and then, all of a sudden, Kim too. We were probably a club now. By that I mean the Broncos were no longer simply about young men playing footy — we were now also about relationships and friendships in all forms. Tragedy can do that to a group of people.

Kevvie was brave through it all, very courageous. He and Kim launched the Kim Walters Choices program, which to this day is offering support to cancer sufferers and raising money for research into breast cancer. Kevvie is a patron of the program and does a lot of work for them.

They were childhood sweethearts and had been together pretty much since I first set eyes on him at age 16.

Kim Walters died on 6 February 1998.

CHAPTER 20

THE WILL TO WIN

At the end of the 1998 season I was a shot bird both physically and mentally. I couldn't sit down, couldn't hold a conversation and I knew I could never do what I'd done that year again.

I had been on the brink so many times with big games, most of which we pulled off. Been in so many camps, with the Broncos, Queensland and Australia. When I finally came home, people would try to talk to me and I'd just get up and have to walk away.

For the first time in my life I had a middle ear infection — I don't care what they write in the medical books, it was caused by stress and stress alone.

We won Origin for the first time in a long time. We won the grand final. When I took over the Australian coaching job we were one down in the series against New Zealand and we ended up winning that too. Beat the Kiwis at Suncorp and in Auckland.

Adrenalin will get you up and pump you through the day, but come nightfall it all begins to fall apart around you and mentally you become an absolute slob. You don't enjoy anything, because you know you have to make so many decisions that affect the lives of so many people, and it all mounts up.

It was not until New Year's Eve that I got to putting my thoughts down on paper. 'I have not felt like it until now,' I wrote at the beginning of my coach's notes. 'I have had a good holiday and am feeling mentally and physically the best I have felt for months. I felt terrible at the end of the Test series. I feel the old enthusiasm is back and I'm keen to do things again.' I continued ...

THE BRONCOS

The 1998 season was very special. The most special part for me was the outstanding commitment the players had to being the best team in the rugby league world. After winning the Super League Grand Final in 1997 and the World Club Championship, they knew their season would not mean as much if we did not win the premiership in the united competition. Newcastle and Manly, both grand finalists in the ARL competition, failed to reach those lofty heights in 1998. Cronulla, our Super League grand finalists, failed to make the play-offs. This is part of why I admire this Broncos team — it's their will to win and the will to keep winning, season after season.

We trained well in the pre-season and got off to a great start by winning our first five games. We lost five fixtures all season, and one play-off game. As usual, we struggled through the Origin series. My own coaching had three major highlights: my halftime decisions and talk at Kogarah Oval; grand final halftime talk v Canterbury; and how we rebuilt ourselves and got the confidence to go on after their loss to Parramatta in the first final.

Once again, I kept things simple at the club. I embraced anything that would help us but at the same time never allowed it to get complicated. I allowed players to enjoy their success and didn't become too rigid about a drink after the game, etc. Players must still be able to enjoy what they are doing.

Craig Bellamy was a tremendous asset. He is very good at his job and very dedicated. He is also a very good person. We had the best defence in the competition and the best attack. Our defence continues to improve.

We had a very good defensive system and everybody had confidence in it. It was the one ingredient that allowed us to win in all situations. Our attack, through our many options, back up and ball control still allows us to be the best. Our high level of skill also gives us an advantage. I have made changes to our attack over the years to contain the sliding defence and the up-and-in defence. Our great ability to get players in motion when we were in possession gave us great strike power. We once again spent a great deal of time on our drills. I know it's an area where we have a real advantage over other teams. It allows them to play with confidence.

This is a very good football team. They have in two years won every trophy and minor premierships. They have lost a total of nine games from 55 matches. It's hard to compare them to 1992–1993, because there were some wonderful players in those teams — some of them still make this team what it is.

Stats-wise we are getting better each year. There are fewer mistakes, which says a lot about the way we play.

Our biggest challenge now is the upcoming season. It does not have to be that difficult if we just put that little bit extra in each week and realise that our opponents will be more competitive. We still have a wonderful team. I just have to make sure I keep pushing.

Andrew Gee, Steve Renouf, Allan Langer and Kevin Walters were my senior players this year. The four of them were great. They did an excellent job with the other players. They were a tremendous support to me and they kept driving the team on the field. Forming the senior players group has been one of my best decisions. The other issue has been the players taking ownership of the program and their performances. Again, this has made a big difference and made my job a lot easier because they were co-operating and all working in the one direction.

STATE OF ORIGIN

I believe that this was one of my best ever coaching series. I took on a task that was extremely difficult for the following reasons:

- A lack of trust between the QRL and the Broncos.
- The lack of trust and unity resulting from the 1996 series (the problem was the split in the game — which meant that on one side in that Queensland camp were ARL players plus the coach; on the other side were the Super League Broncos).
- Our opponents, who are generally stronger than Queensland. This series was to be no different.
- Bar for 1995, when the Super League players weren't selected, New South Wales had not lost a series since 1991. They had been dominant, their team spirit had picked up and they believed Queensland could not beat them.
- The number of Broncos who would be selected for Queensland. With me as coach they would not feel that there was anything so special about living in a camp, playing for Queensland. (There were some pluses, but this was a big issue for me. I had to be different ... say the same things but be different).
- An issue I did not put into the equation was that the *Courier-Mail* would be hostile towards me and the Broncos players. They started on us from the day the team was selected and did not let go until after the final match.
- I learnt in the Tri Series games in 1997 that players such as Alf, Kevin and Steve Walters had become so paranoid about New South Wales being so dominant over Queensland in the last seven years that it had an adverse affect on their performance. Mentally, they were not handling things as well as they should.

So why did I take the job?

I honestly believed there was no Queensland coach other than me who could rebuild this team. I was the most experienced and I felt I had the respect of all the players. I was sick of Queensland being beaten.

I also took the job for my players' sake: Alf, Kevin, Steve and co. I felt I owed them for what they had done for the Broncos. I knew how much playing State of Origin and winning a series in their own right meant to them. I believed I could give them the confidence and faith they needed to get the job done on the field.

Thirdly, this was the most important Origin series since they played the first game in 1980. If New South Wales' domination and Queensland's poor performances continued, in two or three years' time New South Wales would be calling for Origin football to be stopped. I believed this was the most crucial of series. Queensland rugby league also needed a shot in the arm and again I believed I was the one who could deliver. I did not kid myself that we could win the series. I had my doubts, but I was certain that I would reunite the team, make sure teams were selected on form and rebuild the team with youth so that if we did not win this year, we would be in with a better chance next year.

My last thought was that I owed it to Queensland to take the job. Queensland needed this team to stand up and I knew I could do that. And Queensland needed to feel good again about its footballers after Super League.

Game One, Sydney

The Broncos had 10 players in the team. We got beaten by Cronulla on the Saturday night before the game on the following Friday. On the Sunday we went to the Bondi Swiss Grand Hotel for the camp. Spirits were down a bit after the loss. Sunday was a day off for us. I got all the Broncos together in the afternoon and told them I expected nothing but the best from them during the week. I asked them to put themselves out and make sure they spent time getting to know the other players. I told them about the need for them to be perfect because everybody on the staff and anybody who had contact with the QRL would be watching their every move and reporting back on them. (I knew they would not be a problem; I just had to make them aware.)

We had a wonderful preparation and a great week. Close to the best week I have ever had. Team spirit was sky high. Everybody made a great effort to train hard and get on. My theme was not to doubt for one minute that we would win the game. Not to give in, regardless of the situation. They trained with great commitment and enthusiasm all week. A good example was on the Tuesday. It was pouring rain, cold and blowing a gale. We trained for an hour — no one complained. They dropped three balls and their attitude was great.

Our game plan was to play the way we did at the Broncos. We did not have much time for anything else. I just had one of those feelings — which doesn't happen a lot — that we would not be beaten and I tried to get that across to the players.

We set ourselves a goal of scoring first. We did. New South Wales got on top later in the half. We came back, let them in again and then we won the match with 40 seconds to go.

The Swans AFL coach, Rodney Eade, sat with me. When we were down at halftime and not playing well, he asked me, going back to our seats, why I did not rant and rave at the break. I told him we were going to win the game and I did not want them to lose confidence — it would have looked as if I did not believe in them and the game plan.

Game Two: Brisbane

We lost Jason Smith through suspension, but Tallis and Brad Thorn were back. We were pretty confident after our great victory in Sydney. New South Wales got a lot of criticism after Origin I for their interchange bench and how it was used. They made a few changes which made them a little stronger. Our training was good but it's different playing at home. There is more pressure. More distractions. I would prefer to play away. I was more nervous for this game in Brisbane than for games one or three. The expectations are much greater — when we got on the bus to travel to Lang Park, the scenes and the noise of the fans heading to the game just made me and the players more nervous.

For the first game I'd done a couple of talks on teamwork and never giving in or giving up. I did not go over the top then, but I did in

Brisbane. After a talk on the Thursday night I realised I had them too excited too early. I talked about Peter Jackson a bit, how he was such a special guy, how his spirit epitomised Queensland for me, but I got it wrong. I went over the top. Deep down, I knew that but I was also daring myself. I wanted to prove to myself again that even at this level they don't play their best when they are too pumped up. I got what I planned for.

On the Thursday, I rang Ron Massey about the referee, Bill Harrigan. I thought New South Wales would try to put pressure on Harrigan and us by slowing the play-the-ball up and being offside for most of the night. He rang back and said he'd spoken to Mick Stone (the referees' boss) and if New South Wales tried that they would be penalised. That didn't happen. We scored first but after that we were never in it. They slowed our play-the-ball down, were offside. We were getting back and letting them up quickly. Harrigan took nil actions against them. We were down 20–6 at halftime. They were totally dominant.

When they got in the room at halftime I knew we could not win this one, but we had to live to fight another day. I told my blokes to give some penalties away if they had to, but hold them down and creep up offside if they could. I also told them not to give up under any circumstances. New South Wales won the second half 6–4. Final score 26–10. We got two penalties against us; they got nil. The defeat was comprehensive.

I had a number of players who did not play well. When I checked with them later they said to a man they had felt mentally flat. My team talks, playing at home, the expectations ... the only thing that stopped us from being flogged was that great spirit. As outplayed as they were, they just never gave up. I said after the game the loss was my fault. I did not mention the mental side, but I said my not encouraging them to slow the play-the-balls down and the offside had cost us dearly. I told them New South Wales were no better than us and we would get it right next game. Just keep your confidence up and don't stop believing we can beat them in game three.

The Broncos' four original board members have just signed the contract that guaranteed their new club admission into the 1988 NSWRL premiership. From left: Brisbane Rugby League chairman Tom Drysdale, QRL chairman Bill Hunter, Barry Maranta, Gary Balkin, Paul Morgan and Steve Williams.

The Broncos' original directors with their partners in 1995. From left: Barry Maranta, Steve Williams, Lyn Maranta, Terri Williams, Gary Balkin, Suellen and Paul Morgan, Lola Balkin.

Above left: Greg Dowling (No. 11) and Gene Miles celebrate the fact that Brett Le Man has just scored the Broncos' first try in premiership football, against Manly at Lang Park on 6 March 1988.

Above right: Wally Lewis with the Broncos' first trophy — the 1989 Panasonic Cup.

The first time the Broncos went to the Canungra army base for a pre-season camp was in 1989, when one of the activities was a cross-country run, conducted first thing Sunday morning. Young hooker Kerrod Walters (left) was the first player home.

Four great rugby league men. Below: Jack Gibson (left) and Ron Massey. Right: With Bob Bax in the week before the 1992 Grand Final. Bottom: With Cyril Connell, Brisbane's long-time recruitment officer, a gentleman I rate as the Broncos' best ever recruit.

Above: With Kelvin Giles, a key figure in our progress towards the 1992 and 1993 premierships, a man who changed the way everyone in rugby league trained.

Left: Broncos CEO John Ribot (left) and director Porky Morgan in February 1995, just weeks before the Super League war began. Behind them is a photograph of Alan Cann and Kevin Walters celebrating Alan's first try in the 1992 Grand Final.

Top: In the week before the 1992 Grand Final, Glenn Lazarus and I found time to visit the kids at Darra-Jindalee Catholic School in Brisbane.

Middle: A few days later, Lazzo was charging through the St George defence at the Sydney Football Stadium.

Bottom: On the bus from Brisbane airport to the post-Grand Final party at Broncos headquarters at Red Hill.

Above left: With the 'Pearl', Steve Renouf, after the 1992 Grand Final.

Above right: Trevor Gillmeister with the Winfield Cup 12 months later, following our second straight victory over the Dragons.

Below: With Chris Johns (centre) and Kevin Walters after the '93 team completed their heroic fight from fifth place to the premiership.

Above: Peter Jackson in the mud at Canungra in 1989. Right: With (from left) John Ribot, Paul Morgan and Wendell Sailor in Cape Town, South Africa, during our end-of-season trip in December 1993. Below: Three years later, (from left) Gorden Tallis, me, Wendell Sailor, Darren Lockyer, CEO Shane Edwards (at back), Darren Smith and team manager Joe Venardos were at the Winter Park resort near Denver in the US.

I joined (from left) Shane Edwards, Paul Morgan and players' spokesman Chris Johns at the media conference in April 1995 when we finally confirmed that the Broncos had signed with Super League.

The Broncos in February 1997, clad in their Super League gear. Standing (from left): Wade Rothery, Darren Smith, John Plath, Michael Hancock, Phillip Lee, Wendell Sailor, Gorden Tallis, Brad Thorn, Glenn Lazarus, Tonie Carroll, Anthony Mundine, Michael De Vere, Darren Lockyer, Peter Ryan, Shane Webcke. In front: Andrew Gee, Kevin Walters, Steve Renouf, Allan Langer, Chris Walker, John Driscoll, Shane Walker.

I said the complete opposite in all interviews to what I have written here. I had made the decision in the second half that we would play exactly the same way in the series decider, but I did not under any circumstances want to show my hand. I wanted to beat them at their own game. I did not want anybody, particularly the referee, changing what had happened. I convinced the selectors to make some changes for game three. They weren't keen but I had the tactics and I wanted the team I knew would be best suited to carry out the plan. I was so confident that if we played them at their own game they would not handle it. I got the right team and the right game plan.

Game Three: Sydney
When we assembled for Origin III the first thing I told the team was that we were going to play New South Wales at their own game and beat them. I told them I knew they all believed we could beat them. I told them the tactics. In short, slowing the play-the-ball up, getting off the defensive line quickly, ball control. (That is all New South Wales had done since the 1992 series.)

I also made a conscious decision to make sure that we did not go over the top with the psych stuff. I wanted them to relax — and there's no better place than Bondi for that. We just needed to get our tactics right, totally believe in our game plan and ourselves, and build the team spirit by enjoying the week with each other. The spirit was already tremendous so there was not much to be done there.

We trained on the Monday afternoon and started on the game plan. On the Tuesday we trained twice. We brought six Canterbury players over to train with us and worked against them in both sessions. I gave them Wednesday off (a great move). We trained on the Thursday and they were jumping out of their skins. I did not go over the top on the mental side of things. Everything went great for the whole week — it was close to the perfect preparation.

One of the best short speeches ever heard came from Chris Close at the final team meeting, just before getting on the bus to go to the game. All he said was, 'If you let Queensland down tonight you are a …' Well, you can guess what he said. That was it. It was beautiful. Could not have been better. My theme all week was for the individual to have his best ever game, to just be committed to not coming off disappointed. So what Chris said was spot on.

To the game. Chris Johns came into the room just as the players left to warm up. He said, 'You won't be beaten tonight.'

I said, 'How do you know that?'

He said, 'I could see it in their eyes as they went out. Even Steve Renouf looks fired up.'

He was right. From the kick-off they never looked like being beaten. They were outstanding. This was one of the most perfect games I have ever been a part of. We made three handling errors for the game. Completely dominated field position. Frustrated them. Played them at their own game and by the end they had totally lost the plot. They could be out there today and they still would not have caught us. Our execution was excellent, attitude spot on, mentally they were wonderful. This was one of my most satisfying wins, so comprehensive, and beating them at their own game made it even more special. Bill Harrigan penalised us twice for slowing the play-the-ball down but that was it. The final penalty count was 4–1 to NSW. The players were absolutely elated after the game. They knew they had done a great job. I felt so happy for Alf, Kevin, Steve and Andrew Gee. Gary Larson, who I didn't know before the series, had been tremendous in the camp. I was pleased for him because he had given a lot.

It was as satisfying as the 1987 series win, and while winning Origin is different from winning grand finals, it's just as good because you know how much it means to all of Queensland. The manner in which we played the series was also of great satisfaction to me. It was a wonderful series and New South Wales made a great contribution to it. I think I will walk away from it now. Job done.

AUSTRALIA

This was a pretty tough assignment. Australia were one-down in the series. It was after the grand final. I approached it the following way:

- made sure we selected players who were fit, in form and had good attitude;
- never mentioned the fact that we had to win and that we were down in the series — they knew that, so it would have been stating the obvious;
- made an issue of the team being mates — everything I did and said was directed towards that end. I knew if they cared about each other they would play for each other. I did not have enough time to coach a lot into them and they were all tired after a long season.

A big issue in recent years with Australian teams has been the lack of mateship. There have been too many egos. I wanted to break that down. My other emphasis was on Australia playing to their potential and making people feel proud to watch Australians and to be Australian.

There is a different kind of pressure coaching Australia compared to coaching State of Origin. For this particular series it wasn't there. It just felt different. But I made sure I kept talking about the right things and coaching flat out.

I kept things simple. I put great emphasis on the defence knowing that the attack would look after itself (if we controlled the ball). The camps were excellent and everybody made a great effort to get on. They became a team very quickly. It was a great two weeks and a lot of fun. Their training was spot on with the exception of two sessions in New Zealand. Again, I did not overwork them at training. The sessions were short but with lots of intensity.

For the Test in Brisbane I asked them to be mentally strong, to not let New Zealand physically intimidate them. We were great. We had two players knocked out and three players received stitches from their illegal tactics. But we never got away from what we set out to do. They could not intimidate us and they could not beat us.

The staff was excellent. Everybody had the same attitude: do everything for the team. If I got the job again I would certainly want the same people involved. Chris Close does a magnificent job.

To sum up: They were a great group of guys who became good mates and they played for each other. That is why we won both Tests and played football that made everybody feel proud. I enjoyed my two weeks with them. I never over-coached them. I just allowed them to be themselves, but also to be a team and play and care for each other. They did all that.

THE BRONCOS HAD NEVER won a premiership the same year Queensland had won the Origin series. Until now. And it did make it special, especially for Allan Langer.

Until this point Alf had never captained Queensland to a series win, though he had been captain for a number of years. They played on this down south. Phil Gould was always mentioning it and it was an issue with us. The second thing was that Alf had captained Queensland and the Broncos but had never had the opportunity to captain Australia — until now.

These were personal milestones and they meant a great deal to him. As Kiwi coach Frank Endacott lamented: 'Langer is great — the sooner he retires the better.'

I also got great joy out of Shane Webcke, Brad Thorn and Darren Smith playing their first Test matches under my coaching. Darren Lockyer had debuted earlier in the year. I had seen these guys develop from 17-year-olds to Australian players and to be with them on that journey ... well, we had won a grand final in 1992 and I didn't think it could get any better. Then we won a World Club Championship and I didn't think it could get any better.

It got better.

CHAPTER 21

WOMEN IN MY LIFE

IF THEY'D HAD A MOTHER of the Year award back then and they'd given it to Trish then it would have meant a darn lot more to me. Because Trish has always been the one.

I was named Queensland Father of the Year in 1998, but it is something I've never dwelled on because ... what do they say? ... for any man to stand tall, he must first have a rock to stand on. Trish has certainly been our rock.

I've been away from home so often. So many weekends and whole weeks have been lost ... and never a complaint. She's always been pleased to see me achieve and do what I have to do. Always proudly supportive and forever there with that smile on her face when I get home. But if Trish goes away for four hours I'm standing at the door, or pacing, wondering how long is she going to be? How long before she gets home?

She's carried the responsibilities of our home. Great character and great smile. Always happy. The people who know us have most admiration for her because they know the price she has paid for me to be able to do what I've done. Yet Trish has never made me feel guilty or suggested I shouldn't have done it. She has understood that

I'm driven and accepted that, and along the way she's raised three beautiful children who all love her dearly.

TRISH KNOWS I HAVE ALWAYS regarded myself as a man's man. That might not mean much to other people, I suppose, but I know what it means to me: I've always enjoyed the company of men — never was as silly as some of them but enjoyed their company all the same.

Don't get me wrong, I never set out to necessarily win their approval but to have a man's respect was always important to me. And if you said to me I had a choice — those guys over there are going to have a game of footy; and those guys over there are going to a party — then I'd go and play footy every time.

If you said those guys are going to do a job and that other group of men are heading for a night out, I would do the job because I know I'd get more satisfaction.

I guess it comes from getting a lot of responsibility when I was young. I didn't necessarily grab it; it was kind of thrust in front of me, but it's like most things in life in that you get to choose. Most of the places and environments and areas of responsibility I found myself in seemed to revolve around men.

But when the rough stuff and hard work was done there was another part of me that found great solace and confidence in the relationships and trust of the different women in my life.

My mother, Pat Bennett, kept the family together under difficult circumstances and in doing so reinforced to me the value of family. Mum was 20 when she had me. She had gone into Warwick to be close to the hospital and stayed with some people she only just knew, paying her way through housekeeping. When she finally went into labour she called my father and asked him to bring some necessities to the hospital. Two days later, he arrived, drunk, with her toiletries, clothes and stuff in a pillowcase. Then he disappeared again. In the sizzling Queensland heat of January, mum finally checked herself out of hospital and, on foot, carried me the five miles to the railway station, where she would catch the train back home.

It's not so much that women were different then; they just did what they had to do, same as they do today. While there's probably more welfare today, there's a lot of people out there doing it just as tough as Mum did. But she never did anything for herself, like buy clothes or treats. Everything she did was for others. For me, with Mum, the word thanks always seemed so inadequate. I felt her reward for all she did for me was in what I became and what I did. More than anything else, I wanted her to never have to worry about me. An underlying influence in my decision-making has been that I never want to let her down, because I always felt she had been let down far too many times.

My grandmother's name was Winifred, Winifred Brosnan, and there were many wonderful things about her. She taught me many things and was a great card player. She came from an era where cards were played regularly. There was no TV. As a young boy I'd sit beside her until midnight, one in the morning, as she played cards. She wouldn't let me play and I didn't want to play because I was playing in my mind, anyway. I'd watch how she handled herself. How she conducted herself. Her sense of fairness. She hated people reneging, absolutely deplored it.

My grandmother was the first person to teach me about patience, just to be patient. A wonderfully caring person with a reputation as a great cook, she'd always have people over for morning tea and afternoon tea, often people who had fallen on hard times.

My mother had the same type of gift in that we were on hard times but she was still trying to help others who were worse off than her. In previous times, they might have been better off but she would still give them the shirt off our backs if she had to.

There was my Aunty Noela, my mother's twin sister. For lots of reasons I spent a lot of time with her. I wasn't a good learner at school but I was a good learner about life, and she had this great sense of responsibility. She taught me things others didn't — simple things like how to tell the time, do up my shoes. Aunty Noela was probably the first one to come up with a consistent type of discipline. Always fair-handed but you knew if you got on the wrong side of her that wouldn't be a smart place to be. She always had time for me and I always felt I could trust her. When I was sworn in as a policeman I went and lived with her for a couple of years. Here's this big policeman living with Aunty Noela. I loved it — it was one of the best times of my life.

She used to watch me play and still comes to the footy. We all have influences in our lives and we all have to know where we come from and my personality was probably more shaped by Aunty Noela than by my mum. Like me, she is introverted, prefers her own company. Doesn't need the crowd. We can spend a whole night together and barely talk. It is wonderful.

Then there was Betty Phelan, Basil's wife. Basil never scared me, had a real kindness about him, and Betty did too. At the same time, she scared the hell out of me but she also made me better for being in her company on the farm. She was all over me if I had bad manners. If I was rude. She was all over me if I wasn't having a go, being a bit of a sook. I got cleaned up by a horse one day and came in full of tears, full of sorrow, and she picked me up and said, 'You get back out there and get on that horse.' That was the last thing I wanted to hear as I sobbed away. She physically grabbed me, took me out and said again, 'Get back on that horse.'

I was eight, maybe nine, and I'm pleased she put me back on that horse, because I have fallen off many times since and every time I remember and say to myself, 'Get back up, Wayne.' That's what you do in life — you get back up. They knock you down but you get back up.

There came a day when I knew she cared about me. When they are that tough on you, you convince yourself they don't care about you. But they do care about you; that's why they're doing it. You just don't understand. So I was bringing some cattle home, I'm nine or 10, and Baz wanted to go to the races. It's about three miles from home and I'm quite capable of getting the cattle there, there's no dramas. He went off to get himself ready for the races and, anyway, there's this gate left open and the cattle go into this other guy's oats paddock. Rather than take the horse in there and make a bigger mess in his paddock, I got off and left him outside the gate. Usually, this horse is pretty quiet but because Baz's horse has already gone home, he decided to follow at a canter. So I'm on foot, no horse. I get the cattle out, I'm bringing them home and all of a sudden Betty comes back with Baz.

They thought I'd been thrown off, that something bad had happened because the horse had arrived home with no sign of me. She was quite upset about it. I thought, gee, she does care about me.

WHENEVER I'VE BEEN IN UNFAMILIAR territory or searching for direction in life I have sought the wise counsel of others, people like my mother-in-law Jean Veivers and her sister Nola Gray.

And Trish.

At times they have given me counsel I didn't want to hear.

Women have a sensitivity that men don't. Most times they are stronger and more loyal to the family and the concept of family and kids. And their communication is more open.

When it comes to raising the family, they certainly pay a greater price than we blokes pay. I know I couldn't have done what I've done without that type of support. The kids wouldn't be the people they are today without Trish's work. There were times when I was out of order and getting a bit too selfish and Jean would quickly pull me into gear or Nola, in her nice subtle way, would say something. They were never over the top, but they always said enough to set me straight when I needed it, even if my initial response was to think, I don't want to hear that.

Even with my public image — they'll say, you should have done this or you should have done that ... you were out of order there, Wayne. It's always wise counsel without talking down to you. Never bitter, just genuine, they want to help with the direction and subtleties of life you don't usually get from being around men. The caring and trustworthiness. I love their openness and admire their courage.

OF THEM ALL, IRENE DUGGAN was the bravest. As a boy I was friends with her sons. She had arthritis all through her body and was in pain every minute of her life, but she remained this remarkable woman who was very good to me and treated me like one of her own kids.

She always had a smile, always happy, despite being in horrific pain, crippling pain, long before the medications of today. You're a little boy looking for direction and here's this woman of great courage setting out to be happy and not to make everyone else around them feel miserable because of something they have no control over.

There is a side to me all of these women have influenced in different ways, a side not many people see and a side to me that has nothing to do with being a man's man. The sensitive part of me is the part I hide more than anything else, not because I'm embarrassed by it but because the world I live in and work in requires a certain type of manliness. As you mature and develop in your aim to be a better person, you come to see life a little clearer. Women have helped me along that journey.

I WASN'T USED TO hearing girls cry. In the beginning, when the tears came, I'd say, 'Hey Trish, what do you do here?' I have to say my daughters, Elizabeth and Katherine, are not sooks, they don't cry a great deal and I got better with my responses. I remember one day I cried with Katherine — I'm not even sure what it was about, maybe something about school — but we both sobbed our eyes out. I said, 'Kath, things will work out. Don't worry about it.' Whatever it was, she never did worry about it again; she just got on with her life and went on to build a wonderful career.

They were about 10 and 12 when I first realised I couldn't dress myself. 'Dad, you're kidding!' they'd shout. 'You can't wear that with that.'

At other times, I'd get home, walk through the door and they'd be into me about something I should have done but didn't. They have a great sense of logic about them, and honesty. Katherine is brutally honest with me. She just looks at me and says, 'Dad, that's not the way to do this.'

I spend a lot of time with the girls. They love to take me shopping and, of course, I pay. But I cannot win a fight at home anymore. It's three against one. On occasions, Justin will stick by me but only at times because he's a bit of a swinger — he can be manipulated by his mum and the girls.

Beth is me. It scares me. I ring her up and it's like talking to myself. I look at her and I look at me. I recognised that early in her childhood. She was digging her toes in, being stubborn, all the traits I have, and I didn't want to be butting heads with her. Instead, I'd say, 'Trish, they're your kids.' We have a wonderful relationship, Beth, Kath and me. We can sit in each other's company and barely talk.

Whenever Trish was away somewhere I'd take them out to dinner and we'd sit there, order our meal and wouldn't talk. Come home and say what a lovely night we'd had.

They have a lot of their mum's characteristics. Beautiful manners, highly organised, everything in order — and they'll stand up to you and put you in your place without ever raising a voice. While they have never been afraid to give their opinions, their wise counsel, they have always been behind me — whatever decisions I have made — and that's about all you can ask, isn't it?

CHAPTER 22

FAREWELL TO ALF

NONE OF US REALISED what the hell was happening with Alf. In my end-of-season notes I said it was the right decision, but in hindsight it wasn't.

All his life he's carried this weight of expectation. Plus he's an incredibly competitive person ... and he loves you to like him. You put all this together and it means that when he isn't playing well, he doesn't know how to handle it. He hates letting people down and he feels that when he isn't playing well, nobody likes him.

I knew he was struggling. When he got picked to play for Australia in the Anzac Test match I knew he shouldn't have been there.

There's this honesty with the great footballers. They know when they shouldn't be there but they are and they know when they should be but they're not, so they usually take the good with the bad. Alf knew he shouldn't be there ... he didn't even want to be there.

He didn't enjoy that Test and during the game against the Cowboys in Townsville two nights later I pulled him off the field. In the past, whenever I'd tried to give him a rest during a game, he'd blow up — he'd never come off willingly. He'd tell the runner to go and get stuffed. 'And tell the long neck to get stuffed too,' he'd add.

This night in Townsville we were down by 10, or something like that. I sent the trainer out and Alf just dropped his head and ran off. He was happy to come off. Genuinely happy to be off the field. The trainer had said, 'Oh, no, not Alf — he'll blow up.'

I said, 'Just get him off.'

And then, with about three minutes to go, the Cowboys' Noa Nadruku did something stupid. We were gone but he tried to throw a big long pass and we ended up picking it up and scoring in the corner to get us within two. Ben Walker kicked conversion from the sideline to get us a point and everyone cheered except Alf.

He hadn't said anything to anyone but I said to management, 'Make sure you sit me next to Alf on the plane going home. I'm going to find out what's happening here.'

He just opened up. We've always had a wonderful relationship and I could certainly talk straight to him, so I said, 'What's going on?'

He just said he'd had enough. He didn't want to play any more and he was sick of letting his mates down and couldn't find the enthusiasm to play. I realise now we all go through that, we all have those days. Most guys mask it but Alfie was so upfront.

We came home and I left it for a day or two so we could both think about it. With hindsight, I should have just sent him away for two weeks. Sure, we would have copped some criticism but it's what I should have done. I didn't realise the extent of the expectation and sense of responsibility that was weighing on him, crippling him.

In the past, he'd handled it well and always maintained his motivation to play, but because of the huge successes of 1998 and now we'd lost six of our first seven, he was suffering worse than ever. He kept trying to get the best out of himself, to get the passion back into his life and his game but it just wasn't happening. He was a bit more honest than the rest of us.

So he had that terrible press conference when he said he was going to retire. It was our lowest point emotionally, with the exception of the funerals of Peter Jackson and Kim Walters. It was a very low week.

We kept him involved and he was paid his contract for the rest of the year. The club was wonderful with him. We knew he was in a tough place but we didn't realise how tough that place was until it was too late. I suppose we could have sent him to a psychologist or something like that, someone to have a yarn with him, but Alf was never one for that. He'd never had a lot of problems. He'd always just handled himself. If we'd said we were going to send him to someone he would have just dropped his head and walked away.

We were all struggling but he was the captain; he had all the responsibilities. Being a Broncos captain is a huge responsibility. I watch them all the time. It wears them down … the demands, the commitments, the way they have to carry themselves, the number of people asking for a bit of their time. It's life-changing, actually. It would be the same at Manchester United or the Australian cricket team — at all the places with any tradition and success. The Broncos have deliberately made it an important role and the club has kept a lot of stability with its captains and leaders. It's not something we took lightly or gave away without a lot of thought and consideration.

A couple of months later *Big League* magazine named Allan Langer the number one player of the 1990s. And they were right: no one did what he did. No one. He was such a diminutive little guy — 75 kilos he weighed — but he played flat out every week. Hardly ever had a bad game. He was a bit like Roger Federer and Tiger Woods: so good that you never know when they are having a bad day.

THIS WAS ALSO A SEASON in which salary cap restrictions were beginning to hurt. On 12 August, Andrew Gee signed to play with Warrington in England. Less than two weeks later, Alf signed too. They were great mates — still are today — and Alf would have gone anywhere with Andrew. He had a great offer from Wigan but he chose Warrington because of Andrew and because another Queenslander, Darryl Van de Velde was coaching there. I always thought he was only going there to get his pension. Even when he retired I always thought he'd play again, though probably not in England. Alf just had to settle, get himself sorted out.

In 2002, when he came back to play with us, the same thing happened. He'd done all the pre-season training with us and was keen to play, and we were keen to have him. The hardest part for Alf was always the training but he'd got through the early stuff. Now his favourite part, the playing, was about to begin.

But he rang me in late February and said he couldn't make training. I said, 'Why not?'

He said, 'I don't want to play any more.' This is 2002.

I said, 'What?'

He said, 'I don't want to play any more.'

I said, 'You're kidding me. You love playing.'

He said, 'No, I don't feel I should play.'

I asked whether the weight of expectation was coming back on him. He said, 'Yeah, a bit.'

I told him he couldn't go out that way: he had to come to training, if only to say hello to all the boys. 'Don't ring me up and tell me you can't,' I said. 'Get yourself in the car and get to training this afternoon.'

Then I rang Phil Jauncey, our sports psychologist, and told him to get to training. 'As soon as Alf gets there you're having a meeting with him,' I said. 'He wants to retire again but I know what his problem is. All the expectations have come back on him again and he thinks there is so much responsibility and so much required of him, even though he's not the captain now. Phil, when he comes in the door I'm going to send him straight to you and don't come back telling me he's going to give up football because he's not. We rely on him and he has to go through with it.'

When Alf walked through the door I was waiting for him while Phil was hiding out the back — Alf still wasn't big on sport psychs, even though he liked Phil. I said, 'Mate, I've been thinking about your problem and I reckon you need to spend five minutes with Phil. If you still want to retire after that, then I'm happy. You're lucky because he just happens to be out the back — he just called in to see me. You go and see him. I've got a team meeting to conduct now.'

I grabbed Phil, gave him a wink and said, 'You're on. Come back and see me when you're done, boys.'

Fifteen minutes later, Phil poked his head around the door and gave me the thumbs up. And Alf had a great season.

THE 1999 SEASON WASN'T so good. Not only did we lose the first five games; we also lost Mick Hancock and Steve Renouf to injury in game one and at season's end Steve went to Wigan, Peter Ryan went to rugby union and the Brumbies, Andrew Gee went and Alf went. Lazzo retired after winning the comp down in Melbourne. It was a changing time.

The end-of-year presentation was a very sad night for me and on the way home I remember telling Trish that I felt like not going back. They were a real part of us, those guys. Andrew had been with us since 1988, Lazzo had been a wonderful player for us, Alf of course, and Steve Renouf, the Pearl — they weren't going to be around any more, sitting in their seats in the dressing room, coming with us on the bus, sitting where they always sat. You get over it, but it takes time.

They were my family, part of me and part of all the things I did. I might be in a different place every night but they were always there, whether it be with the Broncos or Queensland or the Australian side. I had challenged them so many times. This wasn't just another football team, a normal group of guys. We'd done so much together over a decade and it had become more than simply a coach–player relationship. Trish and I had been to their birthday parties, to their weddings, their kids' christenings, the way family members do.

Having favourites was always an issue. My old mate Bob Bax used to say, 'Yes, Wayne, I do have favourites — and they are all bloody good footballers.' I know exactly what Bob meant.

They were all different. In terms of friendship I had favourites, but not when it came to playing footy and being in that club. They all meant as much to me as each other. Some wouldn't realise that, but I know how I felt. If I could have done something to help Allan Langer I would have, but I would have done exactly the same for the guy in the club no one knew. I didn't differentiate.

BESIDES ALF, WHEN I think back to 1999 there are three Broncos I immediately think of. One is a bloke we had to let go. The other two are men I rate among the toughest I ever coached.

Following the Super League settlement, all clubs were faced with problems trying to keep under the salary cap. If a player had an existing contract there wasn't a drama. For example, he might have had a contract that paid him $400,000 a year, but under the salary cap he'd only be valued at $250,000. The problem came when he came off contract — if he didn't want to take a hefty pay cut, you had to release him.

We had to lose players, it was that simple. I was happier knowing they were going to good clubs, and Wigan in England was a good fit for Steve Renouf. He was unique, Steve. I never saw Reg Gasnier play, but the old guys reckon Steve ran like Reg Gasnier did. I've been coaching for 21 years in the NRL and I haven't seen a player run like him. He had great balance and timing and anticipation. He could score the impossible try and he worked hard to learn how to play tough.

Steve wasn't always tough. When he arrived at the Broncos he was this thin little Aboriginal boy, but he proved to be a great credit to himself and his wonderful wife, who was very supportive. He hated training. Steve had nightmares about training, truly he did. He'd tell me about them. From about midday he'd be in a mess thinking about the pain he would have to go through at training that afternoon. He never won anything at training and never wanted to. But he turned out to be a good trainer in the end and even today he keeps himself in good shape. You often find that — the worst trainers tend to do more exercise than the good ones after they retire.

We had a bit of an issue with his defence early on. Even the board said something and I told them what I always told them: they should stick to running the club and I'd coach the team. One night during a match a player told me to get Steve off the field, but I wasn't going to let some player tell me to do something I knew wasn't right. It was the only way we were going to get him where he wanted to go. With a unique talent, sometimes you have to pay a price before it turns out great.

YOUNG PETERO CIVONICEVA HAD now become a regular first grader and while he was a caring sort of guy, what Petero didn't feel was pain. I didn't like doctors X-raying him — it was only going to give us bad news. To this day Gorden Tallis believes Petero is the toughest man he has played with.

In the early years I couldn't work out why Cyril Connell had recruited him but, as I've already said, then you'd see this flicker of light. This something. Petero just kept growing on me and Cyril kept telling me to persevere with him, which I did, even though his workload and ability to carry the footy were nowhere near what they are today. He would play well one week and badly the next two weeks, but he was a great learner and with time turned himself into a wonderful, wonderful footballer.

TO ME, KEVIN CAMPION WAS our stand-out player in 1999. Kevin was the David Stagg of his day: when the team's playing well you never notice them, but when the team is struggling they always get the player-of-the-match award, because they play that way every week.

In 1997, my brother-in-law Greg Veivers told me about this guy playing in Adelaide he'd been watching.

I said, 'Who is he?'

He said, 'Kevin Campion.'

I said, 'I've never heard of him.'

He said, 'I'm telling you, he is a good player.'

I was coaching Queensland in the Super League Tri Series back then and we were short of players for the game against New Zealand in Auckland. So I brought Kevin over and put him in the team. He was pretty sensational. He was a hell of a hitter and one of the few guys who could come in cold and play alongside Alf and Kevvie. He picked up their styles straight away.

This guy is a bit special, I thought.

Rod Reddy was coaching the Adelaide Rams but he thought so little of Kevin Campion that he put him back to the local league. When I heard that I jumped on the phone and said, 'We'd love you to come to the Broncos.'

He said, 'I would love to come to the Broncos.'

You talk about Petero being tough; this guy was as tough. He had disc problems in his neck and the doctors used to run the other way whenever he ran out. Once he copped a cut to his face and it became infected. We were in the middle of a bad trot, and he turned up with the whole side of his face swollen and just refused not to play. We were at ANZ. He had his gear in his bag — it was a Saturday — and he said he was playing, by hook or by crook.

Our doctor, Peter Friis, looked at him. Peter really cares about the players. He said to me, 'This guy can't play today. If that gets busted again he can get septicaemia. He just can't play.'

The doc and I went and pleaded with him not to play. 'No, he said, I'm not letting the boys down today. I'm playing, I'm playing.'

We listed the ramifications. 'I don't care, I'm playing.'

The doc said, 'Well, it's on your head, Kevin, if anything goes wrong.

'That's fine with me,' he said. 'They need me and I'm playing.' He went out and won the players' player.

I HAD NO IDEA WE would begin the season as badly as we did. Our pre-season training was limited but good and our first two trial games were good solid performances. So to only win one of our first nine games was a great shock. The biggest disappointment in this period was our 48–6 loss to Melbourne in round 3. The rest were no fun, but at least we competed. After Melbourne, we lost a lot of confidence and it was a hell of a job to get it back. I believe our finish to the season was our finest as a club. It took something special to do what we did, particularly with Alf retiring, the Pearl injured most of the time and Kevin Walters either injured or, sadly, out of form.

This season had a lot of similarities to 1994. In February, I read a book where the author said, 'If it is not broken, break it.' Next time I'm part of a premiership I'm going to take his advice. While we were losing confidence our opponents could smell we were down and picked up their intensity on us. Our attitude was not right and it took a lot of beatings for the players to get it right.

The day we began to turn our season around, against Balmain at Leichhardt Oval, my instructions were, 'Tackle anything that moves in front of you and don't worry about passing the ball — just hold it for six tackles every time.'

We won 12–10 and it was one of the worst games the Broncos have ever played. They scored from an intercept and we scrambled over for two tries. We simply had to get a win up to make the guys feel better about themselves and their team-mates. After that, we won 11 out of 13 games and we had some great victories against quality teams.

The main reason for our bad start was the hangover from the 1998 season, when we won the premiership, the Origin, the Test series — so many Broncos were involved in all of that. I know that when I came back for the '99 pre-season I was not as enthusiastic as I normally am. I just felt I needed more time to enjoy 1998. That was one of the main reasons I gave away the Origin and Australian coaching positions. I just did not have the drive. And I only coach — they play.

In the end, though, I think 1999 turned out to be one of my top five coaching years. I had to pull out every bit of experience I had to keep everything together. The players lost a lot of confidence in themselves and each other, while I remained very positive and showed a lot of confidence in them. I cut team meetings back, worked them hard but fairly, and did not overreact to any of the crises going through the place.

At the start of the season too many of the players were not prepared to give 100 per cent. There is not a big mathematical difference between 100 per cent and, say, 80 per cent or 90 per cent but it is the difference between winning and losing. In every game, except the one in Melbourne, we put ourselves in a position to win but we found a way to lose.

As the team stayed at or near the bottom of the ladder, I came to realise what losing coaches go through. I knew what was costing us games. I was going to training and having them practise things time and time again, and then the game would come along and they would make the same stupid mistakes. I just kept at them. That is a good example of the importance of attitude: because their attitude was not good enough, they could not complete the tasks on the field properly. The ability was there, though — that never left them.

A decade earlier, I would not have been able to turn the season around. This time, I took my personal feelings out of the win–loss record; those stats did not matter to me. If they had, I would have handled things badly because my ego would have got in the way.

The great thing about this team was that they never turned on each other. I told them they had to cop the criticism from the fans and press and not make excuses. They did that. I'd stuck a cliché on the wall of my room which said, 'Losers assemble in small groups and whinge and bitch about the other players and coaching staff. Winners assemble as a team.' They stayed strong and never let each other down. I don't believe any other team in the competition had the class and character to do what they did. At one stage they were so low they even looked forward to the bye ... because it guaranteed them two points.

I wrote in my end-of-season notes that I felt that the 1999 season had set us up well for 2000 and beyond. The players who stayed now knew they could win without Alf and company. They just had to keep working hard in a positive manner and things would turn. I was confident we still had a team and a game plan that would win us football matches. But they only win when the attitude is right and the game plan is executed right.

Attitude and the will to persevere are everything. Both need a fair bit of character. I have always wanted players with character in the team, but of course you never know how much until you hit a crisis. In 1999, none of them failed the test.

'I HAVE OFFERS TO COACH at two other clubs, and am probably as close as I have been to moving on,' I wrote in my notes. 'However, it will not be until the end of 2000. There is much to be done in 2000 and I am looking forward to it a lot more than I looked forward to 1999. I may not take the offers, but they both have a lot of appeal to me. Particularly England. We shall wait and see.'

Our last game, a 42–20 loss to Cronulla in the first week of the finals, was a major disappointment, but I had no doubt our players were just happy to make the finals after such a tough season. That is the way they played on the day.

This is how I concluded my notes for the year: 'If our attitude is right and we get our execution right on the field, we will be very competitive in 2000. Actually, we can be more than competitive. I'm looking forward to it.'

CHAPTER 23

TO A MAN THEY WERE MAGNIFICENT

THEY DON'T RELY ON the brilliant individual but instead on each other being as committed as they are to the team. There is no price they won't pay for their mate.

At training, off the field and in battle lives a bond you cannot manufacture but one you can certainly build. They give themselves to the team no matter the ask, whether it be a positional change or a different, less fashionable role or simply more work. You won't catch these guys bitching and whingeing.

Not when they truly are a team.

THE 2000 BRONCOS HAD the minor premiership won four weeks before the end of the season. The last team to do that was Eastern Suburbs in 1975. We had the best defence and the best attack at the conclusion of the premiership rounds. In the play-offs we conceded 14 points — three tries — in 200 minutes of football — the second half against Cronulla (won 34–20, after we were behind 20–6 at halftime), the preliminary final against Parramatta (16–10) and the grand final against the Roosters (14–6). I know that if you just look at the individuals, this was not the Broncos' best ever group, but I have no doubt this was the best team the club had produced to this time.

How did this team, a team that not many gave a chance before the start of the season, go on to be a premiership-winning team? There were a number of factors, but many of them related to the same thing: confidence.

Our first four matches were away from home but we came through those games unbeaten, which gave everybody a lot of belief in themselves and the team. During this period we had a number of injuries to our backs but our forwards carried the team. They stood up then and they continued to do so all season, never worrying about how anyone else was playing. They just came ready to play.

We practised our game plan every week for 26 weeks, so when we got to the semi-finals there was a huge amount of confidence in what we had to do. We made no changes throughout the finals. In the Broncos' first 13 years we won three minor premierships and four premierships. Every time, we followed our game plan all year, so that by the play-offs everybody has great confidence in it and in the team. In the years we didn't win, one of our problems was that we weren't able to reproduce our game plan under the pressure that is exerted at finals time. We didn't get it together consistently throughout a season and then we folded under pressure. In 2000, the team had it right and no amount of pressure could make them crumble.

On and off the field this was a terrific group — great mates who really cared about each other. Mick Hancock, Kevin Walters, Wendell Sailor and Gorden Tallis deserved most of the credit for this. They did a superb job building team spirit.

Another positive which was huge was what I called the 'self interest' factor. A number of guys in the team were either retiring or going overseas to play at the end of the season, and they were committed to finishing with the Broncos on a winning note. They had been winners all their careers and they wanted to leave the club in a winning position. To a man they were magnificent. In fact, this was probably my easiest coaching year at the Broncos. I just had to get them on track and keep everybody focused and happy. The players did the rest. They enjoyed everything about the season and so did I.

But most significant of all, in my view, was the pre-season camp at Canungra. We went up there as individuals and came back as a team.

THE CANUNGRA EXPERIENCE IN 2000 was a special time in my life. Canungra is not a pretty place. It is an army training camp about as far as you can get from a Queensland resort. Australian soldiers have been doing jungle training there, preparing for battle, since World War II.

It is dark and wet, hot and steamy, thick scrub and huge hills.

The Broncos went there before the start of the 2000 premiership to be denied food, shelter and sleep over a 36-hour period and it was the best team-building exercise I have ever experienced. Our first exercise, or obstacle at least, was a dark tunnel half submerged in water. It scared the hell out of me. We went through it in teams ... until it came to a kid named Wilson and Phillip Lee.

They wouldn't go through it. They couldn't. There was just absolute fear. The rest of the guys in their team tried, but they couldn't talk them through it.

So we moved on.

Another great challenge was the pitch black tunnels where the camp facilitators left us and we had to find our own way out.

Many of us live in a comfort zone. This is especially true of football players, with the accolades and the rewards they receive, the facilities they train in and the conditions in which they live. It is not always real. At times it makes sense to take them out of that zone, introduce them to another world, get them to tackle things they don't think they can do.

Not that I went to school much, but in Grade 5 there was Brother Bible. He was the best teacher I ever had. He got more out of me than any other teacher because of two things: he challenged me, and I knew he cared about me.

Brother Bible cared about all of us. If you don't care about people you can't challenge them. I felt like I was an exceptional kid in his classroom. That's how he made me feel; that's how he felt about all of us. He is still my friend today.

Whether I was a player or a footy coach or a police cadet or an instructor at the Police Academy, anybody who challenged me made me better. Meeting a challenge gives me more confidence. Today, I'm 58, and when I go to the farm I'm challenged because I'm out of my comfort zone, so when I get things done there I feel good about myself.

I love training and I love training with people, yet I spend most of my life training by myself because, owing to my work hours, it is difficult to find people to run with. The point is, I can't replace the feeling I get when I go out and run with somebody, particularly players I work with, because that makes me feel so much part of the team. It's the best buzz.

I loved playing. I wish I still could. I always tried to be a good team-mate, and the bond that comes with being part of a good team stays with you for life. You only have to go to a reunion to know that bond is everything. Footy careers don't last long but memories do.

In 2008, I went with the players to The Gap in Brisbane for the big hill run. I'm working with the slower ones now because I'm not at the front any more. I accept that. I felt that I didn't want to do it, didn't want to be there, all the normal feelings. What was I doing this for? And I know that's what they were feeling. You do it because you don't want to let down that guy beside you. Pretty simple philosophy, but it works.

Another year in another camp it was midnight and we were walking up a very steep hill. We had been at it for 24 hours straight. They were carrying a stretcher with 80 kg on it and water bottles and kits and God knows what else. This player, who shall remain nameless, looked at me and said, 'What's this got to do with me being a good football player?'

I didn't answer him because I didn't think it was the right time to answer him, thought we might get into a big verbal exchange. So I just shut my mouth. But when we came out the next afternoon to have a debrief I told the players how so-and-so had asked how did this camp experience relate to him being a better football player?

I said, 'It doesn't. It won't help one of your skills one little bit. But what I hope it has done is given you more confidence in yourself. And if you become more confident in yourself, you'll become better players.'

The greatest learning experience is to be challenged with something you are required to do but don't think you can do — and then do it. Overcoming obstacles and challenges makes you better. It changes your attitude and builds confidence in yourself.

At Canungra in 2000, 36 hours after Wilson and Lee had refused to go through that half-submerged tunnel, we came back to the very same place. They still didn't want to go into the darkness. As they stood there, baulking, the rest of the guys talked to them, encouraged them and challenged them. All of a sudden, they were coming out the other side.

What changed in 36 hours? They felt they were part of something, part of a team. Now they didn't want to let their mates down.

FROM THE BEGINNING, TEAM-WISE, the 2000 Broncos outfit was the real deal. We didn't lose a game in the first eight rounds.

The 18–2 loss to Penrith at Penrith in round 9 was our worst performance of the season, the first time the Broncos had not scored a try in a game since 1995. Penrith had seven players out and we were close to full strength, on paper at least. The following week, without Ben Ikin and Kevin Walters, we drew with Melbourne in front of 30,000 at ANZ Stadium.

We suffered so many injuries in that game. Tonie Carroll played five-eighth and the kids — Dane Carlaw, Ashley Harrison, Darren Mapp and Danny Bampton — were magnificent. Ben Walker had to leave the field after only two minutes with a dislocated elbow, meaning Harrison and later Kevin Campion played halfback. They showed more commitment than the Broncos of old, setting a new standard. It was a tremendous achievement against the reigning premiers and we had them beaten until Gorden Tallis had a misread on Brett Kimmorley late in the game. Gordie came in instead of holding his line and Kimmorley jumped on the outside to set up a try and make it 18–all.

Our players still talk about that night with a fondness not usually in keeping with a draw.

Against Canberra, when we had seven players missing on Origin I duty, Justin Hodges became our youngest ever first-grader, at 17 years 348 carefree days. He was a good kid but not a big fan of training, Justin. He was then, and still is, an athlete. He has this big loping stride that makes him look as if he isn't running fast ... but he is. Most top athletes are short striders and you see their legs pumping quickly. Justin might look slow, but he covers the ground better than most. Paul Hauff, who played fullback for us from 1990 to 1996 and played for Australia in 1991, was the same.

Our premiership march in 2000 would not include Petero Civoniceva — he broke his arm in the return game against

Melbourne in round 16. The big fella came off at halftime and the doctor said, 'Petero, your arm is broken.'

Petero said, 'I'm going back out.'

'You can't,' said the doctor, horrified.

'I'm not letting the boys down,' said Petero.

We finally talked him into coming off with 10 minutes to go and lost the match right on full-time. Mick Hancock, who'd come off the interchange bench, was now in the back row. We'd been practising goal-line defence for a week, two weeks, three weeks ... with a minute to go he turned in and they put a play on us and scored under the goalposts. Broke all our hearts. I forgave him, eventually.

ONE OF THE KEYS TO 2000 for us was Kevin Walters and his return. He had been injured for the early part of the season and when he came back I told him we needed him if we were to win the premiership. I said, 'We won't win without you.' I don't think he made a line break in the period he played this season. He didn't have to, because he had lots of good players around him. We just needed his direction and calmness out there. Kevvie was outstanding as a captain and did a hell of a job for us.

Calmness in football is not splitting the team with panic talk or calling plays that are going to put them all under pressure. The calm players have a belief in themselves and a belief in the guys around them. They keep driving and doing the things they know will win. They do not spook players or verbally abuse them or try to intimidate them into performing. Instead, they work with them and lead by example. They continually display a calmness which in turn calms the rest of the players, so they can all perform somewhere close to their ability. They have an ability to stick to the game plan. Sure, it might not be working at the moment — we might be under the pump, maybe 12 points behind. But the calm players stick to the things they know have made the team successful, the things that work for them.

But they're all different. Wendell Sailor didn't know a lot about calmness at the best of times and certainly not during the round-24 match against the Dragons at Wollongong. He nearly incited a riot.

He loved the occasion, the Big Dell, and the crowd was revving him up and he was revving them up. I thought they were going to jump the fence at one stage. We were all pleased to get out of there in one piece, because people either loved him or hated him and on that day there wasn't a lot of love for him.

Wendell knew I was never a fan of him revving up the crowd, but I knew it got the best out of him at times. He was in the southeast corner at WIN Stadium and they were all on his back. Then he got the ball and ran 95 metres to score this magnificent try. The silence was deafening. 'I think if you came to the ground today you would have to walk away realising you have probably seen one of the best players in the game,' I said afterwards. Just recently, all these years on, I saw him bump two guys off, step between another two and then outsprint everybody to the tryline. It was just another of the incredible tries Wendell has scored.

He and Lote Tuqiri both scored 18 tries in the premiership rounds in 2000, which they wouldn't have done if Steve Renouf had still been playing — even those two he wouldn't have needed. But we had some great wingers at the Broncos, from Carne to Hancock, Sailor and Tuqiri … what a wonderful decade of wingers.

WE FINISHED MINOR PREMIERS and played eighth-placed Cronulla in the qualifying final at ANZ Stadium. They nearly did us that day, leading 20–6 at halftime.

I was already filthy coming down the stairs for halftime. And then Cronulla scored another one on us and it set me off even more. We had played into their hands. Cronulla were pushing up on the outside of our go-to players and we just played dumb … didn't divert and go through the middle of the ruck on them, mix it up a lot more. They were just racing up and picking us off. We'd lost confidence.

First I gave it to Ben Ikin. I said, 'Ben, everything you're doing I detest. You are playing with no vision, no thought — and I just hate that. You've got a choice here: either get your game together or get off. You'll be off that quick you won't know what hit you.'

So he was sulking.

I turned around to all the forwards, naming them one by one. I said, 'If one of you guys passes the ball in this half I'm going to pull you off the field.'

Then I turned to the captain and said, 'Kevin, if you pass the ball to Ben, you're coming off too. I want you all to run direct and over the top of them, not around them.'

I was not happy, and said a few more things you can't print.

They went back out and scored 28 unanswered points. They were magnificent, getting on top through the ruck, taking control.

Petero was long gone with his badly busted arm and Shane Webcke had not played since breaking his arm in the same game Wendell scored that try against the Dragons. We knew winning the premiership would be much harder without Shane, but the doctors didn't want to clear him. It was five weeks since he'd suffered his injury, and I approached him about playing. He said he wanted to play, but the doctors weren't keen. He knew he could rebreak the arm but he said that was no big deal, he'd get it right for the start of the next season. He just wanted to finish this one.

So he started preparing for the preliminary final against Parramatta, with his arm all taped up and a big armguard on, but during a training drill we heard a crack and thought he'd broken it again. Fortunately, X-rays cleared him. Three days before the game we were sitting in a hotel debating whether or not he should play.

Shane had demons going through his mind, but he went out and faced the Eels and then he played against the Roosters in the winning grand final team as well.

Magnificent.

DURING THE FINALS SERIES Brad Thorn decided that in 2001 he would go to New Zealand and play rugby. He had always talked about playing for the All Blacks and Brad is a guy who lives his dreams. He's a very strong personality.

Wherever he has been he's been a winner.

It's no fluke he went to Canterbury, the toughest and best provincial team in world rugby. He was offered a lot more money to go to other places, so he took a hell of a pay cut to go to Canterbury, but he went there because, as he said, if he could make it there he would have made it in rugby. Best teachers, best players … best result.

And that pretty much sums up Brad Thorn. Most guys would take the money and look for the soft option. He took the hard road and then when they first picked him for the All Blacks he said he wasn't ready, wasn't good enough, and withdrew.

Today he is an All Black and the best forward in New Zealand rugby.

I don't use the word 'principle' about many people, but he is one of the most principled people I've ever met.

In 2007, he captained the Broncos when the Origin players were missing, we won the game, and then during the post-match press conference a journalist asked how he felt leading the club to victory. Brad looked down at the Brisbane Broncos emblem on his chest, touched it with his hand, and said, 'This jersey means everything to me. This emblem means everything to me.'

And at day's end that was enough said.

SO THE CLUB WON ITS fifth premiership in nine years and celebrated by waving goodbye to Kevin Walters, Michael Hancock, Brad Thorn, Kevin Campion, Harvey Howard and Tonie Carroll — all at once.

It wasn't getting any easier. I thought I might go too.

The salary cap means that when good players get big offers from other clubs often you either can't match them or you don't want to match them, because to do so would impact on the depth of the playing squad.

In this instance, Tonie Carroll was the one I was most disappointed to lose. I was shattered, but otherwise I felt great about the fact that they were all farewelled with a premiership. I was particularly happy for Kevvie and Mick. They had been with me since they were kids. Mick Hancock had never had another first-grade coach.

Kevvie had never been in Alf's shadow, because he was a great footballer in his own right, but Alf had been the dominant player and got most of the recognition. Kevin got plenty of accolades too … but it was still nice seeing him standing there with the trophy. Proudly standing there with his kids.

Every time I look at that NRL trophy I see him holding it up. Still gives me goose bumps.

CHAPTER 24

NO WAY WAS HE GOING TO FAIL

WE WERE IN ENGLAND for the World Club Challenge against St Helens when the telephone message arrived in the middle of the night. Paul Morgan had died.

I couldn't believe it, so I quickly made a call and had the message confirmed. Some people you never think of as being vulnerable or fallible or even mere mortals. To me, Porky Morgan was always 10-foot tall and bulletproof. But on Australia Day 2001 his big heart stopped ticking.

For 24 hours we just sat around reflecting. I was lucky to have guys there with me who had known and loved him the way I did, people he had helped enormously. They write songs about people being always on your mind and it was like that — the things he had done, the influence he'd had on all our lives, the type of guy he was and the tragedy that he had been with us for such a short period of time ...

Porky was only 52 and just beginning to change the world.

There are times in life when, no matter what emotions you might be feeling, the show must go on. This was one such time. I'm not saying we were in a war, but our situation was like that of a soldier in battle, who sees that his best mate has just been killed, but he must keep his grief in check and keep fighting. We had a game to play and a job to do, and only then could we get ourselves home.

THEY COULDN'T FIT THE MOURNERS into Brisbane's biggest cathedral. When Paul picked me up in 1988 I could not have done the eulogy but as a result of his encouragement and the confidence he had given me, I could do it that day.

There were people better qualified but his family wanted me to do it. So I did and it was an honour. It wasn't as if he was someone who was hard to talk about. So much to say in so little time.

> Paul Morgan — where do you start? To say 'larger than life' is a cliché, but those of us whose lives he touched were dwarfed by his caring, his generosity, his honesty, his time for you and his fierce loyalty to family and friends and anything Queensland.
>
> I first met him in 1970 in Toowoomba. Me a young policeman and Paul working for a fertiliser company. We were both playing for All Whites. That was the last year Toowoomba won the Bulimba Cup against Brisbane. Paul was in the team and I was on the bench. We became friends very quickly. I would call and see him at work and he would tell me his dreams. I have never seen anybody physically push themselves harder than Paul at training and most nights he would vomit towards the end of the session. He left Toowoomba just after the Bulimba Cup win to return to Brisbane and play for Redcliffe.
>
> I got into coaching and he got into business to fulfil his dreams. I would read about him in the business section and he would sometimes catch my name in the sports section (usually in an article about my inability to coach).
>
> Then 1987 was upon us quickly and someone mentioned that Brisbane were to be admitted to the NSW Rugby League, and in

charged Paul with his partners, Steve Williams, Barry Maranta and Gary Balkin, to form the Broncos. I was all settled in Canberra when the larger-than-life figure arrived at my home at 8.30am with my accountant in tow. I answered the front door and there's Paul, holding this big port. I asked what he was doing and what the port was for. 'You keep rejecting my offers to coach the Broncos,' he said. 'I am staying at your home until you say yes ' Four hours later, with a headache, I went for a run by myself and decided that I would take the job. I have said it before: Paul Morgan was the only person who could have convinced me to break a contract. I still regret that to this day; however, I don't regret the next 13 years I was to spend with Paul and the Broncos.

So what did I learn in those 13 years with this character who wore his heart on his sleeve, who could be intimidating, who could get cranky and say things that would hurt, but whose human weaknesses you would forgive immediately? You would try to do your absolute best for him, because you knew he would not let you down and you did not want to let him down. Why? Because he was your mate, that's why.

He was a leader among leaders. School captain at State High, and regarded as the best ever School Captain. Kids from grade 8 to grade 12 thought the world of him, and still do. Great leaders make decisions and very rarely change them. That was Paul. Leaders don't blink. I saw him in a lot of tight situations and a couple involved me. He never hesitated. He knew what had to be done and he did it. Leaders also know that only time will vindicate their decisions. At times you can't justify or explain why you do things and sometimes you know that only time will prove you right. Paul got a lot right.

Paul was also a great dreamer and unlike most people who dream all night, wake up and trudge off into another day of drudgery, Paul would bounce out of bed after a few hours' sleep (too busy dreaming) to toddle (barge) off to turn his dreams into reality. He dreamt of the Broncos being the best and made the statement after our first premiership — 'This is the start of the Broncos dynasty.' I nearly choked him for that. He just replied, 'You don't whack it up 'em enough, Wayne!' He dreamed of Paul Hogan wrestling fake crocs all the way to Hollywood. He dreamed about Morgan Stockbroking being a leading company in this state, at a time when he employed only two people. Morgan Stockbroking became a national company.

Most of all, however, he dreamed of success for others — usually Queenslanders, many of whom he barely knew. He loved this state, but most of all he loved the people who make it what it is, and wanted them to dream and become better too.

He hated seeing young talent wasted and he was always on my number about the young Broncos and what they were achieving away from football. We shared that bond.

All good people have skill, dedication and ability. Paul had a little extra — he had determination. And that is what made the difference for him.

Over the years, Paul gave away bikes to triathletes, bought rowing eights and fours for State High. The school wanted to dedicate these to Paul but he would have none of that and told them to dedicate the eight to his former principal, George Lockie. Paul was a very generous and humble man. I hated his knockers because they sought perfection from him while being imperfect themselves. It was his imperfections that I loved most in him because I saw how much he gave, asking for nothing in return. In my eyes this is what character is. It has been said that a man's character can be judged by what he does for those who can do nothing for him — that makes Paul 'Porky' Morgan one of the great characters of our time.

I vividly remember looking around the church and seeing old people and young people, businessmen and footballers, and thinking how many lives he touched. The gathering spilled onto the street, and I swear I saw kids sitting in a tree to get a better view.

I still miss him today and would love to pick up the phone and give him a ring, just to say, 'How are you?' and to get his thoughts on some things. I mightn't agree with him, though. It's his company I miss. As you get older and your friends start to go there's an emptiness even beautiful memories can't fill.

THE YEAR WAS FULL OF the greatest highs and the greatest lows. The 2001 season always seemed to be completely full on. Everything was changing — from the way the game was played to player management and the salary cap, which was really beginning to bite.

It was a new world and I soon realised I was going to have to make changes to myself or it would go past me. As Bill Gates once said, and I continually remind myself of it, 'The world is going to change with or without you.'

The change probably began in 2000, when we suddenly had exclusive access to a new statistical computer system that was being trialled. It coughed up information on everything from player stats and traits to data on kicking games, strengths and weaknesses. We called it VID Man. It was designed for cricket; it's in every football code as well now. It's a coach's banquet and we had the opportunity to use it before anyone else in rugby league knew about it. I have no doubt it gave us a huge advantage in 2000. But as use of that system spread we were all suddenly under more scrutiny than ever before.

Then QRL chief Ross Livermore knocked on the door asking me to take on Origin again. If it had been just about me I'm not sure I would have come back, but I knew the players wanted me to do it and they had had a horrendous representative season in 2000.

So I told Ross things needed to change. First off I wanted the QRL to form an association with the Queensland Academy of Sport to ensure a good, strong supply of young men for future State of Origins; they needed training, planning and mentoring. There were people in the game suggesting Queensland would never compete in Origin again, let alone dominate it — we needed smarts more than sympathy.

It's one of the very few times I've lied to my wife. We were on holidays at Christmas time but I had to go and organise camps for Origin and I had already been away from home a lot. I knew it was a bit unfair ... actually more than unfair ... but I also knew that if I didn't do it it wouldn't be done to my satisfaction. So I made up some story about having to go and see someone for a few hours, and jumped in the car and drove to Brisbane to spend the day with Tosser Turner and Gene Miles. When I came home I felt so guilty I owned up. But I suppose I'd only told a white lie because I knew I had to get this done and I just didn't want to get told I was out of line ... which Trish hardly ever did. She was entitled to say that to me, you know, because I was giving up more time for rugby league.

It was important for Queensland: that was the bottom line. We needed to improve and to do things differently from the way they'd been done since Origin began. Change the selectors, change a whole lot of stuff. Revamp. I only intended to stay one year.

Then Wendell rang and said he'd had this big offer from rugby union. Under the salary cap we just couldn't offer him what he was worth to our game. We went to see the NRL but they were in the same position then as they are today — all the bosses and the clubs were telling us there were plenty of Wendell Sailors out there, we'd just find another one, but that's rubbish. He was one of the highest profile player in our game, yet we waved him goodbye and gave the keys to the city to rugby union. 'There you go, chaps.'

A couple of years later, this guy's telling me he went to Wallabies training and all these schoolkids turned up and the only autographs they wanted were from league converts Wendell Sailor, Lote Tuqiri and Mat Rogers.

ONE PLAYER WHO WOULD never have considered switching codes, a man who is 100 per cent loyal to our great game, is Shane Webcke. But Shane had a difficult situation of his own to handle at the start of 2001, which came about after he picked up a knee infection during our trip to England for the World Club Challenge and went to hospital when he came home to have it treated. The infection went away, Shane played in our opening premiership game, and not long after the NRL's Dr Hugh Hazard rang to tell me our champion front-rower had tested positive for the banned substance Probenecid. I nearly fell off my chair. At around the same time, Queensland rugby union winger Ben Tune entered hospital with a knee infection, was similarly treated, and then — after he told the drug testers about his treatment — was prevented from playing until the drug left his system.

Shane's doctors had given him Probenecid to aid the antibiotics he'd been given in doing their job as quickly and effectively as possible — it is banned because it can also be used as a masking agent for steroids. But there was never any question of Shane or Ben Tune using it for anything other than therapeutic purposes. I think rugby league handled Shane's situation better than rugby union handled Tune's case. The NRL took the word of a man who doesn't lie, ruled that Shane was not guilty and the matter was not made public. In doing so, they allowed him to avoid the negative headlines Tune endured when news of his use of Probenecid broke in 2002.

THE BRONCOS LED THE COMP up until just before Origin I and then off we went to prepare for New South Wales. I was pretty disappointed with what the Queensland reps had done in 2000. I thought wearing the maroon jersey didn't mean a lot to them any more. So I was very careful, made sure I got the right support and

NO WAY WAS HE GOING TO FAIL

put in 10 new guys who had never played Origin. It was a huge gamble but I had to send out a strong message to everybody.

I wasn't confident going into the series but I wasn't going to let my trepidation show. The one thing I knew was New South Wales would be cocky, that they'd be full of themselves. They'd won the series 3–0 in 2000 and won the third game by 40 points. Our best chance would be to bounce them early in the game, get on top, and if we did that with this young inexperienced side, then we'd just have to hold our breaths.

I picked guys I thought could get the job done. It was Petero's first game and Lote's and Kevin Campion's too. I included John Buttigieg from the Cowboys. Paul Green came back; I knew he would do the job for us. We had Carl Webb, Chris Walker, Brad Meyers, Daniel Wagon, Chris Beattie. And we jumped 'em at the kick-off.

Lote scored pretty early in the piece, which gave us some confidence, some real momentum, and then Carl Webb scored a sensational try right on halftime. They came back really hard at us in the second half, which we knew they would, and we just had to hang in, not give them a sniff.

About seven or eight minutes into the half, Shane Webcke wanted to come off. He'd copped a head knock and couldn't see the football. He was as important to us then as he'd ever been. I sent a message out: 'Can you see the blue jerseys?' And the message came back, 'Yes, he can see the blue jerseys.'

I said, 'I don't need him to see anything else, because all I want him to do is tackle. I don't need him to see the ball, so tell him not to bother calling it. He is not coming off. He is staying out there.'

About 10 minutes later we were back on top. John Doyle, our hooker, raced out of dummy-half and picked up Gorden Tallis. Gordie made a great bust, as only Gordie could, and the hooker backed up to score and put the game out of their control. Geez, John was a hell of a player, but he was always busted up with injuries.

AT THE TIME I COMPARED Lockyer and Tallis to Wally Lewis and Arthur Beetson and it was a pretty good comparison. It was as important a series as Queensland has ever played. They are all important but for this one we were looking over our shoulders, wondering where we were going to get the players from. There weren't many stars around, but Lockyer and Tallis stood so tall, giving the kids around them confidence and carrying Queensland.

Between Origin I and Origin II Gorden got a serious injury. We were playing St George Illawarra and he took a bit of a high knock, seemingly no more than he'd copped many times in his life. But then the pins and needles came and within a week he was operated on. His spinal column was pinching the back of his vertebrae, so it was season-ending, almost career-ending. All of a sudden, the Broncos had lost their captain and Queensland had lost their captain and spiritual leader. Darren Lockyer took over both roles.

NEW SOUTH WALES AMBUSHED us in Sydney. We weren't full of ourselves; we were just doing the best we could without Gorden, without our intimidating factor. They jumped off the defensive line all night, beat us up, but when Shane Webcke and Petero Civoniceva can't go forward for you, you know there's something going on. It seemed to me that in defence they were allowed to go before the ball had been played properly.

We weren't good enough to beat them that night anyway, but I rang the referees' coordinator in the week afterwards wanting to know why referee Bill Harrigan let them jump the way he did. And they admitted they got it wrong.

I came away disappointed we had lost but pleased that we had hung on even though, without Gordie, we didn't have our strongest team. While it was the best team we could have put together, it certainly wasn't going to beat New South Wales in Origin III.

I was thinking, what am I going to do here? Racking my brain. When you're one-all in the series, you can't just walk away. We're back at the Swiss-Grand in Bondi and I'm semi-depressed. We probably haven't got the players to win game three and we certainly haven't got the quality in the right places — in the halves.

I'm thinking, thinking ... and all of a sudden I'm thinking outside the square. I said to myself: 'Well, why can't we bring Allan Langer back from England? What's wrong with that idea?'

I found Darren Smith, a player I respected, and asked him, 'Who are the most inspirational players you ever played with?'

He said, 'Gorden Tallis, Kevin Walters and Allan Langer.'

I grabbed Darren Lockyer and he named the same three, but with Alf at number one. I knew Kevin Walters put Alf at number one too. I thought, we've got to get him, we've got to get him home.

For a couple of days I kept it to myself and thought the process through. Then I put things in place — and it turned out to be the biggest Origin III ever, I reckon.

For seven days every paper was full of it. Every headline, every news service. I had talked to Andrew Gee in Brisbane (he was home from England, having an operation on his shoulder), asked him about Alf's mental state and form, and Andrew said he was the fittest he'd ever seen him and was enjoying his footy. So I rang Alf and said, 'Mate, how would you feel about coming home and playing Origin for Queensland?'

He said, 'What's taken you so long to ask me?'

I said, 'Are you up to it?'

He said, 'Do you think I would come home and embarrass myself?'

In life, you sense missed opportunities and afterwards you wish to God if that opportunity ever comes again you will not fail, that the emptiness inside will somehow, belatedly, be filled. Anyway, I swore him to secrecy.

New South Wales were really good about it, I have to say. They

OK'd it. I had a bit of a problem with one of the Queensland officials but Ross Livermore was on side. The other bloke argued we should have been blooding a young player but in truth we didn't have a young player to blood. We had to do everything we could to win.

People said it was a gamble. It was never a gamble. I don't gamble, but I will take risks. And I knew the risk was minimal because Alf was not going to embarrass himself. Champions hate failure and I knew he wouldn't have agreed to come back if he didn't think he could deliver.

Alf arrived in Brisbane and came straight into camp. I had never seen him train better. He was never the greatest trainer but he was always fun at training. This time, he wasn't quite as funny because of his absolute focus — no way was he going to fail. We did a bit of fitness work on the first day and he showed everybody that he was up to the standard. That was the message he wanted to send to all the players.

The rest is history. We played at ANZ Stadium and he was outstanding. Absolutely outstanding. He should have been man of the match but I think sections of the media who had criticised his selection couldn't bring themselves to vote for him. It was supposed to be the great Brad Fittler's last game for New South Wales and everyone in the Blues set-up kept saying they had to do it for Brad, but it didn't happen for them. I'm not into that stuff, anyway. Alf led from the front, as he always did, and proved to be the inspiration that lifted Queensland to a series win.

THE STATE OF ORIGIN GAMES were played on Sunday nights in 2001. We turned up at Newcastle on the Friday night after that game three and got beaten by the Knights 44–0. So many of us had been involved in Origin and it was just so hard. I understood where the players were. Origin had been such a high, such a night, such emotion and you really can't come down from there in just a few days. We had a young team, which didn't help, and we embarrassed ourselves in Newcastle. It sounds ridiculous to say it took the gloss off Origin, but for me it did. I didn't blame them, though. They were just a bunch of kids. It was too much for them.

Gordie was gone for the year, the injuries were mounting and it was getting harder and harder. Kevin Walters came out of retirement and we beat the Warriors the following week, but soon after that he busted his cheekbone against the Dragons. We lost six games straight before getting a bit of form back in time for the play-offs.

IN THE MEANTIME, I'D DROPPED Justin Hodges. We had taken him to England with us early in the year and he knew we were grooming him to become the first-grade winger when Wendell left for rugby union at the end of the season. He then got a hell of an offer to go to the Roosters, which he accepted, but our club had never been built on that kind of thing. Sure, Wendell was going for the money as well but I could accept that with the older players, those who have done their time with us.

Justin had come to us as a kid. We brought him down from Cairns, brought his parents down, put in a lot of time and effort, and I just believed they owed us a couple of seasons. That's what I believed then, and still do now, whether it's right or wrong. We spend a lot of time giving them our expertise and helping them. I believe the club should get some reward for that.

The other thing, perhaps an even bigger issue, was that we had a lot of good kids at the Broncos at this time — Corey Parker and Brent Tate, for example — who were going to be wonderful players. We knew that the Bulldogs wanted Brent and the Storm wanted Corey, and both players had been offered double the money the Broncos could offer. But still they stayed with us. They were the same age as Justin. I wanted to make a statement to everybody in the joint: if we put time and effort into you we expect something in return. This is what I was standing up for. If you don't do that, that's your choice, but I'm not going to play you in first grade.

We were losing games and everybody was all over me, carrying on, wanting me to put Justin Hodges back in our top side. I gathered all the players together and told them I wasn't going to sell the club out. Not for a short-term gain. Players like Corey and Brent had stayed for the right reasons. To me, if I put Justin back in the team, it would have been like I was being unfaithful to all of them, because they were all playing for less money than they could have earned elsewhere. It's a fine fabric that builds organisations and you have to know what that fabric is ... and sometimes you have to stand up against public opinion. I certainly had the media all over me about it. How many of them had been in a successful organisation, I don't know, but I do know the majority of them had never walked in my shoes, yet they were trying to tell me what I should be doing and what I should not be doing. That wasn't going to sway me, I can tell you.

We held our nerve. Justin went off to the Roosters and the Broncos moved on, winning our last regular-season match, against the Northern Eagles. I couldn't be more proud of the way they finished the season.

WE WERE BEATEN BY CRONULLA in the first play-off game but came back the next week against all odds to beat St George Illawarra. Beat them comprehensively. However, by this stage we had a huge number of injuries to deal with, as well as everything else that was happening at the club.

During the last training session before the preliminary final against Parramatta, we lost Ashley Harrison and Carl Webb, so

Shane Walker, a back-row forward, played five-eighth for us in a patched-up team missing 11 first-graders. We could not have played any more bravely. Despite and in spite of a couple of tough calls and a lopsided penalty count, we almost overcame all the odds. That day was to change the obstruction rule: we had a try scored on us which was definitely an obstruction and I carried on a bit afterwards, bringing it to the attention of the NRL. I said if this is going to be the way people score tries in the future it is going to change the face of the game.

Another thing that was changing in the game was the wrestling, which was becoming more prevalent. This was the beginning of working tackled players on the ground, preventing them from getting to their feet. Clubs were already coaching and encouraging what we live with in football today. Game plans were getting better and there was a lot more structure about the way we were all playing, partly because of this slowing of the play-the-ball. Decisions were being made that changed how we were going to coach and what we were going to coach.

It was a season where we were never beaten in the mind or the heart, only by injury. At season's end, Wendell went to rugby. Brad Thorn had gone to rugby (though he was to come back). Peter Ryan was in rugby and the drums were beating for Lote.

CHAPTER 25

SINGO

ON 29 NOVEMBER 2001, John Singleton launched a takeover bid for the Broncos.

I like Singo — he's another Porky Morgan. They just do the unexpected. Have no fear. They are generous people and they challenge you enormously. They never think like normal people. They expect and demand your best but you don't mind that because you know they will reward and appreciate you.

Singo is a guy I would love to work for. He would stir up the rugby league world, which is what Paul did when it needed it. The game needed it then as it needs it today, but the people at the top don't like that. They like the status quo. They don't like these guys who rock the boat.

Singo specialises in it. That's why he's built empires, that's why good people want to work for him. That's why and how Singo makes things happen. Porky was the same.

Singo loves football and he loves football people, because he knows they are real. Why do you think he's been a great sticker for Tommy Raudonikis and those other guys from Newtown, guys who can laugh at themselves in life? Singo has always been there for those guys. I've seen him at functions and he kills himself laughing at the footy yarns. Loves them. Can't get enough of them.

That's right, he gets it. Every time I see his name mentioned about coming to rugby league I get half excited because I'd love him to be involved.

He approached me when he was going to set up the team on the Central Coast. Wanted me to go there and coach. He said, 'I don't care what it costs me, I don't care what the obstacles are — you are the coach. You can do what you want to do.'

I knew he didn't mean that. I knew he'd be putting his two bob's worth in every day. That's him. Once you have his respect, however, and he has yours, you can tell him to piss off and he won't get offended. But he still can't help himself.

Guys like Singo and Porky bring out the best in you because you hate letting them down. You know they're tough businessmen ready to make tough decisions and you understand the rules. If you are not doing your job you pay the price — and if you don't understand that you are a fool.

You know a bloke is fair dinkum about having a football team when he goes and buys a stadium first. But the League keeps denying him, keeps knocking him back.

It's incredible.

He says he's given up now and walked away, but I reckon he will have one last throw. If the right people went up and gave him a cuddle, said, 'Mate, we've got a deal for you …' he'd be in, because he's like Porky — once you mention the word 'deal' they can't help themselves.

These guys don't give up their dreams, they don't lose — they just get disappointed. They hide inside themselves and pretend. Then they live the lie because they are sick of being knocked by people who don't share their vision. They get sick of beating their heads against a brick wall and spending all their time and energy trying to make it happen for those individuals who can't see because of small-mindedness and pettiness.

People like Singo, and there are few, never walk — they run. They tell you never to learn patience. When the rest of us can't recognise what they can do, we are better off getting out of the road so they can keep going. The irony is the people who can't see are the ones putting the obstacles in their path.

CALL ME A DINOSAUR, BUT I could never see a whole lot wrong with the all-conquering St George and South Sydney eras, with the building of dynasties. Clubs have a choice when rivals are successful. They can ask, 'What are they doing differently? How do we have to change? What do we have to do to get to that level?' Responding to those challenges is the hard option.

The soft option is to pull the competition down to your level. There are people at some rugby league clubs who don't want teams winning three and four comps in a row because it's too hard for them to reach those heights. It's much easier to pull it all back down to a lower level. That's why we see a lot of sameness in league today, with everybody doing the same thing. You turn on the TV and you'll see so many teams playing the same way. The only difference is the colour of their jerseys.

We have to stop lying to ourselves: if it doesn't happen in my era it's still going to happen — all the teams will be privately owned. It's inevitable. That's the great tragedy of locking the doors to the John Singletons: they're the only way we are going to get the cream to the top. We need these self-made guys coming in and driving the agenda. They know you have to fight hard for success and they refuse to harbour the reverse psychology of finding fault and pulling the standard down to make us all the same. We have more multi-millionaires in this country than we have ever had and all they need is some love and encouragement, some direction.

Look at Premier League soccer in England. Manchester United have been a hell of a team. I got the coaching job here the same year Sir Alex Ferguson was appointed as manager at Man U and I've watched them become the most successful team in the world. They have won lots of competitions and they have also inspired others — Chelsea and Arsenal, for instance — to try to reach them and knock them over. That's one of the reasons why the Premier League is such a great product.

I look at the AFL model and see some of the biggest names in Australian business as chairmen of clubs and in other significant roles. Yet every time someone with a bit of a profile shows an interest in our game we run the other way. We make excuses and apologies and end up finding a way not to have them. That's why the Broncos were initially the bad guys. Paul Morgan and co. were pretty outspoken, pretty upfront and wanted to run the club as a business. Their parting of the ways with rugby league has taken us back to the 100-year-old tradition of committees running clubs.

LOOK AT WHAT SINGO AND his mate Gerry Harvey have done in horse racing with the Magic Millions. The growth in those sales and races, which only started in 1986 but are now among the most important events on the thoroughbred calendar, has been phenomenal. I went to Strawberry Hills, his horse stud on the Central Coast, and he took me to the top of a paddock where his expensive yearlings were running around, six or seven of them, their coats glistening.

'Wayne, I love this area on the hill,' he said. 'I call it the Hill Of Hope.'

'Why's that?' I said.

He said, 'Well, mate, I get a six-pack of beer and I come up here, sit on the grass, drink the six-pack and hope like hell these yearlings bring me a million dollars each at the sales.'

Everything he does he does with passion. Porky was the same. If they believe in something they are passionate about it. If you don't share their belief and passion they blow you out of the water but if you are just as passionate about your own beliefs they will recognise that, listen, and often jump in with you so quickly it doesn't matter.

People without passion feel intimidated by them. If you walk into a room with a half-baked belief you'll last less than a minute with these guys, and it's no use walking away sobbing because you didn't have commitment in the first place.

People like John Singleton and the late Paul Morgan are teachers in a different way from most of the people who stand out the front of class at school. When they challenge you it is immediately up to you to decide whether or not you are up to it.

Where I come from, that's the best place to be.

CHAPTER 26

TURNING UP, READY TO PLAY

DON NISSEN WAS CHAIRMAN of the Broncos when News Limited became our major shareholder in March 2002. After Paul Morgan and before Donny a former News employee, Peter Chegwyn, had been Chairman. Peter, known to us all as Cheggers, was extremely supportive of me, the staff and the team.

Cheggars got to love the Broncos, as they all do. For a man who had reached such lofty heights in the business world to end up being a water boy at a football club says a lot about life, doesn't it? We roped him into carrying the water for the boys at training and he did it with purpose and joy.

Don took over in 2001. He had been head of the Commonwealth Bank in Queensland and was a former footballer, cricketer and golfer. He was an affable guy and like the chairmen before him a great believer in the Broncos and their culture. He never interfered greatly, just encouraged us and built relationships around town. The players accepted him and liked him a lot.

One day, I was in a hotel foyer and I saw Donny walking past carrying Tonie Carroll's gear. Next week, he walked past me at training, carrying Tonie's gear again. And the next time we were away for a game, same thing.

This had gone on long enough. I had to ask. It turned out Don had lost a bet to Tunza and had to carry his gear everywhere for the next 12 months. There was Tonie Carroll with nothing more than a can of cola in his hand ... and there was the recently retired head of the CBA, huffing and puffing like a packhorse. That's what sport can do to otherwise clever, clear-thinking people.

THE BRONCOS DIDN'T LOSE A game in the first nine rounds of 2002, a sequence that culminated in Lote Tuqiri's scoring a club record 26 points from three tries and seven goals in a 50–12 win over Northern Eagles.

Then Origin hit, as it always does, like an angry locomotive.

I wasn't going to do Origin in 2002 but Chris Close told me I had to do it, that there was no one else available and that everyone thought I was going to walk out again after doing only one series. He talked me into it — again, I thought I owed it to the players, the state and to him. Chris Close is an exceptional person and I have a wonderful rapport with him. Phil Gould was back for his first Origin series as Blues coach since 1996, and before game one he had a swipe at me about my apparent reluctance to promote the interstate series, adding that I ran the QRL. I never saw myself running anything but the perception out there had me running everything, and Gould fed off that. All I was doing was my job. I'd probably been too busy to realise fully, but deep down I knew from the day of Gould's appointment that the '02 series was going to be a pretty tough one.

Coaches can make a difference at Origin level. Just the way they prepare the teams. They can't make players do something they have never done before, but some can prepare teams better than others.

Gould has a huge record in Origin and his teams have always been well prepared. He was probably made for Origin. He loves the occasion, all the theatre. I'm told he can address a team like few others and his record proves he's more than just talk.

So I was certainly on my toes.

NEW SOUTH WALES WON ORIGIN I. During the game, Gorden Tallis was sin-binned for dissent by referee Bill Harrigan, who later conceded he should not have made the decision they argued about. Talk of a feud between Harrigan and Gordie dominated the media in the build-up to Origin II and at one point I said the ref wouldn't have sent our captain to the sin-bin if he was a New South Welshmen. Gould then accused me of 'stooping to the lowest depths'. It was getting pretty fiery.

At the same time, Lote Tuqiri had been cited for a dangerous throw against St George Illawarra, an offence that carried a one-match suspension. And here was the coup ...

As it had been for a few seasons, if a bloke was picked for Origin he couldn't play for his club team the weekend before the state game. So the Queensland selectors named their side for Origin II with 'TBA' (to be announced) as one of the wingers and the Broncos selectors named Lote to play Wests Tigers on the following Friday night (the Friday night before Origin II). When Lote was found guilty and suspended, he was able to serve his one-game ban in the club game.

All hell broke loose. I think they've closed that loophole now. Meanwhile, the Broncos went to Campbelltown without 15 regular first-graders, including Lote. There were two 17-year-olds, an 18-year-old and two 19-year-olds. The average age of the team was 21. Only Phillip Lee hadn't played for our feeder club, the Toowoomba Clydesdales, at some stage that season, and many had to ask their employers for a day off work to fly to Sydney for the Friday night game. The result? Broncos 28, Wests Tigers 14. Craig Bellamy, who coached them that night, said in the following morning's paper: 'Our players just wanted to come down here and continue the Bronco tradition of turning up, ready to play, every game.'

WE JUST HAD TO WIN ORIGIN II in Brisbane. It was a tough affair, as they always are. This was the night Justin Hodges made a couple of awful errors passing in our own in-goal, which led to two NSW tries.

Justin did it once in the first half and at halftime I tried to build his confidence and show some faith in him. But the same thing happened with about 30 minutes of the game to go. He tried to pass the ball in an impossible situation and New South Wales scored. The whole grandstand in which I always sat for matches went silent. There was hardly a sound until some guy yelled out: 'He's got to go now, Wayne!'

I got on the two-way straight away and said, 'Get him off.'

The fan was right. I don't normally listen to the fans because if a coach listens to them he usually ends up sitting with them, but this guy had nailed it. We got Justin off and we won the game. For the series decider three weeks later, Brent Tate was selected for Origin III after playing only 14 games of first grade.

IF YOU EVER WANT TO talk with authority about highs and lows in the one night, the one game, go look this one up.

With a quarter of an hour left on the clock in Origin III 2002, with Queensland leading 14–12, we kick the ball into the NSW in-goal and a flying Darren Lockyer somersaults and also miraculously grabs the ball and forces it inside the field of play. No one to this day doubts that the ball was forced — no one except video ref Chris

Ward. I got into trouble for describing the no-try call as the hottest decision I'd ever seen but six years on and nothing has changed.

New South Wales came back at us hard and all of a sudden, with five minutes to go, they were four points in front. Darren Lockyer did a short kick-off that allowed us to regain the ball. We played out our set of six and then defended extremely well, which meant we got the ball back in a good field position. With 30 seconds to go Alf found Dane Carlaw running wide and Dane went 40 metres, beating two defenders to the tryline.

Lote was goalkicker that night. We were trying to take some responsibility off Locky so Lote got the job but he didn't kick well. He certainly missed a couple that were kickable.

We were at 18–all, no time on the clock, Lockyer was walking back with the ball and I saw him throw it to Lote. It was a kickable goal. Lote missed it …

I have never … look, Darren Lockyer is such a good guy you never get dirty on him for anything. And I wasn't dirty on him that night. I just walked up to him and said, 'Locky, why didn't you take that goal kick?'

He said, 'Coach, I didn't have to. The game was drawn so we got to keep the shield.'

I also knew we had the shield won with a draw because we'd won it the previous year and there was still elation, though not from me. I had an empty feeling. I thought this would come back to haunt us. The only way against New South Wales is to beat them. They don't understand anything else.

Locky knew the ramifications of a draw and keeping the shield was the important thing to him. But I've always regretted that moment. That's how we finished up with the 'golden point', where if the scores are level at full-time you keep playing until one team scores. They used that Origin game as the reason why we should have golden point extra-time in the case of a draw at full-time.

I WAS CRANKY WHEN Lote Tuqiri signed with the Australian Rugby Union on 15 July. No one wanted him to go, but I'd have to say the powers that be were a lot quieter about his departure than they would be in years to come with the likes of Andrew Johns and Mark Gasnier.

The problem was that we were the Broncos, we were strong, which meant that the other clubs wouldn't support us no matter what angle we came from. The consensus at the time was that the game would find another Lote Tuqiri. 'There are plenty of them out there,' they said. I detested that statement.

The things I know are coaching and what makes football players. I can assure you that the majority of chief executives don't know about these things. If they did, they wouldn't be CEOs, they'd be coaches. There are lots of young men you see out there who you can certainly make into footballers, but there is a small group of rugby league players and sportsmen and sportswomen who have that God-given ability to be exceptional at their chosen sport. I use the term 'God-given' because that's what it is. It's in their genes. You can't go out and find someone else just like them because they are different from other people.

Lote is a wonderful athlete with a fair bit of toughness about him. He is exciting to watch when he gets the ball because of his footwork and great leg speed. He was made for our game. He's a wonderful, wonderful talent.

I've spoken to him lots of times since he made the decision to change codes, but he can't come back to rugby league because he is too well paid where he is. At the time, a couple of Sydney clubs tried to do a deal with him but he was never going to play rugby league somewhere else. He was never interested in that. If he couldn't play rugby league at the Broncos he wouldn't be playing it anywhere.

SO LOTE WAS GOING, AND in round 20 against Parramatta Alf suffered a broken thumb, which was another big blow for us. We were just out of Origin and trying to gain some momentum, but his injury put us on the back foot for a while. At his age Alf needed to play every week to have his match fitness right and the finals were quickly approaching.

I incurred a $10,000 fine after that game, because I said this on the night of the match: 'I've said it before and I'll say it again — when there's a tough call it will go against us every time. That's been going on for a long period of time. The officials' job is not to prejudge; their job is to make the right decision.'

It was pretty harsh, but again, nothing has changed. We know now that referees are given tip sheets on individuals in teams — that's prejudging. Players have to play what's in front of them on the night and referees should be doing the same. But I do understand the difficulties of the referee's job, and in recent seasons they have definitely become more professional.

After 26 rounds we finished third on the ladder, out of 15 clubs. Alf was back and we beat Parramatta 24–14 in the qualifying final and then had a week off before meeting the Roosters in the preliminary final.

We'd lost 28–18 to the Roosters in Brisbane in round 22. They had been in indifferent form before that but they turned it up that night and Justin Hodges had his best game since joining them. He scored a couple of tries, and the final scoreline flattered us. They were all over us. We clawed our way back, as we always did, and kept trying which is part of our culture, but I came away from that game realising the Roosters were the team to beat for the premiership. They were defending extremely well and were good with the footy. When you're making your premiership run late in the season there is always a defining night when you just know what's coming — and they nailed us that night.

So I knew we'd have our hands full in the preliminary final. I was pretty confident that whoever won this game would be premiers.

IN THE END WE SCORED two tries each, but we didn't get a penalty until the 70th minute and before that the penalties were running 8–0 in favour of the Roosters. At that level of footy, with two good teams competing, it's very hard to overcome such odds.

It was not unlike the Chris Ward video-ref decision in Origin III, with the most crucial decision in the game coming with 15-odd minutes left on the clock. We kick-chased and our young centre Casey McGuire tackled a Roosters player. They were 20 metres from their own line and Justin Hodges came up, grabbed hold of Casey and threw him off the tackled player, physically threw him. Casey jumped to his feet, swung a punch and knocked Justin over. Referee Bill Harrigan blew the whistle: penalty to the Roosters. That has never happened before in rugby league. Anybody who knows the game knows it's Justin who should have been penalised. He was the instigator.

We were already getting flogged in the penalty count. We had no history of ill discipline … we were a team that played by the rules.

So the preliminary final was over. We lost. The moment and the year were gone.

The next two or three days were very tough. I'd walk in and tell Trish I was going for a drive and I'd just drive down the coast for a few hours. Another day, I drove a couple of hours in another direction. I was probably as disappointed as I've ever been about losing a game of footy. I knew we had not beaten ourselves. I knew the penalty count had made a huge difference. I knew the players could not have given any more; I wasn't disappointed with them at all. I was fuming, just down. All these emotions …

IT WAS SOME MONTHS BEFORE I could stomach looking at the video of the game but when I did, I did it three times — to study the penalties and the reasons for them, that kind of stuff. Then, in the new year, I asked for a meeting with Bill Harrigan. I told the new referees' boss, Robert Finch, where I was coming from and what it was all about.

They are very good at stonewalling and making you feel like an idiot, telling you the reasoning for penalty after penalty, and you kind of have to live with that. Then they got to the Justin Hodges throw and I knew I had him on this one. I just knew. I knew there was no way out for him.

Harrigan looked at me — this is the most experienced ref in the game, regarded as one of the best refs of all time — and he said, 'Wayne, I had a brain explosion.'

I felt shattered before I went in there but now I was even more filthy and shattered. I just shut my mouth. People at that level shouldn't have brain explosions. It's like the best player doing something stupid in the big game. It shouldn't happen. They've been there too many times.

To this day, I don't know what the real answer was. I'll never find out, obviously.

I've moved on, but to suggest to me that a ref with all this experience — grand finals, State of Origin games, Test matches, just about every refereeing record in the history book — had a brain explosion ... we might not have scored the try, we might not have won the game, but that excuse was completely unacceptable to me.

AT SEASON'S END, SIX DAYS after the Roosters beat the Warriors in the grand final, Gorden Tallis captained Australian in the Test against New Zealand in Wellington. He was a proud man and rightly so.

Who would have thought? Going from where he came from to being captain of his country was a great effort.

Gorden is a guy who went into battle for me many times on the field, and we had our battles off the field too. That's Gorden. Just getting back on the field after that neck injury he suffered in 2001 was an achievement in itself, but he came back and quickly resumed his place as one of the most damaging forwards in the game. Volatility is who he is, the way he is ... and the way I like him to be. He could get you into a stink. Publicly, I always stood beside him but we had some interesting private discussions. With passionate, aggressive people the trick is getting the balance right, making sure you're not getting out of kilter.

Captaincy is a major commitment for all parties concerned. At the Broncos we are proud that the fine men who have captained the club have more often than not captained their state and country too ... from Lewis to Langer, Tallis to Lockyer.

I STARTED THIS CHAPTER WRITING about one of our officials and I'll end it the same way, because 2002 was the final as Broncos CEO for Shane Edwards, a bloke who'd taken on that role when John Ribot took the Super League job back in 1995. Shane had joined the Broncos as our marketing guy after working at the World Expo in Brisbane in 1988, and from day one he faced some pretty tough times. In the end the relentless of the job wore him out and wore him down. Porky and the board started selling shares in the business and the novelty of playing at ANZ Stadium began to dwindle. Crowds were declining and the salary cap was now a dark force.

I didn't envy Shane his job. I realised how lucky I was to be a coach who trains his team all week then gets a result one way or another every weekend. A CEO can work months or even years and still be waiting for a result.

But his commitment to me and the team was resolute. That was one of the great things about Shane Edwards: you never ever had to look over your shoulder; you knew where you stood with him. That was important to everyone, particularly me. He always gave whatever he could. He was totally supportive and a real footy buff. Shane loved his footy. Where John Ribot had been a player and represented his country, Shane was simply a fan brought up on the game.

Just the other day I ran into him and I reminded him of what he said to me when he was leaving. 'You know, Wayne,' he said, 'the Broncos' best years are in front of us.'

CHAPTER 27

IT'S ALL ABOUT THE TEAM

AS MY COACHING CAREER evolved, the guys I came to respect the most were those who weren't blessed with a God-given talent. Rather than the so-called superstars who might develop their natural talent just a little bit, it's the guys who get there by hard work and refusing to give in who I admire more. Guys like Michael De Vere and Andrew Gee top the list with me. Both played for their country and in Origin, but it was more than that. There were times I didn't think Mick was going to make it at all but he did everything in his preparation and lifestyle that he possibly could. He never lost the dream, got picked for NSW in 2001 and made his Test debut two years later.

My upbringing centred around rugby league, and the heroes of my early days were the guys in the local footy teams of Allora and Warwick. There were the Phelan brothers, Max and Brian, and a little halfback named Johnny O'Connor. They played with no resources, just a pair of old footy boots and a jersey that was probably two or three years old, because clubs couldn't afford new ones every year. They just played with passion and the other guys in the other teams were all the same.

When I was seven or eight they took our whole school to the movies to watch the Melbourne Olympic Games. It was the old newsreel stuff. We only had a small school and if I close my eyes today I'm still in that seat in the old picture theatre watching the athletes coming out.

There weren't too many TVs around Allora in those days and it was some months before the film of the Olympics hit town. We saw the opening ceremony, and while I don't remember the names of most of the runners, I clearly remember watching them run. I remember Betty Cuthbert. I liked anything Australian and hearing the crowds cheer.

The next thing for me was just wanting to play footy but my mother didn't want me to play. 'You are going to finish up like your father,' she'd say.

As I neared adulthood, I was inspired by the challenge of playing for Australia. Eddie Brosnan had played for Australia and when I was 12 or 13 he took me down to a Test in Brisbane.

From that day on I knew what I wanted. I had no doubts about it — I wanted to wear the green and gold. We played very little organised junior football at that time, but I still made a promise to myself that I would do the absolute best I could. I didn't know if I could play or not and didn't have a father around telling me. I didn't have a mother around supporting me in that regard either, though she supported me in things apart from sport. I was pretty much a free agent, out there enjoying my sport and trying to work it all out.

As a young boy growing up I'd noticed that when someone in rugby league did something wrong it wasn't 'Joe Bloggs' who was in trouble, it was 'Joe Bloggs the football player' or 'that footballer'. I didn't like that because there are a lot of wonderful people who play football. I thought it was unfair that when one bloke made a mistake all the league players were put under the same umbrella. People who didn't play or weren't a part of it seemed to think they were better than the men who did.

I had seen good men — and not so good men — represent our game and as I was growing up there was always a part of me that wanted to represent the game well. I was always between these two places, wanting to talk properly, to be able to get up and make a speech if I had to ... the ability to conduct myself appropriately at all times and in all places so people couldn't criticise the game. That's always been a driving force for me.

I WAS PRETTY YOUNG AND naive and playing in Toowoomba when I was picked to represent Australia in 1971. I learned a great lesson about myself then.

When I came back from New Zealand I thought that because I had played for Australia I had to be something different — not different as a person but different on the field. I thought I had to be able to show more skills and do more things. That wasn't the case; it was just me being stupid and immature. I didn't have to be different.

We were only away for nine days but in that time half the Australian team didn't want to know me. That didn't bug me. I just got on with life. It was just the way it was, but I made sure when I coached Origin and when I coached Australia that didn't happen to any players in the squad.

I was extremely introverted back in '71 and I'm still introverted today. It's always been a great dilemma for me. I have a public profile but by nature I don't want to be out there in the public eye. People think I can be rude and uncooperative but I would just prefer not to be in the limelight. Lots of times I would pay any price not to be part of it but I also realise that because I coach I have had to change enormously. But the introvert is still very much there. I've had to compromise myself with regard to my personality and be more out there, say things, take positions.

People don't understand that introverts are just happy being part of the group, not having to say one word, not being the centre of attention. I am happy to sit in the corner, but you wouldn't believe the number of times people come up to me and say, 'You look unhappy tonight, Wayne.' I'm not unhappy, far from it. I'm happy on the inside but I just don't show it.

One of my greatest achievements has probably been to overcome this introversion. One of the reasons I survived 21 years at the Broncos was that we usually had a winning football team, but beyond that the Broncos have always been about the team and I was just one part of the team. I'm very proud to have been part of the team. All the players have been in the same boat. It was never about the star player. It was always about the team.

MORE THAN ANY PLAYER, THOUGH, even more than blokes like Mick De Vere and Andrew Gee, the thing that inspires me most about rugby league is the game itself. I'm inspired by the opportunity the game gives young men and I know I wouldn't be who I am, or where I am today, if it wasn't for rugby league. I want other men to have the opportunities I've had and be part of that experience — and you don't have to play for your country, you don't have to be a great player, to get that.

One of my greatest recent thrills concerned a guy named Peter McIlwain, who was a cadet at the Police Academy, one of the first kids I ever coached. He played a bit of football and then spent his life giving so much back to the game. The Queensland Department of Main Roads repossessed land which had been the home ground of the Wests Centenary Junior Rugby League Club and were going to run the Ipswich Motorway upgrade through it until Peter went to work. He had been one of the people instrumental in building the club. Part of the deal that was eventually struck between the club and DMR was to build a $6.5 million rugby league facility at nearby Wacol and they named it after Peter. I went to the opening in 2008 and someone said, 'Is Peter McIlwain dead?'

'No,' I said, 'he's only a young man, about 45 years of age.'

This great facility that he was at least partly responsible for will give so many young men the wonderful experience of being part of a team sport. There's so many good things that go with being part of a team. And it is true, rugby league's a tough sport. But it's one that makes you feel like a man every time you play it.

CHAPTER 28

COULDN'T BUY A WIN

FROM 2000 TO 2005 the Broncos kept losing quality players to injury. Scott Prince was one. He broke his leg in 2001 and never fully recovered while he was with us, suffering another leg break and then a series of groin injuries. The Broncos never saw the best of Scott but every time he played you sensed his pure quality. Ben Ikin was another. He was also seriously injured in 2001 and was never the same player again.

Making it even harder for us, we made the wrong decision at the end of 2001 by letting hooker Luke Priddis go.

Under the salary cap you have to make decisions and, you know, somebody has to go. Everybody wants a little more every year, which means the salary cap is designed for clubs to keep losing some of their top players every year. I make this point now because what happened to us in 2003 was a repeat of what had occurred in previous years at the club. We kept losing key players through long-term injuries; we just didn't seem to be able to get away from the damage these setbacks caused.

The trend was that we would lead the competition — or be in the top two teams — until the Origin series but from there the extra workload on the players and added commitment needed to get through this time of the year would combine to make us suffer as a club. At the end of the season we struggled.

Our fade-out in 2003 was probably our worst. We lost our last eight games straight. The Broncos were leading the comp in round 17 but didn't win another game.

In round 19, post Origin, we went to Melbourne. We got to 22–all at full-time and as the referee blew his whistle for golden-point extra time I was sitting there thinking, they sure know how to kill our elite players. Our best guys hadn't wanted to train, hadn't wanted to play and the next day they were scheduled to go into camp for a Test match.

We lost Locky with a foot injury in that Melbourne game and after that we lost our way. Time and again the players couldn't have given more; they were tremendous. Webcke and Petero and those guys, they put their hands up every week. But we lacked that bit of class, that bit of direction Darren Lockyer always provided.

We just couldn't buy a win. Penrith beat us 13–6. There was nothing in the Wests Tigers game (12–10). Parramatta won 16–14. Against St George Illawarra in our last game of the regular season, we were leading 25–24 and two minutes off winning it when referee Tim Mander pinged us for being offside 45 metres out. Mark Riddell stepped up and kicked the goal. I was never more disappointed for a group of guys — I just wanted them to have a win. The feeling that comes from a win would have meant anything could have happened from there.

So we finished eighth and went to Penrith for the qualifying final. We were absolutely magnificent. They were to go on and win the premiership, but we had them down at halftime, playing in hail and a gale and the penalties were 12–4 against us. It was ridiculous what happened to us in the penalties that day. Again, I thought they were just refereeing one side.

We were pumped up and did our absolute best but it wasn't good enough. The best thing about the end of that season was that I didn't have to make any more losing speeches. It's not easy trying to get them up every week, trying to make them competitive, when the wins aren't coming. It's not easy on them. It's not easy on anybody. I'd be trying to find the right words yet knowing that the best thing that could happen to them was to have a win. But we couldn't buy a win. Couldn't buy one.

Darren Lockyer went on to captain the Kangaroos in England and won the Golden Boot award as the game's leading player. Gorden Tallis stood down from rep football. Scott Prince went to Wests Tigers. And Andrew Gee and Phillip Lee retired. It was a hell of a year.

THIS WAS MY THIRD YEAR in a row as Queensland Origin coach after I hadn't wanted to come back in the first place. Origin I celebrated the reopening of Lang Park (now known as Suncorp Stadium) and it was Phil Gould bringing New South Wales north so it was the same old story in terms of knowing what we were up against. The game belonged to them, 25–12, though we were a bit stiff. There was nothing in it until well into the second half, when Steve Price went for an intercept, missed, and left a hole in our defence.

So we went to Sydney, not lacking any confidence, knowing we weren't too far out of it. It rates as the most disappointing Origin game I ever coached. To this day, I still don't know what happened to us. I don't know where we were coming from or where we went to, but we certainly never went to the game that night. We were never in the contest. From the beginning we were flat and we never got any better. New South Wales looked like giants and we looked like we couldn't play.

They were full of it now, New South Wales. We'd won the previous two series but now they were 2–0 up. I wanted to do everything I possibly could to avoid the whitewash. We were better than that. Everybody was calling for big changes, but I thought with one exception we'd already picked the best players. And in the one instance where we'd got things wrong it wasn't the player's fault, it was our fault because we picked a guy who just didn't suit the balance of the team. We brought Cameron Smith in. Apart from that I convinced the selectors to hold their ground because the best thing we had going for us was the fact that the players were still hurting, still extremely disappointed in themselves.

I knew Gould would be looking for the whitewash. They would be coming back to Suncorp committed, absolutely switched on. And I wasn't wrong. The game was, in my opinion, up there with the best Origin games.

New South Wales threw everything at us. They'd come to finish us off, but we dug so deep it didn't matter. The night before, I'd given this speech. We were staying at the Sheraton, as it was known then, and I told them quite candidly that if they played the way they did in game two a stack of them wouldn't play for Queensland again. I meant it too. I didn't know what position I'd be in to enforce that, but this was about pure pride. I also went down that line with them. I also reminded them that they had what a lot of people don't get in life — a second chance. Don't blow it.

To their credit, they didn't. They were outstanding, winning by 30 points. It was tight for a long way but for the last 20 minutes we brought Cowboys fullback Matty Bowen on and he opened the game up. New South Wales had given everything by that stage, we surged and they folded a bit.

I heard Gould was absolutely filthy after the game. They reckon he carried on a treat. That made that series for me. They'd won the series fair and square, but I recognised how desperate he'd been to put the whitewash on us and pump up his bags at our expense. Denying him that was the only satisfaction I got all season.

I RESPECT PHIL GOULD AS a coach, he's a fine coach. But coaching does make you extremely competitive. I'm competitive anyway, but it still brings out the worst side of me. Most times in my life it hasn't got personal, but with him it's a bit hard not to get personal.

If you aren't ready to play and your team is not well prepared and you haven't got all the bases covered, he is going to revel in whacking it right up you. He's the best coach New South Wales ever had in State of Origin — you only have to look at his record.

While he had some fine players under him, in my opinion they never played great football. They just went out to grind you down, wear you down and beat you up. To Gould, Origin football isn't about entertaining; it was about winning. It was about humiliating your opponent. When they won a series 3–0 one year, they all boasted, with him leading the way, that they'd never made a change, that they'd played all three games with the same 17 players. One of them came up on crutches, he was so wounded, but they were just whacking it up us, trying to embarrass us. Of course, this is one of those things that makes Origin great.

So Phil Gould brings out the worst in me. From time to time he'd have a shot at me about not promoting Origin. That's the greatest heap of rubbish I've ever heard, coaches having to promote a game. You promote the code, you promote the game, you promote your team by the way they play. If they can't play it doesn't matter what you say, the fans aren't going to turn up. They're not going to be interested. They don't go to hear coaches. It's good morning-coffee debate at work to say Bennett and Gould had a bust-up today, but if Bennett and Gould ran out and played no one would go to watch. Nobody is interested. It's about what the players do and the concepts of those games and the passion they play with, that's what gets full houses.

What if I did come out mouthing off? I don't have to play. The players would probably back me, but they'd be backing me with their blood and pain. It would be none of my blood or my pain. I couldn't do that to the players, be a big mouth and goof off and get the other team all pumped up. Nobody does that in sport any more. We all realise the ramifications.

I've always said the game is about the players. It isn't about the coaches and it isn't about the administrators. It's about the men who play the game. They are the ones people go to see. The less I say, the blander I can be, the less reason other teams have to be pumping themselves up about us and getting themselves more excited to play us. They are excited to play us anyway.

CHAPTER 29

OPERATION SUCCESSFUL, BUT THE PATIENT DIED

THE THING ABOUT LEADERSHIP is that only time will justify your decisions.

I never tried to explain my position when I moved Darren Lockyer to five-eighth at the start of 2004, just shut my mouth and did everything in my power to make it work.

Locky was the world's best fullback and maybe one of the great fullbacks of all time, so the switch to five-eighth was always going to cause an uproar. But I've already explained how little I care about criticism. As my mate Mike Young, the fielding coach for the Australian cricket team, often says, 'Wayne, they don't understand.' And they don't. You know the thought you have put into a decision and the reasons for it, so you understand. When you are vindicated, don't waste time waiting for them to come up and tell you they were wrong.

Funny thing is, I'd been criticised many times over the years for not switching Darren Lockyer to five-eighth. It's not something you could do late in the season or on a whim, because the two positions require different fitness levels. They're totally different. The switch would take time, because we had to get Darren right. We had to swallow the pill and make sure he had the confidence and belief in me and in himself. He wanted the challenge and was ready for it, never hesitated. 'If that's what you want me to do, coach,' he said, 'I'm happy with that.'

Not many players I've coached have been so unselfish. He weathered the storm with me and now we never hear anything about it. The silence is deafening, as they say.

WE HADN'T EVEN HAD a chance to dust off the No. 6 jumper when the 'Coffs Harbour scandal' broke in late February. A number of Bulldogs players were alleged to have been involved in a sexual assault. Soon after, we went to a sportsmen's lunch in Brisbane to raise money for charities, but it turned out to be a very disappointing day. In front of 500 people, the compere — one of Brisbane's more respected journalists, a guy I quite like — began proceedings with a crude joke.

Darren Lockyer was on a panel out front. Earlier in the day someone had rung him with another crude joke, this one emanating from the Coffs Harbour scandal. Darren thought it was funny and repeated it for all to hear at the lunch. The media went into a frenzy and he got beaten up badly for it. He'd made a mistake, picked the wrong time and the wrong place.

There's no right in any of this, and while I'm not condoning anything the point I want to make is that the landscape has changed forever. These sportsmen's lunches have been going for 20, 30, 40 years, probably longer, always on the understanding that what's said stays in the room. A respected journalist can say what he likes at such an event and he'll be protected by his fellow journalists, but now there are different rules for prominent sportspeople. What was fun in the past isn't fun any more.

It's the same at presentation nights. You know the media is going to be there and that everything you say is going to be reported so you don't tell it how it is, you just stick to the script and walk away. Some people have paid a lot of money to go to that night and they go away bored stiff.

Darren Lockyer is not a bad man and he's not a crude man. He's simply a young man who makes mistakes from time to time and who learned the hard way that he can't tell tasteless jokes in public. Which is fair enough. He also now understands it is not a level playing field out there.

I WAS APPOINTED AUSTRALIAN coach in February, after Chris Anderson stood down. For my first game in charge, the Anzac Test against New Zealand on 23 April, Locky was picked as five-eighth and captain, and he celebrated by cracking a rib and playing on in a starring role. Talk about tough. When most people talk about tough footballers they're talking about the guys who smash them up and throw the first punch. I've coached a lot of tough guys and Locky's in the grand final for the toughest. I've seen the injuries he's played with, watched the doctors shaking their heads and the crowds cheer as he races into open spaces. I know we won the Test 37–10 but what I'll never know is how he played with that rib.

The following week we played the Bulldogs and he lasted 50 minutes. Suddenly the Broncos were without Lockyer, Webcke and Shaun Berrigan, and the following week against Canberra we lost our young halfback, Brett Seymour, for the season.

Next up, in round 10, the Knights came to Suncorp for what turned out to be the first golden point match on free-to-air television, with Kurt Gidley booting a field goal after three minutes and 26 seconds of extra time. My feelings on extra time were well known. I remember thinking, well the operation was a success, but the patient died.

Newcastle won 17–16, but they had their own dramas, with persistent rumours that Andrew Johns was about to switch codes to rugby union. Knights coach Michael Hagan, who had taken over from me with the Queensland Origin side, had called to ask if I would ring Johns. I just couldn't comprehend Andrew not playing rugby league. I didn't want to comprehend him not playing rugby league. Guys like Andrew Johns are icons of the game; they've gone past being simply greats. For guys like Andrew and Darren and a few others who have served their country and been rewarded in so many ways, if they'd switched to rugby it would have sent all the wrong messages. They are not your normal football players, or even just good players — they are in an absolute class of their own.

My view is the icons owe the game more than the rest of them. If they left for another code, the fans would be sitting there thinking where is rugby league going? The people of Newcastle would have felt absolutely cheated if Johns had gone. That's how I would have felt.

Recently Locky came out and said he'll never play rugby union. That's Darren Lockyer. He accepts the responsibility he has and these guys have in having been Australian captains, State of Origin captains and captains of their clubs.

So I called Joey Johns. We had a good relationship. I'd coached him in the Australian side and liked him. He's a rugby league kid, you know. I said, 'I know the money is tempting and I'm all in favour of you guys earning a dollar but the game can't afford to lose you, mate. You just can't go.'

He talked about the 'challenge' of being a success in rugby. Let's talk about the challenge, right, let me tell you what the challenge really is. The challenge is to go to work every day and get the best out of yourself. That's the real challenge in life. When you are feeling a bit flat, the challenge is not about finding another horse to jump onto. It's about turning up every day and every week and finding ways to keep lifting the standard. Sure, there'll be drudgery and repetition and there'll be people everywhere wanting a piece of you, but it's a soft option to leave. The hard thing is to stay in the game that has made you an icon.

I ENJOYED THE ANZAC TEST experience, though in my mind I saw it as a precursor to more important internationals later in the year. Not that this game didn't matter, far from it, but they'd introduced a Tri Nations competition for October–November and I was real excited about that. For this Test, which was played in Newcastle, I kept a few notes and here is an edited version …

MONDAY, 16 APRIL

9am: Conducted a staff meeting. Told them what my expectations were and outlined what was required of them.

9.45am: Team assembled. Went for 20-minute walk and then did rehab in the surf. Bus picked me up. Returned to team meeting at 11am. The issues I raised were important to me and the team management: punctuality, behaviour, (representing your country), manners, mobile phones, player managers, tour bonus at the end of the season.

6pm. Told them story about Noel Kelly, a former great Australian player. Talked about ANZAC and why this Test is a little bit different to other Tests. Talked about what it means to play for Australia. Presented Steve Price and Luke Lewis with their caps.

7pm. Went to the Newcastle Gentlemen's Club. Had the presentation of jerseys. Dinner at the club was very good. It was a lovely night. Ron Coote and Wally O'Connell presented the jerseys. Both spoke about what it meant to them to play for Australia. Both speeches were tremendous.

THURSDAY, 22 APRIL

9am. Team meeting. Went for 25 minutes. Discussed the need for us to keep it simple. New Zealand will come out with a lot of emotion. We must not get caught up in it. As the game goes on they will lose the emotion. That is the time that we must take our chances and nail the game. The other message was for Australia to play our game. Keep executing.

Concluded the meeting by speaking about the need to play as a team and play for the guy beside you. The mateship is a big issue with me.

FRIDAY, 23 APRIL

Won 37–10. Did not play well for the first 20 minutes but then we got a bit of rhythm. New Zealand scored in first five minutes for 6–0. Then it was 6–all, 10–6 to New Zealand, 10–10. Darren kicked a field goal right on halftime to give us the lead. New Zealand should have been leading at halftime but bombed a try about six minutes out. Danny Buderus made two wonderful try-saving tackles. Players were very positive at halftime. Our ball control was at 67 per cent. We knew they were gone; just had to make sure we held the back and stopped giving away penalties that was allowing them to get a piggy back out of their half.

We nailed it in the second half — within 15 minutes we had the game won. Our best were Buderus (a fine, smart player), Craig Gower and Lockyer. Our go-forward was excellent, led by Webcke; outside backs were good in Matt Gidley and Brent Tate and co. Everybody played well. It was a very good performance.

Feedback from players about the pre-game was that they felt good and had been looking forward to the game. I told them pre-game I wanted them to play with the Anzac Spirit and explained what that Spirit meant to me: never giving up, overcoming the odds, being a mate and then not letting your mate down. I said it's the greatest feeling knowing that guy on either side of you will not let you down. They played with the Anzac Spirit. I was very proud of them. They all enjoyed the week, as I did. I know this much. There is not as much pressure coaching Australia as there is at State of Origin level. I had a very relaxed week. The staff and players were all excellent. No one was late for anything. Always well-dressed and well-mannered, the players were an outstanding group of young men. I cannot speak highly enough of them. It was a pleasure to be a part of their lives for a week. Look forward to when we all meet again.

Came back to a post-match meal and then a function with families, etc. I got to bed about 1.30pm. Tired and satisfied. (My mind was already on Sunday when we play Penrith).

One thing I was to learn over the next couple of years was that coaching the Australian team for a one-off Test at home was a far different experience — for me and for them — to taking them away on tour for a month or more.

IN THE BRONCOS' ROUND-17 win over Souths a 17-year-old fullback named Karmichael Hunt scored four tries for us.

Karmichael is different from Darren Lockyer, but his achievements from the day he arrived at the club have been similarly remarkable. At the Broncos, he's never trained with anyone but the NRL squad. Whatever challenges we have given him he's met. At times I can't quite believe what he has done. Most of them break down, have some type of problem or drama, but this guy just wants to play footy. He's happy to train, happy to do whatever you ask him to do. I have never heard him complain.

Recently someone was shocked to learn that Karmichael knows little about the history of rugby league or the names of players before him. He knows more about basketball players. He loves the NBA and can tell you more about Michael Jordan than he can about Greg Dowling or Blocker Roach. When he first came to the Broncos he'd spend his down time playing basketball with his father. His father was only 36 years old. He looked so young and fit that there were people at the club who thought he was a current player.

The best advice I gave Karmichael was to stay a 17-year-old, and then an 18-year-old and so on. Because soon he was getting all the headlines and adulation and success, but I didn't want him acting like a 30-year-old. I didn't want him feeling he had to grow up fast.

At training he was as committed as anyone. Even when he first arrived he had this confidence beyond his years. He'd tell the players what to do, he'd tell Webcke and Petero where to run and what to do and they loved it. And in games he'd carry the ball back fiercely and without fear every chance he got.

FROM ROUND 17 THE BRONCOS won six games straight, beating Souths, St George Illawarra, Newcastle, Manly, Cronulla and the Warriors. Then in round 23 we played the Bulldogs at Suncorp. That was the day I knew we couldn't win the premiership.

We were close to full strength and in the contest until halftime, but they really towelled us up in the second half. We had no answer. I knew then that we couldn't win it. Did I go and tell the team that? Of course I didn't. I kept coaching. I tried to get them across the line.

Michael De Vere had torn his ACL at training and would not play for the Broncos again. He left at season's end to join Huddersfield. It's funny how things affect you — let's just say I didn't like seeing the back of that bloke. Three weeks after the loss to the Bulldogs, in the final round against Penrith, Brad Meyers and Carl Webb were injured.

Then Melbourne got us cold in the qualifying final in Brisbane. We led 8–0 but lost 31–14 and someone asked whether I was worried about the team's prospects. I said, 'Worry is like a rocking chair — gives you something to do, but gets you nowhere.' We had to play the Cowboys next and the semi-final had been allocated to the Saturday night at the Sydney Football Stadium. They would have got a crowd of 5000 people, so I'm thinking, God, that can't happen. It was either that night or the following morning when I rang our CEO Bruno Cullen and said we should take this game to North Queensland. The Cowboys wouldn't have wanted to come to Suncorp and I thought the game was more important than the politics. Up there, we'd have a full house and everyone would enjoy it.

They must have been thinking the same way at the NRL because within eight hours the deal was done for us to play in Townsville. I was elated to be part of that. Finals are all about great crowds, great atmosphere. And we'd played there lots of times, so we knew what we had to do. There would be no excuses.

SHANE WEBCKE HAD BEEN MASKING a leg injury, he had a spur on his knee, and when I confronted him about it he told me what was going on. The doctor, Peter Myers, came in and said, 'You need an operation but if everything goes right you're still a chance of playing Saturday. I can operate tomorrow morning.'

We got Shane back onto the park on the Saturday morning in Townsville and when he started to jog around he looked like a broken-down old thoroughbred. He could barely get out of a walk. Within 10 minutes he began to run a little bit normally, so we looked for someone for him to tackle to see if he could still hit all right, still had his leg power. The only one there was a physio, who's 70 kg wringing wet. Shane smashed him all over the ground, just cleaned him up. I didn't think we'd have a physio left for the game.

So Shane played that night, and was nearly our best.

Earlier in the week I'd made a decision: it would be all or nothing. We were in the play-offs and there would be no tomorrow. It wasn't a case of just passively going along and hoping we could cope.

I remember saying to Kevvie Walters and one or two other members of the coaching staff, 'I'm going to bring Gordie off the bench.' There are two things the real warriors want: they want to be in the starting team and they want to play 80 minutes if they can. From the time he first came to the Broncos, Gorden had convinced me — or I had convinced myself — I had to turn him into a run-on player, despite the fact that when he first came into the game he certainly was best coming off the bench. He was a huge impact player. I believe now, when I look back on his career, I got that wrong.

He was at his best when he was explosive and not playing for long periods of time. Playing for long periods, he had to pace himself because when Gorden Tallis ran 10 metres he didn't just run 10 metres like the other guys did ... he ran with every fibre in his body at its absolute max. When he hit you, he hit you with everything he had, using every breath of oxygen in his body.

Our best chance to win this game up in Townsville was to bring him in off the bench. But he was captain of the club, it was his final season of football and he comes from Townsville. I thought, if I go and lay that on him now I'll have an argument all week and that's not going to help the team. We were in the change rooms preparing for the game when I said, 'Mate, I'm going to start you off the bench. The team sheet's gone. I've decided I'm going to start you off the bench.'

He said, 'OK, if that's what you want to do.' That's what happened. Gordie played some of the first half and I remember him getting an injection at halftime. We were not big on injections at our club but it could have been his last game and he wanted to go back out for the second half.

We could not have been braver. I was proud of everyone but we were just shot and the Cowboys deserved their 10–0 win.

THE TRI NATIONS CONCEPT — a three-way competition between Australia, New Zealand and Great Britain — was instigated in 2004, and I said to the team, 'Get this right, boys, and you'll have another Origin series on your hands, because these countries will give so much for their colours.'

In the end, the initial tournament worked out well for us because the Australian team produced a sensational performance in the final, winning 44–4. We led 38–0 at halftime and Locky was magnificent. So was Anthony Minichiello, the Roosters fullback. Early on, though, there were a few shaky moments. We beat New Zealand in London and Great Britain at Manchester, but drew the competition opener, against New Zealand in Auckland, and lost to the Poms at Wigan.

At the start of the tour, I decided to keep a brief diary. Here are a few snippets …

SUNDAY, 10 OCTOBER

Whole team assembled at 5pm at Coogee. Issued training gear and had a meeting on expectations, behaviour, etc. I went pretty hard at them re drugs, alcohol, etc. Told them I was prepared to send a player home if I had to. Told them how the media would be looking to find fault, etc. Banned mobile phones. It was not the most pleasant meeting but I had to start that way. Formed a senior players group: Darren, Craig Gower, Shane Webcke, Danny Buderus, Craig Fitzgibbon.

Allowed team to go to Coogee Hotel — curfew 12 midnight. Most of them home by 10pm.

FRIDAY, 15 OCTOBER

Trained at North Harbour on the main oval. Trained at 2pm. Had a team meeting at 1pm. Read them a short story on 'Mateships'. I found it in a book on the Anzacs. Very relevant. Used the same notes (re what we have to do) that I used in the Anzac Day Test. Still relevant.

SUNDAY, 24 OCTOBER

Travelled Auckland-Sydney, stayed two hours, then travelled to Singapore and London. Arrived in London at 6.35am. Trained on the Monday afternoon after arriving in London on the Monday morning. Trained Tuesday; Wednesday, Thursday off. We trained at QPR oval (home of the Test match) on the Friday at 11am.

Had a pretty good week. First two days in London I went down for breakfast at 6am (jet lag) and there was already a stack of players having breakfast. Over the next few days I was one of the few who kept turning up at the early hours. As their jet lag left them they came later. We trained at a private school ground. It was a good facility. Did a bit of shopping. Took the whole team to the House of Commons. All went on the bus to see the sights of London. Traffic was ridiculous. Played New Zealand at QPR at 6.15pm on Saturday night. 17,000 in attendance. Excellent small ground with a great atmosphere. NZ led us 6–0 after five minutes. Led us 12–8 at halftime. Scored two tries in last 10 minutes — down our right side. Still shocked at halftime. Team was down, not a lot of enthusiasm — did not get into them but encouraged them to do the things that make us successful. Attempted to sort out our right-side defence.

We kicked off to New Zealand in the second half and in the first set they attempted off-load after off-load; by the fourth tackle we had the ball 50 metres from the tryline. By the end of the fifth tackle we had scored through Darren Lockyer. We got some confidence and scored 24 unanswered points against them. In the end it was a very good second half. After the game went with the team to see a boy in a wheel-chair. It was a very moving moment, walking across the field and being with the boy. Gave him a jersey and Willie Mason took his shorts off and gave them to the boy.

Real down moment after the game. The Australian team has no team song. It leaves a big hole after a good victory (intend to do something about it.) I get a real thrill out of seeing the boys line up in their Green and Gold, singing the national anthem. Went out into London after the game but that was a mistake — could hardly move, the city was packed with people — came home on the Tube. It was packed. All went to the 'Church' at 1pm next day. Weird place but it was a good day. It closes at 4pm. Pay £7 and you get three cans, two in a plastic bag. Left for Leeds at 4.45pm on the bus.

FRIDAY, 29 OCTOBER

Now in Leeds. Had Thursday off. Everybody appears to be a bit bored. Decided we would train at Manchester City today and stay in Manchester for a few hours. Fill the day up. It's an hour down and back. Hit a traffic jam coming home and it took one and three-quarter hours. Rest of it worked alright. I am very sick and miserable with flu but have said nothing to anyone. So many players and staff affected by it. Scott Hill has to pull out of Test team because of flu.

SUNDAY, 31 OCTOBER

We started yesterday's game (v Great Britain at Manchester) well — could not score, had lots of field position. They scored 80-metre try against the run of play — then led us 8–0. We scored right on halftime to go in 8–4. Scored in first 10 minutes after halftime to be at 8–8. Scored right on full-time, 30 secs to go to win 12–8. Deserved a draw, lucky to win. Nathan Hindmarsh made a huge play to stop a field goal and allow us to win the game. We defended well but failed to play well as a team with the ball. Our halves did not combine at all.

FRIDAY, 4 NOVEMBER

Had a night out after the Great Britain game and on the Sunday went to Harry Ramsden's fish and chips restaurant. Went from there to a pub. Trained Monday — running, ball work, weights. Gave the team four days off until training at 9.30am tomorrow. Lot of the players went to Prague. Staff and that went in different directions. I went to Cambridge University. Had a couple of good days. Went on the train — stayed with a Professor Bill McDonnell. Came home to a Huddersfield Old Boys reunion. Had a lovely afternoon, met up with former players. Went to the George Hotel and looked at the History of Rugby League museum. This is where the game was first formed.

MONDAY, 29 NOVEMBER

Tri Nations final. We decided to attack Great Britain down their left side. In the two Tests they had stopped all our attack on that side. They had defended different to anything we had experienced before. However we felt that we had some answers to that style of defence.

We decided to do three plays:

Play 1: A grubber kick in behind — their winger came up to lock and their fullback was poorly positioned. First try Australia. Ball goes wide, Anthony Minichiello puts grubber kick in (kick was spot on). Matt Sing scores, Shaun Berrigan could have scored as well. Six points.

Play 2: The idea was for Lockyer to attack back around the play-the-ball area with his passing or running game on their left after we got a quick play-the-ball. Try two. We start a break down our left, ball comes back through the ruck and with back up we go 40 metres and play the ball on their right side. Play-the-ball is quick. Lockyer gets back at first receiver; on the right reverse passes to Minichiello, who is coming down through the play-the-ball area. (exactly where he was required to run). Six points. 14–0.

Play 3: The idea was for Lockyer to run wide, then turn Berrigan back in at the play-the-ball area. He was not to get caught with the ball. They did it perfectly down our right and Berrigan passes to Minichiello who scores under the posts. 20–0. All over at the 20-minute mark. Felt great.

CHAPTER 30

DOING WHAT'S RIGHT

WHEN HE CAME BACK to us he was all of 36, which is a young man in most walks of life but an old man in football. To me, as a footballer, Darren Smith was ageless. A remarkable guy.

But his form had been indifferent for a long time. Alf and Kevvie would see me with him in the weights room and they'd say, in jest, 'Oh no, we've got the wrong Smith here. We should have Jason here.' They were referring to Darren's journeyman brother, who shared the ageless gene.

Darren did take time to grow into the club and the way we played our footy. He was originally from Easts in Brisbane, and he came to the Broncos in 1995 after playing some terrific football for Canterbury. He became extremely valuable because he didn't take a lot of coaching and just got the job done every week, no matter what position you played him. He stayed with us for four years, then went back to the Bulldogs before going to St Helens in England. In 2004, he was back at Easts playing in the Queensland State League and we were beset with injuries, with Tonie Carroll and Petero at the top of the list.

I rang him up and said, 'What do you think?'

And he said, 'Oh yeah, I'll give it a shot for you.'

He'd play, then it would take him a full week to recover. And then he'd play again. In 2005, he played 16 games for us before finally giving the NRL away. I wish to God he'd never retired. He was in the Mick De Vere category, a really good professional.

DARREN LOCKYER WAS THE OBVIOUS choice to be captain in 2005. He had already established himself as a footballer in the Alf mould, in that he led from the front and had the respect of the players but never said a whole lot out there. Darren is an extremely introverted bloke. Early on, being captain wasn't easy for him, but being such a learner and always wanting to do what's right for the team, he developed his communication skills.

If you don't know him now you'll never know him, because part of being an introvert is not wanting people to know who you are. Most of them are very comfortable in their own skin; they don't do things in order to be better known.

Who is he? He's reserved, soft-hearted, very balanced. A very clear thinker and a tremendous accumulator of knowledge. He is a perfectionist — that's what he is first and foremost. He's always looking for better ways to do things and to do them properly. Just look at the way he has grown into the captaincy. Locky was always talented as a footballer but I can tell you the captaincy wasn't something he was naturally talented at. Like most introverts, he understands how to deal with criticism. It doesn't faze him too much, he takes it on board to make sure he develops himself. And there is a bit in him that likes to be extroverted, which gets out when he has a few beers. The other Darren Lockyer arrives. He is a fun guy. Completely different personality.

He's certainly one of the best team players I've ever coached because his whole being is about the team. He will make a very good coach if he chooses to go down that path.

THE 2005 SEASON WAS VERY similar to the ones that preceded it, in that we played our best football up until Origin, lost key players to injury and just faded out of the competition ... limped out. We lost eight games from nine at the end.

The round-22 game against Manly was the turning point for us. We had worked through the Origin period, from rounds 12 to 19, with six wins from seven games, and were six points clear at the top of the table. In the latter part of every season there is a point where you either turn good or you turn bad and this day against Manly we had two guys miss the bus to go to the game. That was the beginning. They were downstairs playing the poker machines and we just couldn't find them. No one thought to look there.

A few hours later, we had the game won, as everyone had predicted, but then got soft and let them back in. Manly won by a field goal, 21–20, and then the injuries started to come. Locky did his hammy against St George Illawarra and the following week we were heartbroken at Penrith. We went down there with three or four guys missing but began with a magnificent Justin Hodges try. Hodgo had come back to us at the start of this season. He soon set up another try but then he did his knee — an injury that would keep him out until the final game of the play-offs — and I made an error by putting him back on that night against Penrith. He thought he was going to be OK. I knew he wasn't 100 per cent but we were short on the interchange and needed a body out there, I thought, to seal the game for us. There were only a couple of minutes to go and Penrith went at Justin, who just couldn't run. They scored: 22–20. It was my mistake and I told the team afterwards, took full responsibility. So Hodges and Lockyer were gone until the finals. Shane Webcke was also missing.

I never received as many emails and letters and phone calls in the 21 years I was at the Broncos as I did when Justin Hodges came back to the club. All the correspondence was negative. Even certain members of the staff weren't keen, but I knew the kid who'd left the club in 2002 was a good person and I had great faith in him. In his first couple of games back, whenever he got the ball, there were some boos but it wasn't long before they were all cheering for him.

In the early days we could win a premiership despite heavy injury tolls, but in this era of salary caps we didn't have the same number of quality of players to back up when we lost lose the key one. We brought in a teenager, Berrick Barnes, and he was playing so well the Australian Rugby Union soon took him off our hands, and we had the Eels beaten in the final round of the comp until Fuifui Moimoi knocked Berrick out and he couldn't come back. Fuifui got seven weeks and we got sent to purgatory. Instead of being on the rise going into the play-offs we were on the downslide.

Rule interpretations made by the NRL have taken us down a road where the team making the fewer unforced errors invariably finishes on top. What happens when you have a lot of young guys who are not regular first-graders, or are yet to experience a lot of first grade, is that they make errors at crucial stages of the game. The continuity is not there. Someone doesn't turn up on his assignment somewhere. It costs you and you can't overcome that. From about 2003 on, whenever the injuries hit, that was something we often struggled with.

SO WE WERE GETTING TOWARDS the end of the season and it was all falling apart again. We got to the play-offs as the third-placed team but lost to Melbourne in Brisbane. Then it was the semi-final against Wests Tigers at the Sydney Football Stadium, a place we love to play.

There were three crucial moments in the first half that night against the Tigers. First, Darren Smith was over the line but Benji Marshall saved a try. How Benji got his hands under the ball I have no idea. Then Darren threw an inside pass only to see it miraculously intercepted by Benji, who raced 90 metres to score. While all this was going on Tonie Carroll tore his hamstring. Lockyer was on the field but he wasn't fully fit, certainly not in match condition.

The third moment came right on halftime. Brent Tate was caught with the ball on the last tackle. Changeover. He put it on the ground, they played it on the halfway line and straight away passed wide to their captain Scott Prince. We had not re-formed in defence. Try time again.

I had never been in a more depressed dressing room at halftime. They'd given everything and knew they deserved to be in front. But we were down 10–0.

We went out in the second half and made a charge, but in the end, as my old mate Ron Massey keeps saying, 'Wayne, the bridge is too far.'

I came home bitter, dirty, depressed, eating chocolates like they were going out of fashion. They are my anti-depressants. I never like looking at the last game, particularly when we lose, but in the end it got too much for me and I had to go and watch it. I had to watch it for one reason only: everybody was telling us how hopeless we were. We knew we were out of form but I did some stats, which told me at halftime we had broken their line five times, they had broken ours once. We just couldn't finish it. In the second half, we broke their line three times and they broke ours seven times, yet they won the match 34–6. The stats and the video showed that there wasn't much between the two teams but the scoreboard didn't reflect that.

They won the game, deservedly so, and they went on to win the grand final. They were a great team to watch, the Tigers, played some great footy.

WHEN WE GOT TO THE end-of-season reviews I knew I had to do something. I knew if we kept doing what we had been doing for the past three years we'd keep getting what we'd always got. I didn't want to go through that again.

The first thing I had to look at was myself. I asked a few questions of a few people who don't always tell me what I want to hear, people who have known me for a long time. I try not to accumulate people around me who pat me on the back. I'm not interested in that, it doesn't help, doesn't make me better.

Had I lost the eye for coaching elite footballers? The passion for it? I was confident that wasn't the case. Losing certainly dulls you but it doesn't make you a worse coach. If anything, it probably makes you a better coach because you have to look at yourself and your ways a lot harder. I wanted to stay, but I came to the conclusion that we had to change our culture with regard to the way we trained and played.

We trained great, don't get me wrong. We never had a problem with training in our club, and we've certainly had some great guys as trainers, from Craig Bellamy to Steve Nance, Kelvin Giles to Gary Belcher. But we had to change. How do we get fitter? The game requires its players to be fit all the time, but how could we achieve that without working harder than we already were? I realised I had to go outside the game to achieve this. Kelvin Giles had come from outside the game and it was time to do it again. That was point one.

Point two was the way we played. The game was changing, with the wrestle becoming dominant, play-the-balls getting slower and refs having more of a say in things. We had been playing ad lib,

Right: I loved playing, wish I still could … Broncos training, July 2008.

Below: With my grandchildren, (from left) Bella, Will, Joey and Grace.

Left: Crowd surfing at Red Hill after we defeated Cronulla in the Super League Grand Final in 1997.

Below: A group of Broncos in the home dressing room at Brisbane's ANZ Stadium in 2000 after beating the Sharks in a qualifying final. From left: Kevin Campion, Michael Hancock, Tonie Carroll, me, Kevin Walters, Brad Thorn and Harvey Howard.

Allan Langer was a great footballer, great captain, great Bronco ... best of all, he and I are great mates.

Above left: Alf during his fantastic return to Australia ... Origin III, 2001. Above right: The Maroons a year later, after retaining the Origin shield. From left: PJ Marsh, Allan Langer, Shaun Berrigan, Lote Tuqiri, Andrew Gee (at back), Brent Tate, Gorden Tallis (in front), Robbie O'Davis, Steve Price.

Centre Stuart Kelly (left) embraces Robert Tanielu after our 19-year-old prop scored in our round 12 win over Wests Tigers in 2002. Scott Prince is at right. We had 15 players out because of Origin and injuries, but the 'Baby Broncos' did us proud.

The people I admire the most are the ones who reach the top by working hard and never giving in. Men like Michael De Vere (left) and Andrew Gee (right).

Right: With the Tri-Nations Series trophy at Elland Road, Leeds, after Australia thrashed Great Britain 44–4 in the 2004 final.

Below: Our mood was very different at the same ground 12 months later, when we lost the final 24–0 to New Zealand.

Shane Webcke (left) and Petero Civoniceva in the dressing room at the Sydney Football Stadium in 2006 after we came from 20–6 down at halftime to beat the Bulldogs 37–20 in a preliminary final.

Brad Thorn in Brisbane after the 2006 Grand Final, proudly showing the premiership trophy to Broncos fans.

In 2007, when the Broncos celebrated their first 20 seasons, the club formally recognised 20 of its finest players. Seventeen of these men attended the function when the names were read out. Back row (from left): Gene Miles, Michael Hancock, Chris Johns, Steve Renouf, Glenn Lazarus, Andrew Gee, Gorden Tallis. Front: Kerrod Walters, Michael De Vere, Petero Civoniceva, Tonie Carroll, Shaun Berrigan, Allan Langer, Shane Webcke, Darren Lockyer, Kevin Walters, Brad Thorn. Absent: Wally Lewis, Terry Matterson, Wendell Sailor.

Justin Hodges scores the first Broncos try of the 2006 Grand Final. Karmichael Hunt is in the background.

The highs and lows of our great game. Above: With Darren Lockyer after the Broncos defeated Melbourne in the 2006 Grand Final. Below: Two years later, the Storm scored a last-minute try at Suncorp to knock us out of the competition. Locky couldn't believe what had happened to him. None of us could.

playing what was in front of us, and while we had structure, we had never allowed it to dominate the way we played. Did we have to change to the way other teams were playing? Did we have to block runners and choreograph everything? It's like a big dance company now, with every movement choreographed. I had seen other teams doing it to break down defences, because defences were now so much better — even though the defenders weren't any smarter, I can tell you that. (Rugby league, by the way, is the only football code in the world where referees determine the speed of the game.) So we had ended up with this brand of footy where everyone knows where they have to run, when they should run and who they should run at. This was the major thought in my mind, that we could no longer play the way we had always played.

The two crucial positions we had to work through were hooker and halfback. Barry Berrigan had been great for us at hooker in '05, playing 20 games. I just wish he'd come to us when he was 18. His younger brother Shaun had been playing some outstanding football for us since 1999, while Barry had played at Canterbury. I didn't know much about him. After the Bulldogs, he played a bit in the bush and finally came back to Brisbane with Redcliffe, which was when Shaun tipped me to him, saying simply, 'My brother goes OK'. I finished up grabbing him but his time at the Broncos was plagued by injuries. He kept doing his neck in, had a problem not unlike Brent Tate, who had to wear a specially designed neck brace after he was injured in 2005. So we were trying hookers out and nothing was working for us.

At the same time, I was trying to make Brett Seymour a halfback but he was really a five-eighth. He tried hard for us — there is no criticism there. But we were struggling in that area too.

Combine that with the injuries and we were in a hell of a fix. So we needed a new guy to run our fitness program and I wanted to change the way we attacked.

The fitness guy was Dean Benton. Kelvin Giles helped me find him. Then another guy, Jeremy Hickman, came along, initially as a rehabilitation coordinator, which was another new trend in the game. Once the players finish physio, these guys get them back into shape, with running and training and weightlifting.

Ivan Henjak would be the new assistant coach. I'd coached Ivan at Canberra in 1987, had employed him as State League coach in the early 1990s, and I'd brought him into the Broncos set-up in 2004, helping Cyril Connell with recruitment. I knew he'd be a good fit. Peter Ryan would be the defensive coordinator. Peter had turned up late in the season and done a bit of defence with us. He convinced me I should employ him. I'm being a bit facetious: Peter is very good at what he does.

But before any appointments were made, I had to tell Glenn Lazarus, Kevvie Walters and Gary Belcher. Glenn Lazarus had been coaching the Under 18s, Kevin was my assistant coach and Gary was the performance coordinator.

I have to say this was my most traumatic time at the club. It was very, very difficult and I nearly left myself. The reason I didn't go is that I knew we had to change and I didn't think there was anyone more capable than me of orchestrating that change. If I thought there was I would have stepped aside.

It's never been about logging up 21 years at the Broncos. It was always about being able to do the job, getting the results and keeping the club in good shape. I knew I was employable, so that wasn't an issue — if I wanted to continue coaching it didn't have to be at the Broncos, it could be somewhere else. A long time ago I accepted in my mind that my career probably wouldn't finish at the Broncos.

I knew what I had to do. How should I do it? When should I do it? I let it go until after the presentation night, which we have just after the grand final. I didn't want to rain on everybody's parade. I wanted everybody to enjoy that night ... but I have to say I didn't. It was a terrible night for me, knowing what I had to do the next day.

It was just so sad. We have all since got on with our lives, but that day — 7 October 2005 — will always be one of the lowest times in my coaching career. It's just the way it's going to be and I can't get away from that. As always, I did what I thought was in the best interests of the Broncos. It hurt some guys who were really close to me, I understood that, but I still had to do what I believed was right.

The thing I've learned from making tough calls all the time is that we all have to be ready for the tough call, to be able to handle it and get on with our lives.

THE NEXT DAY, AS THE news of all the changes at the Broncos was breaking, I was in Sydney with the Australian side for the start of the Tri Nations series. The Kiwis were up for the game and played great footy. We were underdone, got beaten, and I had to go to the post-match press conference. The previous year Australia had won the Tri Nations playing some outstanding football, but this time we had turned up under-prepared, with some guys still recovering from the grand final, and the first thing they wanted to know was when I was going to resign. What's wrong with Australia?

Losses do happen. If they keep happening, fair enough, that's another issue, but we all fail from time to time. You win the next week and the same blokes who were after your scalp are now convinced they are the reason why — you won because they motivated you.

And we did win the next week, beating the Kiwis in New Zealand. It was something special. We had to dig so deep. I thought New Zealand would come off the boil and be full of it after beating us in Sydney; I banked on that a bit but in fact they were as committed as they'd been in Sydney. It was Joey Johns' last game in the green and gold, so we had to stand tall and we did. We were magnificent. I could not have been prouder of an Australian footy team or of the sheer quality of that Test match.

AFTER THE GAME IN AUCKLAND, we went to Wigan and beat Great Britain 20–6, then to France to play a one-off Test at Perpignan. On the way there, we were training at a rugby union ground in Paris when Locky picked up the ball and suddenly collapsed on the ground with a broken bone in his foot. His tour was over. He was a great leader of those guys and now he was on crutches. There was no Shane Webcke either. We went back to England, to Hull this time, and beat Great Britain again, 26–14. We had to win that game to make the final against New Zealand, who were already through.

I was struggling with the tour — I was certainly not myself — and was looking forward to going home. Physically I didn't feel great and mentally I was terrible. I probably needed to be home, in my own environment, more than anything else. I didn't need any more pressure. One of the things that was happening was that the media were calling for change at the Broncos — after I had implemented the changes I'd decided on. The change they were talking about was me.

I felt like I was disguising my worries pretty well on tour. I kept to myself more than I normally do but made sure I did everything I had to do coaching the players. I almost always enjoy my own company, but this time even my own company wasn't that good. But I had a job to do. It was no use sooking about it and carrying on, even if what had happened at home was still with me and not going away.

So we got to the last game. I have the notes here ...

MONDAY, 21 NOVEMBER
Beaten 24–0 at Elland Road, Leeds, in the final against New Zealand. Completely outplayed and out-enthused. One of the most

disappointing games of my career. We just did not want to be there. Tried to rally them at halftime but they just couldn't lift. New Zealand were very good and played with great spirit and a very good game plan. They kept kicking for the corners and were very aggressive defensively and didn't allow us to get out. Their ball control was also excellent, they were certainly ready for the match. They deserved their success. I was extremely disappointed that I could not rally them at halftime. I didn't think we could win the second half but I knew we could play a lot better than the first.

I decided with about 20 minutes to go that I would not coach Australia again. I wanted to coach them until the World Cup in 2008, in rugby league's centenary year in Australia. I wanted to coach a team that would be a lot more consistent and play with stability. I think I achieved that in about 50 per cent of our games, but it would not improve unless we approached things differently.

I felt that my continued involvement with the Australian team would impact on the Broncos and I was not prepared to do that. So I decided I should go. I resigned a month later.

The ARL wanted me to stay on but I did not. I did not meet my own standards.

I only finished these notes on Saturday, 20 October 2007. Took me a long time.

THE MOST DIFFICULT THING you do as Australian coach after being beaten like that is go to the media conference. I always feared this day, because the Australian team has enjoyed so much success in the last 30 or more years. I didn't want a heavy defeat in a big game to be on my watch, but that is the risk you take.

I stayed longer than normal at the Elland Road post-match conference. I was pretty open and candid because I knew it was the end of my time as Australian coach and I wanted to give them a comprehensive overview of my thoughts on the game. It was all over for me. When I walked out of that press conference I decided that I wasn't going to talk any more about the Australian team. I had done my time. Said all I had to say. So no one was going to get a word out of me.

When we came home in 2004, after winning, we flew into Sydney and then Brisbane. When I went through Sydney airport there was not one journalist there. When I arrived in Brisbane there was one journo who wanted to interview me.

This time around I was thinking no one would be interested in my thoughts. They weren't in 2004 … when we won. Then it hit me … we've lost so they'll turn up in droves and want to whack it up me. But I was strong in myself, so I was just going to say 'No comment' and keep walking. I had the game plan and I was fine.

When we arrived at the airport in Brisbane I was in a pretty good mood … a really good mood, actually. I was coming home to see my family and it was over. I was just waiting on my bags in customs when this Qantas employee came up to me.

He said, 'Mr Bennett, there is a team of journalists out there.'

I said, 'I expected that, mate.'

He said, 'We've got a back door. We'll get the documentation done, they'll clear you and I'll get you out the back door.'

I thought, that's a good idea. That's what all the rock stars do. I thought, what's wrong with that? But I said, 'No mate, I'll be right, it's no drama.'

He said, 'No, you don't need that in your face.'

And I said something like, 'No, I don't.

I always feel rude when I say 'No comment' and keep walking. I know there is a perception that I can be rude, but it's not my nature to be rude and I thought going out the other way would at least save me from that. People wouldn't see me on camera saying 'No comment' and walking off; they wouldn't be thinking, there's that rude bastard again. I said, 'OK, mate, I'll take your offer.'

He went away and I waited and waited, but he didn't turn up for ages. I had my hands on my bags to go out the normal way when he reappeared and said, 'Wayne, out the side door.' So I went out and that was it. Innocent as that.

I nearly got to the car, you know. I don't carry a mobile phone, so Trish was just waiting for me in the normal place in the terminal. I got a message to her via Steve Walters. One of the journos realised I wasn't coming so he followed her and they got a photo of me getting into the car.

When I woke up the next morning I knew I was going to be a headline, never had any doubt about that.

In hindsight, I made a mistake. It was not my style. It really wasn't me. I'm a big boy and have always faced up to what I've had to face up to. I wrote an article and apologised. I was wrong. In the end I would much prefer people did think I am a rude bugger. If that's the impression I give, so be it, because I'd rather give that impression than do a runner again through a side door.

CHAPTER 31

TRUE BELIEVERS

OPERATION HARDEN UP, AS we called it, was the idea of Paul Bunn, our football manager. Paul's a real lateral thinker and we needed something different after all the turmoil over the staff departures at the end of 2005.

I have always been keen on army-style camps because adversity can create bonding and because they put players in a confronting environment, outside their comfort zone. But we had never done a six-day camp, never that long, and we had to hire some battle-hardened ex-army guys to run it. It happened in late November, when I was away in England with the Australian team.

The players were told they were going on a holiday and to bring their golf clubs and surfboards. So they lobbed at the Broncos training facility, ready to rock and roll, but were taken to the middle of the field and told the holiday idea had gone west. They were told to go the sheds and take off every bit of clothing except their underpants. Then they were issued with army clothes and footwear ... as the bus left for Operation Harden Up, locked away back in the sheds was a mountain of golf clubs, surfboards, mobile phones and Hawaiian shirts.

There were some terrible excuses in the first couple of days for why they couldn't do this and that and cries about what they shouldn't be doing. They were four to a group. On some occasions at tea time, each group was given a live chook and six raw spuds. Bon appetit. If they couldn't cook them they weren't going to have any dinner.

So they were challenged in many ways.

This was the starting point for 2006, a time of change. At pre-season training it was obvious working under Dean Benton and Jeremy Hickman was going to be different from anything they'd done before. Dean in particular placed huge demands on them. Just on Christmas we lost Greg Eastwood. He said he'd had enough and went home. Greg had played the year before but was only a kid. We had to send Ivan Henjak to get him back, a process that took three or four days.

Most of them felt like spitting the dummy and going home. The physical work was hard, but Dean was changing their training culture. There were issues they had to address with regard to skin fold, training methods and different sessions in the weights room, where they did a lot of stretching and other things they hadn't done before. A lot of biometrics, a lot of strength work rather than just lifting weights. They trained with huge intensity and the sessions weren't as long as they'd been in the past.

I spent most of January and February trying to keep them together, because they weren't happy. A few of them were most unhappy but I could see where it was going. At different times a few threatened to walk out, but we managed to hold it together.

WE GOT TO OUR FIRST game against the Cowboys and played dismally. They performed as individuals, not as a team, and I quickly recognised why. For the past few months they had spent most waking hours individually trying to survive and please Dean. They were still not happy in themselves, and playing rugby league was the last thing on their minds.

I remember getting them together straight after the Cowboys game and saying, 'Look, guys, I don't know what we will do this year but I know this much — you will be a team. That's one of my specialties: you will be a team. When this season is over we might not have done much in the comp, we might have done a lot, but we will be a team.'

NEXT UP WE WERE TO play the Sharks at Cronulla and during the week I got a phone call. Lachlan would like to meet us. Lachlan Murdoch was our owner now. He would like to meet with me and Broncos CEO Bruno Cullen and would we be available on Friday? I think we were to play Cronulla on Saturday night. Would we be available? Yeah, that would be great. So we did a bit of a cruise on the harbour.

It was the beginning of the end. Silly as it sounds now, I think that's where my departure from the Broncos started. After that day it was a case of when I would leave, not if.

Don't get me wrong, it was a great cruise. I enjoyed Lachlan's company. He's a terrific guy, a great Broncos supporter. John Hartigan, who is Chairman and Chief Executive of News Limited, also came along.

I knew by this stage that we were in for a tough season. The papers had already been into me and before we'd played a game a number of people had written us off, including our ex-captain. Gorden Tallis was quoted saying if the Broncos had a poor season I would have no option but to quit.

Lockyer's captaincy was also in question. Queensland had lost the 2005 Origin series and Locky has never been an arm-waver or finger-pointer ... beautiful demeanour, ideal for a leader. The ill-informed, however, were looking at other guys in the competition who did a lot of yelling and screaming and abusing, thinking that was the way a captain should behave. I never wanted that from Locky and he never wanted to play that role — it just wasn't the way we did things at the Broncos. So Darren was under the pump, or at least his leadership was.

Anyway, John Hartigan was on the boat with us. It was a lovely afternoon and they were great company, but I was still uncomfortable about the year ahead because we had made such a big cultural change. We had a lot of experienced players there, but we didn't know how they were going to react. They certainly hadn't reacted well so far. They'd done the work, but not reacted well.

Not only is John good company, he is also a wonderful success story, having worked his way up from copy boy to CEO of the Australian arm of the most powerful media empire in the world. Once these guys get to that level, though, you rarely see them. They work behind closed doors. Unless you make an appointment you'll never get to see him. As we were getting off the boat I said, 'John, I think we're in for a pretty tough season. If that's the case and we don't finish up making the play-offs, where would I stand as coach? What would be your position there?'

He replied, 'Well, Wayne, I think the Roosters are probably going to win the comp.'

I said, 'Do you?'

He said he really couldn't guarantee me anything with regard to what might happen if we had a bad season.

In another conversation I had with John a couple of years later he refuted this no guarantee discussion, but that was certainly the impression I was left with after that cruise. I came away from our time on the harbour feeling very uneasy. I never asked Lachlan the question because he wasn't the CEO of News Limited — he was on the News board at the time — and I didn't feel he was the guy I should be asking anyway.

SO WE WENT TO CRONULLA and were down 12–0 at halftime but gutsed it out, the way the Broncos can. Got up and won the game. In fact, we won 11 of our first 17 games, including a round-8 come-from-behind result against Canberra. They led us 18–0. At full-time it was Broncos 30, Canberra 28.

We were coming together as a team. I knew we weren't on top of our game yet, but I also knew we were beginning to put some stuff together.

One of the crucial aspects of that year was being given a bye after the last Origin game, which meant we could give the players seven days off. Dan Baker, our strength and conditioning coach, had flagged the idea during the pre-season. We wanted to try to avoid the post-Origin slumps of previous years. Dan said we'd pay a price for it, that when they came back it would be like starting all over again and we would have to ride that for three or four weeks before they'd come good. We lost to Melbourne in round 18 without our Origin players, had the bye in round 19, then lost to North Queensland again, to Wests Tigers, Canberra and Melbourne again. Five in a row, paying the price Dan had predicted.

The media had another half-chance to go me, but this time the problem was that our CEO was buying into it. Bruno started making what I thought were inappropriate comments about the team's future. I suppose the one that got under my skin most of all was the day he was quoted in the papers as saying, 'Wayne future is the furthest thing from the minds of the people who matter at this club.' Then, a couple of sentences later, he added, 'Review time is November ...'

With my contract at the Broncos, because of my longevity, I've always had the understanding that if I wore out my welcome there would be a quiet tap on the shoulder and they'd say, 'Listen, mate, you're out of here.' I reinforced that with Bruno when he got the job.

What I need most of all, as a coach, is for the club to stand behind me. I can cop everything thrown at me — that doesn't bug me too much if I know the club is behind me. What I don't need is them coming out publicly and saying I have their full support. That is usually the death knell. I continually reinforced that to Bruno and to everyone before him. It's like the guy who comes out and says he's retiring to spend more time with his family. That's rubbish. Believe me, that's not why he is retiring. He's been away for 20 years and his family's not home any more.

What I needed Bruno to do was simply remain silent. If not silent, solid would have done. I just needed their support. But I wasn't getting that and each time I fronted him about it he said he'd been misrepresented in the papers: 'They've screwed it around the wrong way.'

'Well,' I said, 'stop going to the papers then. If that's the case, just let it go.'

We had a new chairman, Darryl Somerville, but I wasn't going to run to him and say, 'What's my position here, Darryl?' I had never played that game and I wasn't about to start.

I never wanted to get the sack from the Broncos. I felt that if there was one thing I was entitled to it was a tap on the shoulder. Then I'd say, 'That's fine, I'll resign and walk away. Let's not have a public debate about whether or not I should be here. Let's not have a blue in the papers. The Broncos have always been bigger than that.'

PUNCTUATING ALL OF THIS, at the end of July there was a nightclub incident that allegedly involved Brett Seymour, while back-rower Neville Costigan was charged with drink driving. We had been pushing change both on and off the field, and now we had a 24/7 random drug-testing policy, run independently of the club, just trying to make sure we were on top of as many things as possible. The landscape is continually changing and you can't afford continual stuff-ups by players.

All of a sudden we were having a bad week. Sometimes it happens. Sometimes it has nothing to do with footy. You don't even get to coach some weeks. Leading up to the nightclub incident we'd had some other situations and I was over it. I'd had enough. That morning I walked into the change room and looked at Shane Webcke, Brad Thorn and Petero Civoniceva — they were sitting in the corner talking — and I thought, you guys have given so much to this club, I'm not going to fail you today. Shane was playing his final season and I wanted it to be a satisfying one for him. I know what I have to do. I have to show some direction. That's what I was thinking as I watched the body language in the room. I couldn't stand there that morning and go through the ritual of apologising for bad behaviour and making excuses.

Within 15 minutes I had told the two boys they were no longer required at the Broncos. I remember we went to Suncorp to train that morning and I was a shot bird. I asked other staff to take the session and walked around like a zombie for a while. I hoped those two boys would learn an invaluable lesson and change their behaviour. At times, it's true, you have to be cruel to be kind. I knew it would be tough for their families, and I knew their families personally. It certainly sobered the place up, I can tell you. There was deadly silence in the joint. Over the next three or four hours I received a number of calls from players asking me to reconsider and even offering to help as much as they could to sort the boys out. I said the decision had been made and I was not going to change it. The only thing I felt good about was that I wouldn't have to apologise to Webcke, Thorny and Petero.

Against Melbourne in round 23 we were just so courageous. The team's performance had finally come together. Melbourne, who were leading the comp by six points at the time, was the right game at the right time for us. The turning point.

We played Shaun Berrigan at hooker. We had been talking about it for a long time. Shaun was playing for Australia and Queensland in other positions and he was a great utility player, but I knew what he could do at hooker. I also knew it wasn't a position he loved playing, but he was a bloke who was always prepared to do what was best for the team. The timing had to be right too, because it would take time for oppositions to work out what he did well and what he didn't do well in that position. Four weeks out from the play-offs, I thought the timing was absolutely spot on. We had to make a run now or it wasn't going to happen.

Melbourne beat us 18–12 but we were outstanding. The contest brought the best out in us and it had to, because there was no fallback position. I had never walked into a losing change room and felt so happy. On the scoreboard we had lost but mentally we had won. That's what I convinced them — mentally they'd won and they should forget the scoreboard. They all knew what they had put in, the price they'd paid, and most of all they all knew that if they kept going they could really achieve something.

The following week we beat the Bulldogs down there 30–0. We did a great job on them. We went back to a private function and that's when Petero made his speech. He addressed the playing group and I couldn't have been prouder of him. You are often proud of your players for a whole lot of reasons. So many of them came to the Broncos as kids and I saw them grow as players and grow into family men taking responsibility. People would come up and tell me what wonderfully mannered men they are. How caring and giving they are. There is no one in that category greater than Petero. In every sense he is a giant among them.

He had gone from a shy 17-year-old boy to the man addressing the playing group in Sydney. The things he was saying reflected many of the things we had spoken about over a decade, perfectly delivered in his way and in his words.

The theme was our behaviour over coming weeks, the chance to come together as a group and do something really special. He called for a commitment from everyone to get off the drink, to focus …

I STAYED IN SYDNEY THAT weekend for a meeting with Nick Politis, the Chairman of the Sydney Roosters.

Just before the Melbourne game a close friend had called and said, 'Nick Politis would like to talk to you about going to the Roosters.' The Broncos were struggling at the time and I didn't want to stay at the club if I was the problem. There were no guarantees we were going to win the grand final.

Nick Politis is in that Paul Morgan/John Singleton category of guy, a real achiever. He had been in contact with me on and off over the years but I had never gone this far before, and it excited me a bit. We had a very good meeting, during which he said, 'I think you can win the premiership this year.'

I said, 'I think you're right, Nick, but there are two things that can't happen here. I don't want to rain on Shane Webcke's parade. He has been a wonderful player for the Broncos and if we can win a premiership and he can be part of it, that will be the best send-off he could have. All the players have a chance to win and I don't want to rain on their parade either. This will be the biggest rugby league story of the year. If it gets out before the season finishes, Nick, the gig is off. It's not going to happen. I won't jeopardise the Broncos' chances of winning a premiership because of my own interests.' I needed to make sure nothing impacted on the team.

Nick was very concerned about Ricky Stuart, the Roosters' current coach. He thought the world of Ricky and it was a very hard call for him, but Ricky was out whether I took the Roosters coaching job or not. That was his decision but there is never any joy for anyone in the making of those ones.

I would be there for three years. I reiterated that all bets were off if it became public.

I came home and got on with my life, didn't think too much more about it. It wasn't the time for that — I had other priorities.

PARRAMATTA AT PARRAMATTA IN round 25 was a tough game but again we toughed it out and the signs were great. The players were doing the tough things, the things that win premierships, so I couldn't have been more pleased with them. The other great thing was that we were playing pretty much without injury, missing only Karmichael, who had broken a bone in his foot in round 15 against St George Illawarra. I was putting the same 16 players on the field every week. Then Karmichael came back and it was the same 17 players every week, which was as crucial as anything else we did. Absolutely crucial.

In Shane Perry we had finally found ourselves a halfback. He was 28 years old, had played a bit of first-grade with Wests and the Bulldogs before joining the Redcliffe Dolphins. He was the most unfashionable halfback in the NRL, right, but the guys loved playing with him. He gave them great direction and was a tough little bugger. One of our great wins that year was against Cronulla, when we beat them in Brisbane without all of our Origin players. Shane led them tremendously that day. He did a hell of a job and we realised this guy could get us around the paddock. He'd hurt his leg and been out for a month leading into our bad period, which underlined even further what a crucial player he was for us. Locky had a lot of confidence in him, everyone did.

Some people were questioning why we were sticking with him, saying we couldn't get the job done with him, but everyone at the club believed in Shane Perry and he was living the dream. One day he was sitting down at Redcliffe watching Friday Night Football and the next he was playing NRL with a chance to go to the grand final.

We had Shane Webcke's farewell in the final round at home against the Warriors. It was a huge game. Huge day and huge crowd. Everybody wanted to send him out on top. They played extremely well that day, the Warriors, really whacked it up us, and we had to work hard to beat them. It was a hot day in Brisbane — you can get those stinkers with spring coming — and it took a lot out of us. We played the game on the Sunday and had to back up against St George Illawarra in the qualifying final on the following Saturday night.

When the Dragons came up we were flat; trying hard, but flat. Shane's farewell had been huge. We were all caught up in the emotion of it. And so we should have been — he was our mate. Everyone had played their heart out for him. I was in a losing dressing room after the qualifying final, but instead of being down and kicking the cans, once again I was really upbeat. Told them what I thought, told them what had happened. I didn't tell them before the game, because that would have given them an excuse for not playing well. I never do that with them. Afterwards, though, I had to make sure they still had confidence and weren't down in the dumps because we had another chance the following week and we could get it right.

ABOUT THIS TIME IT WAS reported somewhere I had all but signed a three-year deal with the Roosters. I remember ringing Brian Canavan, who was now the CEO down there, and saying, 'If that's as bad as it gets we'll be OK, but if it gets any worse than that, Brian, I ain't coming.'

We played Newcastle in the second semi-final and got a bit lucky. They had a couple of key players injured and we played out of our skins. We went down there full of confidence and when it all comes together at the Broncos it can be pretty exciting stuff. We did a great job on Joey Johns, kept him out of the game and the Knights were on their way out of the comp.

When that report about me and the Roosters was floated I spoke to Shane Webcke and mentioned it to Darren Lockyer, but I didn't go near Bruno. He came out and made some comments about not believing it would be happening and saying that I hadn't spoken to him about it. At the press conference after the St George Illawarra game I was asked to categorically deny that I had been in discussions with the Roosters, or was it something about committing myself to the Broncos? It flushed me out a bit but I said nothing.

A friend of mine called and asked what was going on. He said, 'You can't leave the Broncos.'

I said, 'Well here's the situation. I'm not going to leave the club in turmoil. I'll get the job done at the end of the footy season, then I'll move on and they'll appoint another coach pretty easy. I mean Ivan Henjak can certainly do the job. There will be no great drama.'

He said, 'What's Bruno's position with all this?'

I said, 'I'm not sure.'

So we organised for Bruno to come out to my house and sit down with me and Trish. I told Bruno my position and why I'd done what I'd done. He assured me that he didn't want me to leave the Broncos. I said, 'Well, mate, I need a commitment from you that you will stop going to the papers and discussing the issue. If I'm not wanted just tell me and I'll go, it won't be a problem.'

I arrived in Sydney later that week and made a tough phone call. I rang Nick and told him I wouldn't be coming because the story was breaking. Neither Nick nor I had made any comment, but the story was out there. I stressed again that I wasn't going to jeopardise the Broncos' opportunity to win a premiership. Nor was I going to harm the club to benefit myself. Nick understood. He understood the rules of our agreement.

THE SEMI-FINAL WIN OVER Newcastle was followed by a preliminary final against the Bulldogs. We went out there a bit sluggish and they got a couple of tries on us ... and a lot of confidence too. The turning point was about seven or eight minutes out from halftime. They had a couple of consecutive shots on our line to score tries. We held firm and were beginning to pick up our intensity. I could see us turning things around, and I thought, if they don't score here we can still win the game but if they score in the next two sets leading into halftime it's all over for us. We went to the break trailing by 14 points, 20–6. In a hole, in a hell of a mess.

But the key part was that as they came down the tunnel towards the rooms big Willie Mason started mouthing off, 'THE BRONCOS ARE GONE ... YOU'VE GOT NOTHING.' Mouthing off big and loud. My blokes came in fuming. I think they were more filthy about that than they were about the scoreboard. I seized the moment and told them this was about the true believers ... true believers win these kind of games, so don't give in.

Shaun Berrigan went back out and scored one of the finest rugby league tries — and certainly the most determined try — I had ever seen. He was living his faith, his belief in the team. Nothing was happening for us when Justin Hodges made a break, getting to the 40-metre line before meeting Berro coming the other way. Determination and belief can't talk and Berro never said much either, but if they could they would have been screaming in unison, 'My team needs this try and I'm going to score it for them NOW.' It gave us the momentum and opportunity to get to the grand final because from that moment we absolutely nailed it. Canterbury went backwards, couldn't get any rhythm. It was all Broncos.

We knew we had our hands full with Melbourne but I was also very confident, as confident as I'd ever been going into a grand final. Not over-confident but of the belief that we had the players and the game to beat Melbourne if we implemented our game plan correctly. One thing about Darren Lockyer, he could really follow a game plan. He is certainly the best I've coached at it. Sticks to the script. He always had great belief in our game plans and could get other players across the line on it.

Locky had come a long way since the criticism of his captaincy early in the year. Back then, we sat down and spoke about it privately. We've always had a really close relationship. More than coach and player, we're friends. Up to the end of 2008 he'd played over 300 games in the NRL and I'd coached him in every one of them. I saw him play at 17, saw him captain Australia in Test series and saw all his Origin victories. Our relationship is not all about football. I had complete trust in him and total confidence in the way he drove the team. I would not see him let down. So we had this private discussion, open and frank, and we agreed on some things that I would make sure happened and that he in turn would make sure it was happening on the footy field. He was worried about some issues in the place. You had Dean on one hand, being extremely demanding, and me on the other, trying to get them to play footy. There was a clash of personalities at times and my management skills were tested.

What Dean Benton had been doing from the beginning was right but it was a huge change for these guys — suddenly there was no alcohol in the change rooms after games and there had always been beer in the rooms. For crying out loud, our first sponsor in Porky's days was a brewery. It's not a big deal to you and me, but it is a big deal for guys who have done the same thing after every game every day of their careers.

So I was in both worlds. I could see where we had to go, but at the same time I had to create harmony and get everybody working together. I assured Locky we were on the right track and he assured me we would get there.

Leading into the grand final I was asked whether this one meant more to me than the other six, including Canberra in 1987. It did, a bit, because there are different ways you can get there and this battle had been huge. Unless you had lived the 12 months with us you could not comprehend it. This wasn't just about football, it was about changing cultures and driving performances higher, driving players to places they hadn't been. I'm talking about 31-year-old and 32-year-old men who had played 40 Test matches for their country and 30 Origins, you know, icons of the game. Greats of the game. At the same time, all the other stuff was going on around me and there were people doubting me. Lots of times you have to walk alone.

As Ben Ikin, now my son-in-law, said to me recently: 'You always do things for the right reasons, Wayne. Sometimes you get it wrong, but I've never seen you do anything for the wrong reason.' It's a pretty fair comment. That's what I built who I am on. I do things because I believe they are right. Sometimes I do get them wrong.

The one thing I never second-guess myself about is the reasons I do something. Did I do it for self-gain? Did I do it because I was selfish? Did I do it because it was about me? I never have to answer those questions.

With the Roosters thing, I got it wrong. It was for the right reasons but I went about it the wrong way. I learned from that and promised myself it wasn't going to happen again. But I had lost trust in the board at the Broncos and following the revelation of my talks with the Roosters I had no doubt they had lost trust in me. What was always in the back of my mind was the conversation I'd had with John Hartigan.

Those guys just make a phone call. They say, 'This guy is on the move.' No one ever comes and knocks on your door. I didn't want that happening to me. I was insecure. I wasn't sure what was happening so I thought, well, it's your move Wayne, you make the play.

I KNEW MELBOURNE PLAYED A certain way. It was a bit like the 1993 grand final against St George. They'd got there by doing certain things religiously. They won't change. They can't change. I knew they weren't going to change on the day, so I came up with a few ideas. The biggest thing we had to do was frustrate them. Take them away from what they knew, what worked for them. I knew I had Webcke and Petero and Thorn up front to do the job. You can have all these ideas but if you don't have the cattle to do it you can't do it. I knew this was their moment. These guys had lived for this moment, they were big-match players.

Lockyer is in the same boat and Berro was playing great, giving them direction. I thought we could mask the areas where they were better than us. And again, when you play a team like Melbourne in the play-offs, you only want to play them once. You don't want to be playing them twice, not in the form they were in. With the St George Illawarra loss in the first round of the finals the draw fell into place for us but it wasn't orchestrated. It could not have been better, because it put us on the other side of the draw to the Storm. The same thing happened in 1985 when I coached Brisbane Souths to an against-the-odds premiership win against Wynnum.

I had been down this path before and I hadn't forgotten it. Wynnum had had all the best players back then — Wally Lewis, Gene Miles and Greg Dowling, a whole host of stars — and were the best team in the comp by miles. I knew we could only beat them once. Wynnum and Melbourne are too good to play twice. They work it out.

On grand final night 2006, the Broncos were magnificent, sticking to their game plan religiously. We got a little bit of luck, and you need that, you need a couple of things in the game to go your way. No big deal. That's footy — it happens every week. We got the luck and we rode it and pulled off an unbelievable win. What made it special was the manner in which we went about winning the game.

And the other great thing about it was Shane Webcke. It was unbelievable that it finished as it did for him, as lots of people deserve things in life and don't get them. He certainly deserved it and I was just elated for him. Everyone in the team was elated for him. He was one reason they played the way they did, they just didn't want to let him down. You have to do it for yourself first but having someone else in your thoughts can give you that little bit of extra strength, that little bit of extra push and motivation when you are feeling tired and exhausted. When you're thinking, bugger it, I'm in pain. If you say you're going out there to do it for somebody else, that's a trap. I made sure that wasn't happening at our club. No one was doing it for Shane Webcke — but deep down we all were.

An old cliché I've lived by is: It's amazing what can be achieved when no one cares who gets the credit. And nobody cared. We just all wanted to be part of it.

Afterwards, I felt different to how I'd been in earlier grand final days, not with the guys, but because we had to stay the night in Sydney. That was a real downer. Previously, we'd always flown straight home but now it was played at night and we couldn't catch a flight home until the following morning.

We went back to the hotel and the boys partied but I didn't want them going home on the plane drunk, embarrassing themselves and the club and the game. I hated doing that because they were entitled to a drink, but they had to be respectable the next day. At the same time, I just enjoyed the victory. But I knew my time at the Broncos was running out. Too much had happened now.

CHAPTER 32

THREE AMIGOS

OTHER CODES AND CERTAINLY other countries honour the memory and achievements of their footballing greats better than we do in rugby league. I have always marvelled, for example, at the way American football and British soccer salute their greats.

There is a chemistry you long for in sport which has little to do with formula or science, a greatness few understand but everyone enjoys.

Some mix better with others while some stand alone.

Mal Meninga and Gary Belcher were sensational together. Allan Langer, Kevin Walters and Kerrod Walters gelled like song. Wally Lewis always went to Gene Miles, whether they were playing for Wynnum, Queensland or Australia. Darren Lockyer and Kevin Walters were wonderful together, the young fullback and the crafty five-eighth or half. Their magic combined in three grand finals and dozens of games for Queensland and the Broncos.

Most of the time these guys didn't have to talk to one another to plan — they just knew.

Others stand alone and inspire whole teams. Chris Phelan did that at Souths in Brisbane in 1981 and 1985 and for Parramatta in

Sydney, where he played in three grand finals in a row and won premierships in 1982 and 1983. Glenn Lazarus did it at Canberra, Brisbane and Melbourne. Steve Walters was in the same category. And Andrew Gee.

Of the players I have coached I have never seen a better chemistry than that built between Brad Thorn, Shane Webcke and Petero Civoniceva. It wasn't so much about natural ability; it was borne more out of them being hard men with a want not to let each other down.

They all came to the Broncos as 17-year-olds and I was pretty much across their lives as they developed differently to become the cornerstone of the club's achievement in 2006, when all their years of experience and playing together came to the forefront. Not wanting to let each other down is an important ingredient. Do your job, do it to the best of your ability and don't let anybody down.

Brad Thorn came into first grade in 1994 with no great natural ability but at 193cm (six foot four) and 112kg he was certainly a hell of an athlete. Knew his job, his role, and played to it — his ethos became his power within the team. He played with emotion. He loved moments when he passed the ball effectively or made a big hit. They were the emotional times for him.

Webcke was just pumped up all the time. He had to rip and tear everything in front of him apart. I once said to him, 'If you slow down a little I can play you a little longer in each game.'

He said, 'Mate, that's your problem. It's not mine. My job is to play flat out for you and when I'm buggered you get someone else on.' It made a bit of sense.

He made his first-grade debut in 1995. Queensland were having a bit of a rough time in Origin around this time and I remember the QRL Chairman, John McDonald, wondering aloud where the next lot of front-rowers would come from. I said, 'John, I've got one at the Broncos.' I don't give my players too many wraps publicly but

Shane turned out to be everything I thought I could see in him. And more. A relentless commitment to excellence. You don't see that in a lot of people. His upbringing was paramount. He had come off the farm where his father had worked him hard, fairly but hard. He didn't know anything else but hard work. He also understood the value of a dollar and couldn't come to grips with how he could be paid so well to do something he loved.

Petero played his initial first-grade game in 1998 after coming from Redcliffe. His body is chiselled out of rock and while he was slower coming along than the other boys, he watched and he learned and in the end became as good as his tutors.

They hung out together. When Brad was on the drink they drank together, though he has changed his ways. They sat in the change rooms together. They sat on the buses near each other.

Not all footballers are men. These were men. There is a great honesty with them. They never sat in meeting rooms or change rooms pumping each other up and telling each other how well they were going to play. They just went out and did it. After the game, they would go back to their corner and at some time they would look at each other and maybe even nod. Nothing had to be said. They knew they hadn't failed anyone.

I saw that so many times with them. I knew when it mattered they were playing for each other. Could see it in their faces. The way they played. One would make half a mistake out there and the other guy would turn up to help him.

A great insight to Petero came when he became dehydrated while we were doing three days at an army camp in pre-season training. It was hot and we were working hard and hadn't had a lot of sleep. It's the last day, early in the morning, and I could see Petero was struggling. They were all carrying 40kg packs and I told him I would carry his for him. He wouldn't let me do that. It wasn't going to happen. So it got to about midday and we were getting as much fluid into him as we could, but the soldier in charge noticed Petero was falling off the pace a bit. He even brought the medical person out to check him but Petero refused the attention. He refused to leave the group and he refused to not do his share.

About 2pm he began shaking and shivering uncontrollably. The best thing we could do — and we did it by accident — was to put him in the creek to cool him down. We got him out as quickly as we could, by ambulance, and later the doctor told him he was about an hour away from frying his kidneys. There is always a fine line here between understanding a player's psyche and not trying to destroy it while at the same time caring about their safety.

Petero spent a couple of days in hospital and it certainly slowed him up for a week or two.

These days I can't watch him play in a Penrith jumper. The day we beat them in Brisbane in 2008, and we beat them comprehensively, I felt so much for him.

At the start of '08 Brad decided he was going back to union again. People were starting to question his age and he said, 'Coach, you know me, if I can't get the job done I will walk out of the game tomorrow. I won't take anybody's money.' Never frightened of a challenge, Brad.

Webcke, his exploits of bravery were unbridled. True to himself always. He was part of four premierships (1997, 1998, 2000 and 2006). Brad was also a member of those four teams. Petero won two but it should have been three. He broke his arm and missed 2000. The doctor looked at it and said, 'That's broken Petero, you can't go back out there.' It was against the Storm. He could hear it rattle as he went back out and played another 30-odd minutes before we could get him off.

To me, anyway, the three of them are immortalised in our game.

I still see their influence at the club. I know the influence they had on a guy like Corey Parker was wonderful and allowed him to grow as a person and player. Sam Thaiday is the same, they had a huge influence on Sam. In 2008, Sam won the most prestigious award at the Broncos — the Paul Morgan Medal — and no one throughout that season gave more for the club than Corey, who developed into a real leader, a far cry from the boy who'd made his first-grade debut as an 18-year-old in 2001.

Webcke, Civoniceva and Thorn — the Three Amigos I call them — and Lazzo, Andrew Gee and Gorden Tallis all played their part in building a tradition that the next generation of Bronco forwards is carrying on today.

CHAPTER 33

A SUCCESSION PLAN

I THINK IT WAS DECEMBER 2006 when the phone message came from Darryl Somerville, the Chairman of the Broncos. He wanted to go to lunch with me.

Never in my life had I lunched with Darryl. The fact is, he had never called me before. I'm not saying he should have rung me, right, I'm just saying how it was. Totally out of the blue.

I'm thinking this is strange, something is going on here. I picked up the phone and said, 'Darryl, why are we going to lunch?'

He said, 'The board wants me to talk to you about the Roosters, and what happened there.'

I said, 'Look Darryl, I don't operate that way. I'll go to lunch with you but I won't talk to you alone about the Roosters. Because if the board has a problem with me and the Roosters I need to talk to the board as a whole about it. I don't need an edited version going back to them, or one man's perception of what I said happened. They need to hear it from me. I said if you still want to go to lunch Darryl, that's fine, but we're not talking about the Roosters.'

He said, 'Then there's not much point having lunch, is there?'

I said there is not, but I'm happy to go to the next board meeting and talk to them about the issue.

The board meeting came around early February and a few questions were asked about the Roosters.

Talk then turned to a succession plan for the coach of the Broncos, a subject we'd been discussing for the previous 12 to 18 months. The only real criticism anybody could find of me centred round the fact I'd been there for a long time, maybe too long. I was watching John Howard prepare for yet another federal election and I was hearing the drums beat. I was reading with interest how it seemed only a matter of time before Essendon parted ways with their long-time coach Kevin Sheedy, how that club seemed to be dividing. Sheedy had begun coaching the Bombers a few years before I began with the Broncos.

I said to the board, 'Guys, if you want me to move on it will be the easiest sacking you've ever had because you won't get a murmur out of me.' I didn't have a ready-made answer to the succession plan and said so, but I did offer the view Ivan Henjak was certainly capable of doing the job. Somebody said, well, he doesn't have a high enough profile and I replied, 'If that's what you're looking for, here's an alternative — Darren Lockyer will make a fine coach. But you are better off having him play as long as you can.'

The plan I suggested had Locky playing through until 2010 (if his body held up that long), him dropping out of football altogether in 2011 before coming back as assistant coach to me in 2012 and taking over at the end of that footy season. I'd bow out but would always be in the background for him. I could become his assistant for 12 months, it wouldn't worry me. My time is done, I'd be happy with all that. I said, 'He is an outstanding guy and will make a great coach but he mustn't be rushed into the job.

It would be great for the club to have that continuity and in many ways the making of the Broncos, a natural progression.'

Again, I reiterated if my time was up here, it was up. 'But I know as much as I've ever known about coaching,' I said. 'I am as keen as I've ever been. As for the question whether I've been here too long, no one asks it more than I do. I don't want to stay here if I'm not effective anymore and can't get the job done. It just doesn't interest me. Right now, the players are still listening to me, I have their cooperation and they continue to work for us. It doesn't appear to be an issue that I've been here too long but that's not my call. If you don't want me here just tell me, it won't be a hassle. You have to make that decision, not me.'

With that I left the meeting.

WE GOT TO ENGLAND FOR the World Club Challenge against St Helens and prepared pretty well. But the game turned out to be the beginning of a very frustrating few months. Some guys were committed, others didn't have their minds on the job and we lost 18–14 mainly through unforced errors. It was to be this way for three months. They weren't committed, their minds wandered, they were looking for soft options and easy ways to win. Some wanted to work hard but not as a team, not as a whole.

Webcke has retired and while his retirement was huge we knew we could manage it because we had to manage it. He was gone. That's what happens in footy — the greats retire like everyone else and leave your club. I have been down that path so many times. It wasn't something that intimidated me or worried me. We were always going to miss Shane Webcke but that wasn't the reason we were getting beaten. We were getting beaten because we had an ordinary approach to the way we played our footy. We won only four of our first 12 NRL matches.

AS A COACH, YOU KID yourself into thinking you can make players do things they don't want to do. Often as not, they will look you in the eye, agree to do something, and then they'll go out and let you down.

But they won't do that to their team-mates. I don't know what it is but when they look their team-mates in the eye and tell them they are going to do something they are invariably, albeit within their powers, true to their word. It has something to do with the potent mix between embarrassment and honour.

The turning point of our 2007 season came against the Bulldogs in round 14. Many of them had played in Origin II on the previous Wednesday night and when they returned for the Friday night game against the in-form Bulldogs they went behind closed doors for a team meeting, which is unusual for them. They obviously made some commitments to one another while in there because they came out and did all the things they hadn't been doing as a team. I never went into any detail about it but noticed suddenly they were looking one another in the eye again. There was real commitment. They wanted to be there and they enjoyed being there. The enthusiasm was back. Broncos 19 Bulldogs 12.

It was the first of five wins in a row.

However, in round 17 against the Titans, just after Origin III, Justin Hodges did his hamstring and then the following week, against the Cowboys in Townsville, Darren Lockyer tore the cruciate in his right knee but stayed out there for two more plays, just trying to get us home. In that short period of time he also damaged his knee cartilages. Brent Tate had ruptured his cruciate and medial ligaments in the third Origin game. After the Cowboys game we're doing a simple training drill and Karmichael Hunt fell to the ground like he'd been shot, tearing three of the four muscles on the back of his leg. His season was gone too.

Still, all the stuff they weren't doing early in the season they were now doing with commitment and discipline. They were trying hard.

But in round 21 against Manly, Shaun Berrigan went in to make a tackle, put his head on the wrong side for whatever reason, and a Manly player's knee collided with his jaw, which led to a fractured eye-socket. That was the moment I knew whatever chance we had was no chance at all.

That we got ourselves into the play-offs is a miracle.

In the second-last round of the competition we had a good win against Canberra in Brisbane, though we did have a couple of calls go our way in the second half when we needed a bit of luck. Then we went down to Parramatta for one of the funniest games I've ever coached. It was weird. We went up about 10-nil, 12-nil or something, and dropped a ball that could have made it 18-nil. They came back and scored something like 60 points against us. It was a day when all the players you expect to make the tackles were the ones that didn't. I remember Brad Thorn and Petero and Tonie Carroll making uncharacteristic mistakes to give them their first 20 points. They were full of confidence, Parramatta, and I knew we were in for a tough time against minor premiers Melbourne in the qualifying final.

Tonie Carroll pulled his hamstring the week leading into the Melbourne game, which led to one of the few bust-ups I've ever had with big Tunza. He trained with us the night before the game but he wasn't right. I knew we were going to be battling anyway and didn't want to send someone out with the boys only to see them have to come off after 10 or 15 minutes. He'd be off the ground and we would lose an interchange player. I knew we needed everybody we could get and had to stand over him and tell him he wasn't playing. He was adamant, but in the end I just told him it was not going to happen. Players like him don't want to let their mates down, I understand their motivation, and admire them for it.

The Broncos were valiant to the end and Petero did a great job, giving us hope and courage and all those things you need, but

Melbourne scored seven tries on us and six of those came through our outside backs.

All the promises and what-might-have-beens in '07 were taken away in the end by things out of our control. The only thing we could control was how hard we tried every weekend and from those five wins in a row right through the back end of the season the players were outstanding.

What happened reminded me that at the end of the day it's the players who most influence the outcome. They drive it. If you have coached long enough you understand that, if they don't want to make the effort and pay the price, then it ain't going to happen regardless of all the speeches you make. On this occasion, I was as proud of those guys as any team I have coached at the Broncos. I wasn't proud of the team at the beginning of the season but I was proud of them at the finish.

A huge presentation night awaited where the club would farewell Brad Thorn, Dane Carlaw, Shaun Berrigan, Brent Tate and Petero Civoniceva — all wonderful clubmen who, in total, had played almost 1000 games for the Broncos.

PRESENTATION NIGHT WAS getting close and I just had a feeling — and it wasn't good.

I fronted up at Bruno's office and said I had a gut feeling about life memberships or awards, whatever.

He said, 'Well, I wasn't going to say anything to you but, yes, we want to give you life membership.' And he wanted to do it at the players' ball, the presentation night.

We spent the next 20 minutes in passionate debate about why I shouldn't get life membership and especially why I didn't want it on that night. The tradition at the Broncos is if a staff member is to receive an award the presentation is done at the beginning of the season, not on the players' night. Presentations nights are for the players, the players only, and I didn't want to be made an exception to the rule. More importantly, I didn't want the life membership.

Barry Maranta and Paul Morgan had offered me life membership of the Broncos a decade earlier and I had told them it wasn't important to me. Now I was telling Bruno exactly the same thing. I said, 'I'm embarrassed by it.' Truth is, I've had many accolades and many rewards, many wonderful moments. And I've been paid well for it. I don't need life membership. And the last thing I wanted was to receive an award on the players' night. I didn't want to impede or impose on their night in any shape or manner. Over the years I fought to make sure that night was preserved for the players. Staff and coaches are part of what the club is about — but not on this night.

One of Bruno's constant replies was, 'In our 20th year celebrations, we have to be seen to be doing something for you, Wayne.'

I said, 'You don't have to do anything for me. I don't think it's going to worry the fans but if you want I'll come out and say publicly I've declined any awards.'

Finally, Bruno gave me an undertaking that there would be no presentation to me at the players' ball. If it was to occur, then it would take place at the launch of a season, which has traditionally been the time when life memberships are given to staff and players. There were other staff members who had been at the Broncos since day one and they were going to be awarded life memberships at the 2008 season launch. I didn't like the idea of being made an exception to the rule. Bruno will refute that such an undertaking was made, but I wouldn't have left his office without it.

On the night, it was magnificent to see Brad Thorn awarded life membership because he had done his 10 years and was leaving again for rugby. We were at the end of the presentations and I was sitting there, relaxed, having spent a good 45 minutes up on stage with the likes of Brad and Petero, all those guys. Thanking everybody. It had been a pretty emotional time for me with all those guys leaving. I might not have shown it but it was there inside me. I'd had enough.

Everyone had had enough. It's 11, 11.15 … Bruno goes up as he always does. The chief execs always go up to finish the night off and his opening line is, 'I know this is not going to make him happy …'

And I'm thinking, oh no, he's going to give me the life membership here. I was so filthy. I don't know if I've ever been crankier.

Whatever he said, I didn't listen. My body language was terrible going up to the stage. I was fighting every fibre not to go up there at all, but knew I had to go up. I'm thinking, how do I accept this? Do I play the game? People who know me well enough, I'm thinking, they will understand. They know I'm not big on giving myself a wrap so they will be fine and the rest can please themselves.

I shook his hand, said thanks, and walked back down.

My only regret was I should have turned around to the mic, looked at everyone and said thanks properly. I was never going to say anymore.

I was just so disappointed and couldn't hide that disappointment. Andrew Gee grabbed me, I'm friends with Andrew, and he told me I should have handled it better. I knew I should have. I knew what I should have done but I also knew what I couldn't do. Couldn't be false, had to be true to myself.

I said, 'Andrew I've never been good at handling accolades and pats on the back, awards. I just love helping other people.' One or two others grabbed me. Mick Hancock. I respect Mick and love him and he was in the same boat as Andrew. I accepted that from those boys but a couple of others grabbed me and, you know, I really didn't care what they thought.

CHAPTER 34

THREE PRIORITIES

THERE IS A GREAT LINE that says if you argue with fools, they will pull you down to their level and then beat you with experience.

Cricket's greatest wicketkeeper, the Queenslander Ian Healy, was our media manager for the 2003 State of Origin series, and I remember him saying to me, 'Wayne, you have to look beyond the camera, beyond the journalist, and see that you're not really talking to them. It's the fans you're talking to.'

I said, 'Heals, I love the fans, but when that guy asks me the question I can't see anybody else but him. So don't ask me to change.'

When I got into coaching we never had press conferences. What we had in the change rooms after a game was a journalist to whom you might or might not give a one-on-one interview. Over the years, though, the press conference has become a formality where we go to a room to be asked questions by a number of people from various media organisations.

One day, after I decided I didn't want to go to a press conference, the NRL changed the rules and made it compulsory for coaches to attend. If you didn't attend they slapped you with a $10,000 fine. But even today they still haven't made it compulsory for coaches to talk at these conferences.

What has changed — and I realise I have to change too — is they're not simply press conferences anymore and it's not just a bunch of journos sitting there. Because the fan at home is now in the room, watching on live television.

I have always had three priorities as a coach: first, the club; second, the players, and sometimes I put the players in front of the club; and my next priority is the fan. And then there's daylight.

I HADN'T WATCHED A LOT of Monday Night Football and until the second last Monday of May in 2007, the Broncos had not been involved in it. But a few weeks beforehand I saw the coaches being televised live after a Monday night game, looked at Trish and said, 'I have to find a way to get out of this.'

I knew I wouldn't be comfortable.

While I do a lot of live TV and am experienced at it, I have never done a television one-on-one after a game, except maybe after a grand final. They make me feel uncomfortable. It's an emotional time. You are either on a high or a low and there's no in between.

I've always been conscious of trying not to show elation publicly after a win or depression when we've had a bad day. Why? Because I did not want to be seen gloating or being full of myself in the demise of someone else, as it will be my turn tomorrow. Kipling wrote about it many years ago, about treating triumph and disaster as the very same beast.

So all that's in the back of my mind as I walked into the room this Monday night. I know it's LIVE. I walk in the door — and I have no rights. No one at the League has advised me that there's a live camera in there and even if they had I wouldn't have the right to say no. I don't have an option. I see a solitary camera there and I realise it's an exclusive interview. I have not agreed to it.

I immediately go into a very defensive position. Body language and thoughts. I sit down and see the same faces I see every week and suddenly the TV interviewer produces a notebook and begins his questions from the top of the list. The notebook interview does not normally happen at after-game conferences. The questions at media conferences just seem to come from off the top of the journos' heads.

I am saying to myself, 'This is not an interview. This is a Spanish inquisition.' I was not thinking about the fans at this stage. I went straight into protection mode — tell them nothing, take them nowhere.

I had told the players before the conference how proud I was of them. How inspirational they were. How the football gods weren't with us at the moment. And in hindsight I would have liked to have said that publicly, for their sake.

But I didn't. I kept myself to one-sentence answers, showed no enthusiasm for the questions. I didn't handle the situation well. I let my emotions take over.

If there's any fan out there given the impression — and I'm sure I did give the impression I didn't care about them — well, I'm not like Fonzie, I can say sorry. That is the only reason I wrote this chapter. I never intended to insult the fans that night.

Those who know me sensed where I was at and what I was doing. Trish rang me an hour later (she does not ring often after matches) and she talked about the television interview.

I didn't feel good about me and I told her so.

It wasn't not answering his questions. I have a right not to answer his questions if I don't want to. I've given worse interviews than this one. After the preliminary final in 2006, when Canterbury led 20–6 at halftime, I could see the headlines: BENNETT GONE. FAILS

AGAIN. BRONCOS IN DISARRAY. I went into the press conference after the game and they said well done but without sincerity. We were into the grand final but there was never going to be any outward elation from me after that one.

I've changed many things about myself over time and now I'm preparing to change this. I'll never be that reticent after a game again. I can still protect the players even at my own expense and I won't be intimidated. But I will always remember the fans are out there watching and they're more important than my own feelings at that moment.

CHAPTER 35

TOGETHER WE WORKED ON IT

I LOVED HIS HONESTY. It's the hardest thing in life — being honest with yourself. I talked to my players about it all the time at the Broncos. When Andrew Johns went on national television and was honest with himself one Thursday night in August 2007 I just hoped all my blokes were watching.

He was sick of living a lie.

Andrew's was the worst kept secret in rugby league. I don't think anybody close to the game didn't have at least a hint of what was happening.

I know on the Thursday morning when we all arrived for training and one of the Broncos mentioned the press release with Joey's name on it that had been put out after he was arrested in London — which featured the claim a stranger had put the ecstasy tablet into his pocket — well, no one was buying into that. How could you not be pleased for him later on as he dismissed the charade, difficult as it was?

At one time or another we'd all talked about his wonderful gifts as a footballer but now he was making a huge step to change the lives of a lot of people away from the football field. Andrew Johns had nothing to hide anymore. More importantly, men, women and children will listen to him on the issue of illicit drugs because he's lived it.

Of course, the drama queens soon went to work, but there were a few things I wanted to throw at them before they completely tore up their nighties and before people began beating up on the NRL or the NRL began beating up on itself. More than anything, I needed them to know our game had done more drug testing under the World Anti-Doping Agency code than any other football code in this country and had been doing so for a long period of time.

They were primarily testing for performance-enhancing drugs but, to their credit, the NRL had also introduced internal testing that was compulsory at every club. Each of us has to do so many tests each year looking for recreational or illicit drugs as well as performance-enhancers. Ironically enough, Newcastle (Joey's team) was the only club not to vote in favour of it.

The only weakness, I believe, in this policy is that the testing procedure is left to the clubs. I see that as a flaw because I believe the clubs should be appointing an external body or agency to do the tests. That's what we did at the Broncos.

During his interview, Andrew Johns alluded to something which might have gone over a lot of people's heads when he said he knew if he played a Friday-night game he wouldn't be tested until training the following Monday. That should never have been allowed to happen.

We tested every day at the Broncos. Less than a week before Joey went on TV, one of our very promising young players was out on a Saturday night after a Friday-night game and was offered a tablet, no different to what had happened to Andrew. I had word of it by the Monday. I confronted this player and he assured me he didn't take the tablet, that he had told the guy to bugger off.

As I questioned him a little more he informed me he had been tested by our independent agency on the Sunday morning. The testing was just a pure coincidence but as a club it gave us great reassurance. One, what the kid said was true; and, two, his innocence was backed up by the testing the following morning.

Pressure.

Expectation.

They are not just powerful words but also part of what we do. We can't get away from them.

Instead of giving lectures about drugs, which the young blokes of today lose interest in after a couple of minutes, maybe we'd be better off teaching them how to handle themselves better, how to handle expectation and pressure. Would that not be helping them for the rest of their lives?

What happened with Andrew Johns will happen again. Don't pretend it won't. It's not just about football. It's about families, work places, schools and nightclubs. All our code can do is keep testing and cornering abusers.

In days gone by, it was drink driving. If you didn't drink drive you weren't having a go in the old days. People still drink drive but the public stigma makes those who do nothing short of deplorable.

Together we worked on it. And that is a good thing.

ABOUT TWO MONTHS AFTER Andrew Johns gave that difficult TV interview I went to England as coach of the All Golds, a team and tour put together in 2007 to celebrate 100 years of New Zealand rugby league, and one of the highlights of the trip came when the New Zealand High Commissioner organised for us to visit Buckingham Palace. I got to meet Her Majesty, Queen Elizabeth II.

I felt really guilty when the big gates opened to let our bus in and we drove past the thousands of people standing outside. I had spent the day practising the names of the New Zealand players because I had to introduce them and had no end of trouble trying to get their names pronounced properly. It was a great honour. The High Commissioner was in the function room, with captain Ruben Wiki, the team, and in came the Queen and the Duke of Edinburgh. I got the names right and all of a sudden about eight corgis came racing down the hallway. The Duke looked at me and said, 'I'm over these dogs.'

They had these magnificent tea urns. I'm introducing the Duke around and there's a guy carrying the tea urn. The Duke looks up and says, 'Is that the trophy you are playing for?'

I said, 'No, that's a tea urn.' Though I have to say it did look a bit like a trophy.

He knew about rugby league and couldn't believe how small our halfback, Stacey Jones, was alongside all the big guys, how he played the game. The Duke was very chatty and very good.

Just the other day, I read an article quoting the actress Helen Mirren, who played the title role in the movie *The Queen*. She made a great point. Said she had great admiration for Her Majesty after playing the role. 'It's a miracle she's never gone mad,' Mirren said. Meeting all those people, having audiences, being briefed about their background, where they are from, always having to do the right thing. Once wouldn't be too hard, but day after day it would add up to a pressure I'm not sure we know ...

For me, the tour had started with two days in Wellington, where I attended a memorial service for Albert Baskerville, the man who organised the original All Golds tour in 1907, and then a luncheon at Parliament House where the New Zealand Prime Minister Helen Clark sent us on our way. I was coach for this leg of their tour and Steve Price, another Queenslander who was playing for the Warriors in the NRL was in the team filling the 'Dally Messenger' role (Messenger had toured with the New Zealand team in 1907).

We flew into the UK in two groups — until the Tuesday, there was me and 10 players; then the rest of the squad, who had been involved in a Test against Australia in Wellington, joined us in London.

We trained every day from Saturday to Wednesday, either at the Wasps rugby club or on Regent's Park, then had Thursday off before travelling north for the commemorative match that was played at Warrington. The training sessions were excellent and the players' attitude and discipline was spot on. They were a happy group, the Kiwis, with a very good team spirit and I had a very enjoyable time with them. We won the game 25–18, after leading 15–5 early on (tries were worth three points, as they'd been back in 1907) and then falling behind 18–15 in the second half. I was honoured to have been invited, pleased I took the job, but as always when I'm away I spent a lot of my time looking forward to going home.

CHAPTER 36

21 YEARS

HAVE I BEEN HERE TOO LONG? Do I still have the passion?

I knew if I left my departure in someone else's hands they'd get it wrong but I also knew from the decisions I'd made over the years that the hardest one would be this one I had to make about myself. More than any other, in the terms of scrupulous honesty, it was the decision I just had to get right.

The license I had been given to fulfil the dream that was the Broncos always made me feel both blessed and pressured in that I knew we could never be simply another footy club. By starting from scratch we had the opportunity to learn from the mistakes of others and make sure we didn't repeat them. The original directors all played football but until the Broncos they were never part of committees or boards so, like me, they marched to the beat of their own drum. John Ribot had never been an administrator, either. We were all given clean space in which to work.

From day one I studied the great clubs from all codes and countries, how they would invariably turn on themselves. How players would turn on the club, committees on coaches … the gossip and innuendo. And I spent a lifetime promising myself I would not stand by and allow this to happen around me.

In the early '90s, when the push came for me to be sacked, that's when it was reinforced to me this club is different. No football club in this country has ever responded to such criticism of its coach by coming out and offering him a lifelong contract. That gesture became a driving factor in so many of my decisions and how I have subsequently handled situations — those directors might be gone but, regardless, I could never stand by and allow this club to turn on itself.

The Roosters in 2006 ... while the leak of the news that I was leaving the Broncos was ill-timed, I reconciled the angst my departure would cause with the fact my leaving would happen at the end of the season and be over pretty quickly. Sure, I expected some nasty comments but they would be directed at me and not the club. On so many occasions I had taken a bullet for the club and I was prepared to do it again to ensure the Broncos remained what we'd always set out to be: different.

BRUNO INFORMED ME IN late November 2007 that he wanted me to come to a meeting of the Broncos' board on 13 December to discuss the team and coaching. I told him, 'I want to continue to coach after '09. Will you pass that on to the board.'

On 7 December, an article discrediting me appeared on the front pages of Sunday newspapers in Brisbane and Sydney. Between the lines I read that News Limited were preparing to move me on. Do I dig in? Do I try to rely on public support? Try to get one or two board members on side? Do I play the game?

On the Monday, I had an early-morning meeting with the Chairman, the CEO and a friend of mine. I told this group that in my view the article was way out of order, that obviously I was being sent a message and I would resign at the end of 2008. They told me they were happy for me to see out my contract, and the Chairman suggested I take some time to 'cool off' before I handed in a resignation letter. The board had a meeting scheduled for early February, and we decided to put off any decision until then.

Essendon fans in the AFL were ropeable when the Bombers told Kevin Sheedy he was no longer required; to his credit, while the fury raged around him Sheedy never said a word. These things often leave long-term scars and friendships are lost forever. Look at the Canterbury Bulldogs and the way they've turned on themselves, the Mortimers and the Hughes brothers, George Peponis.

Look at former Prime Minister John Howard. The only real criticism of Howard — and I'm not saying whether or not I'm a supporter — is he had held the Liberal leadership for a long time.

Can I still do the job? Yeah.

Am I still committed? Yeah.

Am I still passionate? Yeah.

Ticked all those boxes. Not a problem. Do I still want to coach? Yes. Does he still want to be PM? Does he still think he can do it? Yes, yes. What's he doing wrong? Well, he's been there a long time.

John Howard misread the signs. He needed people with conviction to tell him it was time for a change. In my case, taking on that kind of responsibility would be a challenge for the people around me.

I was not getting any feedback along these lines but at the same time I knew it was my turn to make the decision, tough as it may be. I won't deny it was a sad time for me, though there was also a relief inside because I knew the end had to come one day. I had never kidded myself about that. It's very hard to get fairytale finishes in this game. In the beginning at the Broncos I thought I would probably stay three years. I lasted 21. It was a hell of a time. I looked at all the good things, how lucky I had been to be given the opportunity to achieve my dreams and at the same time provide stability for my family. I'm sure the club would have offered me another job if I had just wanted to give up coaching but I didn't want to do that. Coaching is what I do. And leadership is also about knowing when to leave.

When Steve Williams rang me all those years ago he talked about Tom Landry, the long-time Dallas Cowboys coach. It didn't finish the way Tom wanted it to finish. They knocked on his door and said, 'Tom, you're gone, you've stayed too long.'

Same with Don Shula at the Miami Dolphins. He spent 25 years there. Kevin Sheedy. In 2007, when we were in the UK for the World Club Challenge, I bought a book about former Liverpool manager Bill Shankly and Manchester United's current boss Sir Alex Ferguson and it strengthened my resolve about this day coming and what to do, how to handle it. Shankly joined Liverpool as manager in 1959 and took the club to the first division, winning championships in 1964, 1966 and 1973, the FA Cup in 1965 and '74 and the UEFA Cup in 1973. After 15 years the son of a Lanarkshire miner said he felt it was time for a break but he spent most of the rest of his life (he died in 1981) resenting how he had given up coaching. I didn't want any of that.

So I thought I would take the pressure off everybody, make it easy. Do what's right and, most importantly, make sure the club didn't turn on itself.

AS I WRITE THIS, IN September 2008, the only bit of pain or regret I have is seeing the way Brisbane Lions coach Leigh Matthews recently resigned. I would have loved that to be me. At the end of the AFL season he just walked in and said, 'It's over.' No fanfare, no fuss, no parade, no last game, no last moment.

You can't do that in our game because we have this ridiculous situation of being able to recruit players at any time of the year. I knew I had to make my decision public or it would have unfairly affected players either coming to the club or staying. They needed to know who the coach was going to be.

Hence the board meeting that was staged back on 5 February 2008. I actually asked the board to meet the night before the scheduled date because I knew the media would be all over us, and they agreed. I told them candidly my reasons for resigning and asked them, 'Do you want me to stay for the upcoming season?' They unanimously said they wanted me to stay and finish the season so we devised a plan on how we would manage it. I withdrew from all forms of media bar the weekly post-match conferences and the players cooperated in not talking about me or my departure.

MY STRENGTH IS MY CONSCIENCE. See, I don't need someone saying nice words about me, I don't need someone giving me a pat on the back, because if I can't live with myself then it doesn't matter what you say or who says it, the pain is still there. I don't need the parade and I don't need the farewell. I need to know deep inside myself I did as good as I could. I also need to know I never lost the confidence of the players.

If I thought I had done the wrong thing by the playing group, that's the thing that would hurt me most of all. I see their dreams and I see their failures. I am there to guide them, help them and care about them. Does it always end up perfect? No it doesn't. What I have to know is I didn't let them down. Yeah, I've made some tough calls they didn't always understand. However, there is a big difference between that and losing their confidence. You can't coach when you haven't got the confidence of the players and I hope I have never done anything publicly or privately that has betrayed the trust they've had in me. The things that drive me are the players and the fear of failure. Those days when we are doing it tough and not playing well, I'm looking for the answers and struggling to come up with them sometimes. But that's the reason I get out of bed — I can't let them down. And that's the thing that upset me most when I resigned: the individuals. Many of them came to the Broncos because of me; if I showed any emotion it was only when I thought about them and what they mean to me.

What got me through this last season, what gave me the strength, was not wanting to let them down. Only one time I got a little teary. It was early in the piece on a long drive to the bush, along the Warrego and Leichhardt Highways to the town of Theodore. Shane Webcke and Andrew Gee came with me, two of my closest friends. I needed to hear their opinions on certain things about my departure and how I should handle it. These two guys stand up to me, they tell me what they believe and I need that. I don't want to hear it but I need to hear it. I was strong in my opinion as they were in theirs and they were right in most of the things they said. I mentioned the players and got a bit teary. The rest I could handle, but leaving the players … it was only a couple of tears. Five-hour drive. Great trip. Enjoyed every minute of it.

IN OUR PRE-SEASON GAMES WE looked like rubbish. We were lucky to beat a local state league team at Redcliffe.

Darren Lockyer was still behind with his knee and it would be an on-going issue. We got to round one of the premiership and played way above my expectations, beating Penrith. I couldn't believe how well they played, how easily it came together. I honestly didn't know what they were going to throw up, had no idea. Brad Thorn was gone, Petero was gone, Shane Webcke had gone the year before. They were huge losses but the new players stepped up and we got away to a great start to the season, and we were able to maintain that form for a number of weeks.

After we beat the Roosters in round two, however, there had been a further problem with Darren's knee unrelated to the original injury. The team became very resilient, managing to put a number of wins together without him which was a remarkable effort considering how much Locky meant to our play.

Training was an issue for him and the knee was just not responding. Nobody was really sure what the new injury was and we were in a state of flux. Every week he was somewhere between being right to play and not being right to play. In the meantime, my job was to keep the place together which I think I did pretty well, while Ivan Henjak was working himself up about being the next first-grade coach. He was on an emotional roller coaster — huge highs one day, huge lows the next, and every so often he would jump off the coaster altogether.

It is never easy to replace a coach and the Broncos were in a difficult situation. They had gone after Melbourne's Craig Bellamy, which was their prerogative as a club. You have to do what you believe is the best thing. They were also chasing Canberra's Neil Henry, but in the end Ivan did get the job. As a group we managed to maintain our composure and Locky was still on and off with his leg.

I have probably never coached a better team player than Darren Lockyer. He had always put the team first but I quickly realised this situation was different. He really wanted to play for his state and country in the year of the game's centenary celebrations and I didn't blame him for that; he deserved to do all those things. He is such a credit to the game. But it was pretty obvious to me every time a big match was coming up he was trying to get himself on the footy field. Before the Centenary Test match against New Zealand in May, he came and saw me and we had a half-hour conversation about whether he should pull out of the representative program because he couldn't do justice to himself. He left that meeting with a real commitment to withdraw from rep football, including Origin, for the year but at day's end he rang and everything was up in the air again. He'd changed his mind and was in a real difficult place, which can happen at times like this when you so badly want to play.

A week or so later, on the eve of Origin III, I had the first bit of a bust-up I've ever had with him. He made himself available for a club game and I knew why he made himself available — because he wanted to play Origin. He was so underdone it didn't matter. I knew it wouldn't be fair on him and I knew it wouldn't be fair on Queensland. So I let it run down to the last day — D-day — when I grabbed him and said, 'Locky, you're not fit to play. You shouldn't even be contemplating playing.'

He got the cranks with me, slamming his hand on the table. Darren is not an aggressive guy, but he probably thought he was being very aggressive. 'I'll prove you wrong,' he said, 'I'll prove everybody wrong.' And he left the room making a few gestures.

I said, 'Hey mate, I want you to prove us all wrong but you're not going to prove us wrong because you're not right to play, that's what I know.'

I was going to say something to him about putting himself before the club. That's not who he is but it was so important to him … and then in his newspaper column he wrote how he'd been selfish in wanting to play so badly and I thought, well, at least he's being honest with himself.

As a coach, that's all you can ask for, all you want to see.

AFTER ORIGIN WE SET OURSELVES the target of winning seven of our next nine games and came up just short, winning six of the nine. In the interim I had little to do with the media. In previous seasons, after our last training session of the week I'd front for a media conference at our training headquarters at Red Hill but this year I asked Ivan to do it so we could further limit my exposure.

Even so, there were times during this final season when I had to manage emotions, never more so than when a number of players came to me at different times seeking advice after they were told that they would have to find a new place to play in 2009. Blokes like prop Ben Hannant and hooker Michael Ennis, who were having tremendous seasons, were placed in the difficult situation of having to consider offers from other teams. In the past I would have been the one making these personnel decisions but it was no longer my call. That's fine, I'm not criticising the club for any calls they made. It's a great club. That's the point — none of the players ever wanted to leave. Whether or not I was there, it didn't matter. They were coming to me with these great emotions and they were still expected to turn up every week and play to the best of their ability. Somehow Ben and Michael and the other guys who were leaving managed to achieve that.

It was never an issue that the club would fall apart without me or any other individual. The club is bigger than that. We made sure it was bigger than that. No one's indispensable. Still, it was difficult to keep them focused and not lose confidence and belief in each other.

Our saviour was a fit Darren Lockyer. The plan was to bring him back for the game against the Bulldogs, which was played 11 days after Origin III, and that's what happened. He never missed another game and made a huge difference.

Bruno Cullen kept his part of the bargain really well. Thankfully, there was no BRUNO v WAYNE BENNETT or BRONCOS v WAYNE BENNETT anywhere to be heard or read.

INTERESTING, IT WAS, LOOKING FOR a job for the first time in 21 years. So I get a call from the Cowboys about going there. Their coach Graham Murray had been sacked so they were obviously looking for a new one. I had a cordial meeting with their chairman, Laurence Lancini, and CEO Peter Parr, who I had worked with at the Broncos. Trish came. At the end of the meeting Laurence said he certainly wanted me to be the coach there and I thought the Cowboys would be a great fit for me. Queensland-based team. And I'm Queensland through and through. Made sense to me. I like a lot of things about the Cowboys and knew it would be a challenge, which is what you want. There was nothing daunting about the prospect.

Even though I was pretty confident about getting the job, there was one thing bugging me: as he left the meeting after saying I was the man they wanted, Laurence turned, and said, 'I've got to take this back to the board.'

I thought, why would someone in your position have to take this back to the board? You're the chairman, if you're not in control of your board then I don't feel real good about that. I have only worked with guys who can control their boards and make the decisions. The other guys just give them the tick.

Then a penny dropped. I remembered an article written by Roy Masters in late 2007. I didn't take a lot of notice of it at the time but someone told me about it, how Roy had written Gorden Tallis had been appointed at News Limited's prompting to the Cowboys board. Roy also speculated I was going to leave the Broncos and that Gorden would act to ensure I didn't get the coaching job at the Cowboys.

Anyway, a few days after the meeting with Laurence and Peter I got a phone call to say I'd missed out on the job. I was certainly taken aback, not because I thought I should get the job but because they'd sought me out. Intimated as much as you can without signing off on it that I was the one they wanted. When Laurence said I was too old for the job I nearly fell off the phone. So I made a few calls myself and the wash-up was the other directors wouldn't support him. In the end, I thought, thank heavens I'm not going to a club that runs by democracy. Give me leadership over daily democratic meetings every day of the week.

About a week later I got a phone call from St George Illawarra. I was terribly concerned about their coach Nathan Brown, he's a good bloke. A real good bloke. I was assured he had been informed he would be finishing up as coach at the end of the season. So I jumped on a plane and met their chairman Warren Lockwood and CEO Peter Doust. I'd worked on the ARL Foundation board with Peter and have always got along well with him. The Dragons, great club. When I was young I dreamed of coaching there, long before the premiership expanded into Brisbane. I certainly didn't take much convincing. They didn't take much convincing either and we did a deal within half an hour, subject to board approval. A week later, I met the board and the deal was done.

Trish didn't say much. She knows the impact the move will have on our family, me living in Sydney, but she would rather me coaching than sitting home being cranky because I'm not doing what I do best. She has always put everyone before herself, Trish. She is the most unselfish person I've met. She says, 'Just do what you do until it's time to retire.'

Coming into the 2008 play-offs I was feeling very alive, pleased to be there. The Broncos qualified for the finals, finished in fifth spot on the ladder. I knew I had a good footy team. I knew we were getting our game right, our best players on the field. I wasn't overly confident but I knew if things fell for us, little bit of luck and everything lined up, we could get it done. Everybody talks about premierships, but they are so hard to win. Nobody appreciates how hard it is until they are part of one.

THE EASY THING FOR ME to do would have been to have the season off but it would have been a very selfish thing to do. I had to do the right thing by the players. I had to do the right thing by myself as well. The point I have to make is that there was and is a perception — and I think both Bruno and the Broncos board bought into it — that I ran the Broncos. That has never been the case. What I ran was the football department, I make no bones about that. I did it my way and I couldn't have done it any other way. They control the club, the organisation, and I controlled the football. It's been one of our great strengths. I had a great passion for the Broncos but the day I resigned is the day I lost that passion. I didn't lose my commitment, though, because I owed it to the players and the club to remain focused.

For three years I'd deliberately been giving the coaching staff more and more responsibility. Back then I didn't know when I was going but I knew my time was running out, so I stepped back. I had my finger on all the things that mattered to the performance of the football team while delegating more and more. They were suddenly in greater control and thinking, well, we can do without him. That's what I wanted them to believe, the way it should be. How I've built teams over the years is to make them believe in themselves first and foremost and then believe in each other. Okay, we are going to miss you, whether you are an Alf or a Kevvie or a coach, but we are going to get the job done anyway. We are going to do it to the best of our ability and we are not going to fall over. That's the great measure of strong organisations.

You learn. For 21 years I've been learning at the Broncos. Why did I stay so long? First off, I didn't believe I could coach at a better place. It was just such a wonderful place to be, always vibrant, full of ideas and energy. I didn't think I could work with better people. The second thing was I came to the realisation for me to be a better coach the real challenge was to find different ways to deliver the same message. I knew if I went from one club to another, then I could take my ideas with me but I wouldn't grow and that was important to me. Here I am dealing with the same guys for 12, 13 seasons, asking them to do their best and it's the same old voice, same guy, delivering the same messages. The other thing I did was put good staff around me, from Brian Canavan in the beginning to Jeremy Hickman at the end.

I'm a rugby league child, teenager and man. Son, father, grandpa. My grandfather Bennett played rugby league and so did my grandfather Brosnan. I have photos of them at home. My father played, my uncles played and I was born a rugby league tragic. I didn't know anything else from the time I can remember, from three or four years of age, going on bus trips with my father and on my mother's knee. Later on, she sent me to keep my father sober, but that didn't work. Then she sent me to get him home at a reasonable hour, and that didn't work either.

Justin couldn't play rugby league, I wished he could have. I say to all parents I run into, there is no reason why your son shouldn't play rugby league. The thing I love is being part of a team. The other thing that has challenged me more than anything else is the toughness of it. It's not the most pleasant experience, getting tackled. It's a very physical, confronting game and your courage is always being challenged because you know your body is going to be on the line and there is always a chance you might come up not feeling too good. You might come up pretty dusty, thinking, I won't be doing that again, but somewhere in your make-up you get up, find the courage and go again.

I was 20 years of age when I copped my first stiff-arm. I was only talking about the guy the other day. Tears came to my eyes from the pain of it. My head was spinning. I'm walking back to my position, thinking, if this is rugby league find me another sport to play. But the pain quickly went away and I always came back to play that little bit harder and to overcome the fear.

I got into coaching in 1974 because those kids wanted me to coach and I wanted to give something back. I have great admiration for the men I've coached. They are not role models or heroes. Lots of people are quick to find fault with them and that's easy to do but I still admire them greatly. It's been a hell of a journey but it would have been just as good and just as much fun if it had never reached the heights of NRL, state and country. Rugby league has been such a part of me, I wouldn't know what to do without it.

CHAPTER 37

MASS

I LOVE THE SIGHT OF him shuffling in to see me, his wry smile and great presence. Loved it for 22 years.

Ron Massey has loved this game all his life. He was brought up playing rugby league, followed it, coached it, doing everything you can possibly imagine in the game. This is the kind of person I often talk about, the kind you don't want to let down because you know what he's done for the game and what the game means to him.

The kind you know that you are fortunate to meet.

Soon after I arrived in Canberra in 1987 we were playing Cronulla in the first game of the season and the great Jack Gibson had been invited to be the guest speaker at a pre-match luncheon. Mass was with him. Wherever Jack coached, Mass was his coaching coordinator — that's the term he used for himself. They were mates from wayback and Mass was always the guy in the background ... just happy to be part of the team.

I wanted to be at that luncheon right or wrong because I'd never heard Jack Gibson speak at such a function. Ron Massey came up to me in his very frank and forthright way, introduced himself, said he'd followed my career a little bit. It was just a chance meeting, but for one reason or another I got his phone number off him. It was to be the beginning of a very long and valued friendship for me.

I'll never forget Jack's talk. One guy got up and asked him this question, the longest winded question you've ever heard in your life. He kept answering himself, time after time, in what set out to be a question. Jack just stood there, expressionless, the way only he could, paused at the end of the marathon question, and drawled: 'I agree with everything you've said.' It brought the house down. Then someone got up and asked him about selectors. Jack said, 'Well, when I was in America I actually asked somebody about selectors and they said, "Is that the thing in the cars, when you're selecting the gears?"' Jack said the Yanks had no idea what selectors were, and he doesn't use them here anymore, either.

Outside family, over the past 22 years I guess there's been no one closer to me than Ron Massey. No greater friend. It's true, our friendship was put under a bit of pressure in the Super League years. He was very much an ARL person and he'd read a couple of articles where I feel I was misrepresented but we patched things up pretty quickly. Got through it fine.

He makes so many good points on so many subjects. Without a doubt, he is the most ethical person I've ever dealt with.

Mass worked for Jack as a bookie, and knew all the rogues from the '60s and '70s, when there really were rogues. He knew them all. He'll tell you a bit about them but there's a lot he doesn't tell you too, of that I'm sure. Some of the stories he knows will never be told because he has this wonderful code of ethics he lives by and a real strength of character to go with them.

Like all true friends he will tell you what you don't want to hear. He certainly doesn't mind offending me.

When it comes to football and football people his is the wisest counsel.

I've seen him at functions with his ex-players, how they just idolise him, always making a beeline for Mass. Jack had the aura, the persona ... Mass had the feel, the can-do attitude, the discipline, the firmness, and great man-management skills.

He was also a wonderful speaker. Today, he remains so charismatic, people just gravitate towards him. Has an opinion on everything. Loves his sport and knows all sport. Watches every game, everywhere on television, every sport. Picks up things others can't see. I remember him calling me years ago when Australian cricket was at its absolute peak. Australia was fielding and Mass said, 'Hey Wayne, they're the best defensive team I've ever seen.' I thought, no one else would think to put it in that context. Who in the world ever thought of cricketers performing as a defensive team? He said the way they save runs, the way they throw, their strong arms, their support for each other out there. It's the same with American football, golf, swimming, and he's not backward in telling a friend of mine how to produce TV.

That's not quite right — Mass will never tell you how to do something. He will suggest, beginning with, 'I might be wrong but ...' The silliest thing I ever said to him during one of these discussions was, 'Mass, you're losing the plot.'

Now, every time I talk to him, he says, 'I could be losing the plot, but ...' Don't be fooled, underneath he totally believes in himself — knows he's right.

Tough as teak, he is. Compassionate. Caring. Emotional. And he's never frightened to show those characteristics, who he is. Uncompromising. Opinionated. You just know he's in your corner and he's going to be there for life.

He and Jack had a wonderfully close relationship. I remember when Mass was really sick and Jack went to the hospital. The nurse said to him, 'Only family can see Ron at the moment.' Jack just looked at her, and said, 'I am family,' before marching on into the room.

I can see why they worked so well together. Mass has no ego. Jack was the up-front man, the showman, and together they were dynamite.

A friend of mine said recently, 'They'll never make another Ron Massey.'

I said, 'You're wrong, they already have.' His name is Paul. Paul Massey, Ron's son. He has just been appointed the football manager at St George for the 2009 season. The only difference is he's been a policeman for 20-odd years. I've never met a more honest man, but Mass could never have been a policeman, that's not in his make-up at all.

CHAPTER 38

YOU CAN'T ALWAYS WIN

As MELBOURNE WHIPPED the ball along their backline I realised it was over for us. I could see we couldn't defend it. They scored in the corner. No time left on the clock. Storm 16, Broncos 14. On the long journey back down to the change room, with my emotions sadly out of control, knowing it was all over and struggling to make some sense of it all, my thoughts turned to the Broncos' four original directors.

They would have been absolutely elated that we had played such a great game of football in the spirit and commitment they always sought, knowing the fans had gone home disappointed with the result but realising their team had never given up. 'You can't always win, Wayne,' I could hear them telling me. 'We don't want to leave the fans disappointed in our effort.' Porky's big voice echoed off the concrete walls.

I remembered our first game at the old Lang Park, how we'd had 17,000 people there, back in 1988. On this night, the second NRL semi-final, 20 September 2008, the quality of the football was sensational and 52,000 were there to enjoy it.

IN 21 YEARS WE HAD become the football club we all dreamed about and now my time had come. That's what I was thinking getting into the lift to go down to the team, about my time, with a final week of difficulty from off-field incidents adding to the theatre that has always been the Brisbane Broncos. A few days before, I'd seen a headline deeming the Broncos to be in crisis. The Broncos were never in a crisis. Being the responsible organisation they are, as they have shown throughout their existence, the Broncos were doing everything they could to respond responsibly. It would have been better if the events that led to allegations being made against three of the club's players hadn't happened, but they had and nobody was walking away from them. There is a process that needs to take place and, as I always remind myself, if it was my family involved then I would want fairness and the correct process. I view the team as part of my family. If we've done something wrong, then we'll be men about it and pay the price. But the players involved deserve the opportunity to fairness and the protection of their rights.

I have no doubt that's why we fought two World Wars, where too many wonderful Australians lost their lives, so that people like me and younger men and women have the right to be viewed innocent until proven guilty.

WHEN I'D GOT THE information on the previous Sunday that something had happened I made the relevant phone calls to the people I understood might have been involved. I trust their honesty because that is the way I have coached them, the way I have always dealt with them. And they understand I will be more sympathetic and a lot more understanding if there is transparency. So I got the details, checked the story. As a coach, I felt terrible but the first thing I had to tell myself was I haven't done anything wrong.

Because my thoughts are, what could I have done better? Where have I failed them? Is it my fault?

In this case, there was a lot of, 'Why us?' Why did it have to happen to us now? But I had to work through that process quickly because that's just about my ego. About my image. When I got through that, and it took me a couple of hours but I got through it, I began to think with clarity; I realise there is another person involved here, a girl, and she obviously has her point of view and just as much right to fairness. She has to be respected. I also realise there is now a police investigation and we have to be compliant. So I began those processes to make everybody accountable to the police.

GOT TO TRAINING ON THE Monday and, you know, everyone was looking at me. They're not looking but they were. The players, that is. I walked into the change rooms and heard a false laugh, a nervous giggle here and they're trying to create some atmosphere over there but I knew it wasn't real. The only time it was going to be real was when they saw how I was handling it all. For the grace of God go I, because no one else was looking down on them and at the end of the day they are team-mates. They socialise together. On this night, after beating the Roosters in the qualifying final, they all went out together but that's not unusual. It's in their time. Now I know they're feeling for each other. I told them what I had to, didn't elaborate because I didn't need to, because it is out of our hands with the police now investigating and we can do nothing until that investigation is completed. Until we have both sides of the story no decision can be made. I asked them to trust the system and the club and to do what's right by all concerned.

So we went out and trained. But it just wasn't where it should be. I knew everybody was distracted. There was a flock of media there, faces we'd never seen before, sticking cameras in our faces and asking questions we can't answer. I know life was going to be different for the week.

We had to get on with it. The following day things become a little clearer. The players were interviewed by the police, voluntarily attending the interviews. I walked back into the training facility and discovered they were a little happier; I knew I had to pull all 17 together. I expressed my feeling on the matter that morning. I told the players if they have issues this is the time to express them but no one said anything. My feelings are of disappointment but I wasn't condemning. It's not that I'm trying to … look, it's not about me. I feel enormously for them and their families. I'm close to their families as well and I know how distraught their families are. I know the hell these boys have to go through now. They need me to be balanced, and not to jump to conclusions. Not finding fault easily. That's what makes me different.

I've never forgotten my own growing up. Too many older people do. I've deliberately worked hard not to forget that. My friends get older and purer but they have forgotten I was young with them and I was the one who was always sober. I saw the things they did they now forget. I've always had great difficulty living with double standards. It helps me have a balance. Whether I'm talking to the players' parents, or talking to them — and my concern is always for the players.

Every situation is different. And that's how I had to manage it.

WITH THE EXCEPTION OF 1995, the year Super League was born, the 2008 season had more adversity in it for the Broncos than any other. From the day I resigned to the try in the last minute of this second semi-final. The year challenged me as much or more than any other. If I did anything well in 2008 it was to do with my man-

management skills being at their peak. I had to manage so many things and most of them had nothing to do with football. From my resignation to players leaving the club, disagreements within the club, within the team … the list went on and on. And then, of course, we had to play half a season without Darren Lockyer. We had no more Webckes or Peteros, outstanding leaders in their own right. This was a new footy team, a new look, the pack in particular. We didn't expect the start they gave us, the way they played at the beginning of the year, winning six of their first eight. The whole season on the field was a great credit to the players. They overcame hurdle after hurdle, difficulty after difficulty, and I think the qualifying final epitomised how strong they were. We got bashed all over the park by the Roosters in the first half. If we were in the boxing ring someone would have thrown in the towel. Games like this don't happen in the NRL anymore, the brutality of it. Sure, games are still extremely tough but in a different way. This one came from a decade ago. The Broncos stood as tall as any team ever stood. Soaked it up, came back and in the end just took it away from the Roosters.

I mean it when I say this is a premiership lost for the Broncos. At the end of the comp we'd won four games in a row, last three regular-season games and the qualifying final, we'd kept the same side on the park for five straight games, and, football-wise, everything was right in the club. Then we tripped a metre short of the finish line. I've gone into other play-offs knowing we can't win but this year it was right. I could smell it. It wasn't right all season, I wouldn't say that, but that's how it always comes together. It comes together at some magical point, which is what you're trying to do all year. You're trying to fine tune, it's such a delicate thing … with the click of a finger it can come; and with the click of a finger you can lose it. It's like a bit of cotton — it can hold or give. So hard to describe but I know when it's there.

We couldn't have done what we did against the Roosters and we certainly couldn't have played like we played against Melbourne if it wasn't.

We beat the Roosters 24–16 on the Friday night, and the most logical consequence for us was that we'd be playing Canberra at home in the semi-final the following week, or maybe Cronulla if the Raiders could pull off an upset in their qualifying final. I couldn't see the Storm — defending premiers, top of the table throughout 2008 — getting beaten by the Warriors, the team that finished eighth on the ladder, in that first week of finals. Not that any particular result worried me, because we had a footy team here and whatever came our way we were going to be ready for it ... that was the strong message coming out of our win over the Roosters.

High levels of confidence. So the Warriors got up in the last minute and suddenly we were playing the Storm. And I'm happy. I mean, the Storm are a team you only want to meet once in finals football, and because we'd won and they hadn't we didn't have to go to Melbourne. We were the hosts. It's a knockout semi, winner goes through to a preliminary final, loser is done for the year. I'm confident. Even the Monday didn't dent that confidence because I just knew we'd get it right by the weekend. I talked to them about adversity — used Shane Warne as an example because, you know, that guy got through more personal dramas in a week than most guys do in a lifetime. George Best. There was relief in coming to training; there would be even more relief in playing. That's what Warney showed us — every time he went out to play he was walking away from the drama off the field and nobody would play better than him. So I wasn't worried about the playing.

At the same time, I didn't try to make the controversy something that was going to galvanise us or bring us together because this was very personal ... there's a young woman involved here and three of my players. I just made sure the episode didn't pull us apart. And it didn't pull us apart.

The crowd was magnificent when the players ran onto Suncorp, their cheers saying, 'We support you. Let's go, Broncos!' I think they were also saying we know the club will do what's right when the time comes. The fans have great confidence in the Broncos, and so they should.

ON THE FRIDAY MORNING BEFORE the game, at the end of the team session, I said, 'Guys, they can't beat you tomorrow night.' I knew the Storm couldn't beat us; I'd seen enough football and knew they were at the end of their run. They were there to be beaten. 'But we can beat ourselves. If we give up silly penalties ...'

I nominated the areas where referee Shayne Hayne is strong in awarding penalties. I then nominated other areas that could hurt us, such as being too wide of the A defenders and sloppy ball control. 'If we do those things,' I said, 'we'll just give them hope and continually invite them back into the game.'

My last comment to them as they left the change rooms on the Saturday night was, 'Guys, they can't beat you — we can only beat ourselves.'

I don't normally make such statements but that was the belief I had in this team and that was the belief they had in themselves. In the end, though, our ball control destroyed us. Not just on the last play, it happened all night. Our top players made unforced errors, which is just unacceptable at this level. Such mistakes will hurt you at any level but at semi-final time and against an absolute quality team ... we kept them in the game ... instead of being eight or 10 points up at the end, where they couldn't have caught us even if we made the mistake, they were still in with a chance and they grabbed it. I've coached enough to know that. I've coached enough to know what works and what doesn't work.

Late in the game, when I thought our prop Ben Hannant had charged over for the match-winning try, I was really disappointed with myself for the way I reacted in the coach's box. I have taught myself to be disciplined in that box, because that's what I want the players to be. It takes me back to the double standards. I want them to treat the ref with respect, I want them to play in the right manner and I want them to be emotional and passionate about the game but not by being big heads and full of it. I don't want their coach to be carrying on down on the sideline if it ain't working out for him, if it ain't working out for the team. Emotion takes over and you lose control. I need to be composed and I need them to be composed. That's why I hated myself for jumping up when I thought Ben had scored — I wasn't in control for that moment. It's the same reason why the player doesn't get up and play the ball properly. We had four of them on the night. I can cop a bad pass, whatever, but those things like not playing the ball properly happen because the player's mind is not where the moment is. I saw the referee's hand go out and I thought he had awarded a try, but it turned out Ben had been held up. And I disliked myself immensely for the way I reacted, celebrating. For me, it was nearly as low as losing the game. Some people might not agree with that but they don't have to — they don't walk in my shoes.

I went from this absolute emotional high to the bottom of my feelings in four minutes. It made the pain greater. The magnificence and sheer power of sport has to do with it being unscripted. It's not like a movie — no one's writing the finish.

BACK IN THE CHANGE ROOMS I knew the cameras would be on me so I walked in and hid in an area where I knew they couldn't find me. I didn't want anybody seeing me. There is a side of me that knows that for everyone who is disappointed for me there is someone out there who is happy and I didn't want to give them any more satisfaction.

I probably had to show as much courage as I've shown in anything I've ever done, controlling my emotions and my real feelings. It was terribly important in this time of extreme disappointment that I conduct myself in a manner, as hard as it was, befitting a man fortunate enough to have spent 21 years a Bronco.

I didn't see Steve Williams, Barry Maranta and Gary Balkin at the ground but, as I said, I was thinking about them. The late Paul Morgan was there in spirit.

I have my moments but generally I don't say much to the players after a game. This time, I never felt more hollow saying something to them. I just said, 'Thanks. Thanks for the season and thanks for your effort tonight.' That was probably the worst moment. Thanks is such an inadequate word and we say it so much without meaning it. It's a word I never try to use a lot. I try to live it, rather than say it. I feel great despair for them. I knew I wouldn't be there for them again. Five days later, as I write this chapter, the last chapter, I still feel empty about that. I can't go back and pick up the pieces for them, and make them better in the things they need to be better. I can't put my arm around them. It's a different feeling to just losing a game. You feel there's so much to be said, and you can't say it … so much to be done, and you can't do it. And I don't like the feeling but I just have to live with it.

Beyond that, though, I wasn't carried away with the fact that my time at the club was done. It's been a long time.

I ran into Brad Thorn after the game. At times you ask yourself, 'Why do you do it? Why do you put yourself through it?' To see Brad Thorn, he was so proud of the players' effort and commitment. He's never one not to tell you how he feels, Brad. He made me realise that every one of the 163 players I coached at the Broncos who watched that game would have felt as proud as they have ever felt. That's important to me, because it's their club. Brad was shaking my hand, almost breaking it, saying, 'Coach, I was just so proud to be a Bronco tonight. Every other Bronco who watched that game and has worn that jersey, paid the price, would be proud.'

Trish went home early. Justin had been sick and couldn't come to the game. Finally, I drove out of Suncorp into the night and I did so full of the disappointment that came with the loss, but at the same time satisfied I'd made the right decision to leave. I was thinking, I'll be back. It's just that I'll be coming back with another badge on my shirt, as coach of St George Illawarra Dragons.

I'm not retiring as a coach, I'm just leaving the Brisbane Broncos. From the very beginning it was never about just one match. It was about 21 years.

Mission accomplished.

THERE IS NO INDISPENSABLE MAN

I like collecting clichés, sayings, short stories and poems — wise or maybe even funny words that I can refer to from time to time, usually to pick me up or to put things in perspective. I prefer to keep them to myself, though occasionally I'll share them with my players or my friends. A few years back I saw this poem, called *There Is No Indispensable Man*, which was written back in 1959 by Saxon N. White Kessinger, and I went looking for it again when I began thinking about what my eventual departure would mean to the Broncos ...

Some time when you're feeling important,
Some time when your ego's in bloom,
Some time when you take it for granted
You're the best qualified in the room,

Sometime when you feel that your going
Would leave an unfillable hole,
Just follow these simple instructions
And see how they humble your soul.

Take a bucket and fill it with water,
Put your hand in it up to the wrist,
Pull it out and the hole that's remaining
Is a measure of how you will be missed.

You can splash all you wish when you enter,
You may stir up the water galore,
But stop and you'll find that in no time
It looks quite the same as before.

The moral of this quaint example
Is do just the best that you can,
Be proud of yourself but remember,
There's no indispensable man.

WAYNE BENNETT

BORN: 1 JANUARY 1950

Senior Coaching Record: Ipswich 1976; Souths (Brisbane) 1977–79, 1984–85; Brothers (Brisbane) 1980–82; Canberra Raiders (NSW Rugby League) 1987; Brisbane Broncos (NSW Rugby League, Australian Rugby League, Super League, National Rugby League) 1988–2008; Queensland (State of Origin) 1986–88, 1998, 2001–03; Queensland (Tri-Series) 1997; Australia 1998, 2004–05.

Raiders Coaching Record (co-coach with Don Furner): Seasons 1; Games 28 — Won 17, Lost 11; Win rate 60.71 per cent
Finals Series: 1 (1987)
Grand Finals: 1 (1987)

Broncos Coaching Record: Seasons 21; Games 526 — Won 335, Lost 179, Drawn 12; Win rate 63.69 per cent
Finals Series: 18 (1990, 1992–2008)
Grand Finals: Six (1992, 1993, 1997, 1998, 2000, 2006)
Premierships: Six (1992, 1993, 1997, 1998, 2000, 2006)

State of Origin Coaching Record: Series 7; Games 21 (not including the match in California in 1987, which NSW won 30–18), Won 11, Lost 9, Drawn 1. Win rate 52.38 per cent
Series Wins: Four, plus one tied (2002, when Queensland retained the Origin shield because they had won the previous year's series)
Super League Tri-Series Coaching Record: Series 1; Games 3 — Won 1, Lost 2; Win rate 33.33 per cent

Australian Coaching Record: Tests 16, Won 12, Lost 3, Drawn 1. Win rate 75.00 per cent

21 YEARS A BRONCO

Year	Played	Won	Drawn	Lost	Position	Finish	Captain
1988	22	14	0	8	7 of 16	7th	Wally Lewis
1989	23	14	0	9	5 of 16	PO	Wally Lewis
1990	25	17	1	7	2 of 16	PF	Gene Miles
1991	22	13	0	9	7 of 16	7th	Gene Miles
1992	24	20	0	4	1 of 16	1st	Allan Langer
1993	26	20	0	6	5 of 16	1st	Allan Langer
1994	24	14	1	9	5 of 16	SF	Allan Langer
1995	24	17	0	7	3 of 20	SF	Allan Langer
1996	23	17	0	6	2 of 20	SF	Allan Langer
1997	20	16	1	3	1 of 10	1st	Allan Langer
1998	28	21	1	6	1 of 20	1st	Allan Langer
1999	25	13	2	10	8 of 17	QF	Kevin Walters
2000	29	21	2	6	1 of 14	1st	Kevin Walters
2001	29	15	1	13	5 of 14	PF	Gorden Tallis
2002	26	17	1	8	3 of 15	PF	Gorden Tallis
2003	25	12	0	13	8 of 15	QF	Gorden Tallis
2004	26	16	1	9	3 of 15	SF	Gorden Tallis
2005	26	15	0	11	3 of 15	SF	Darren Lockyer
2006	28	17	0	11	3 of 15	1st	Darren Lockyer
2007	25	11	0	14	8 of 16	QF	Darren Lockyer
2008	26	15	1	10	5 of 16	SF	Darren Lockyer
Total	**526**	**335**	**12**	**179**			

Notes
- 'Played' indicates premiership matches played and includes the 1989 play-off and finals matches.
- 'Position' indicates where the Broncos finished on the competition ladder.
- 'Finish' indicates where the Broncos finished in the finals series — 'PO' indicates lost a play-off for fifth place; 'QF' indicates they were knocked out in a qualifying final; 'SF' indicates they were knocked out in a semi-final; 'PF' indicates they were knocked out in a preliminary final.
- Brisbane won the Panasonic Cup in 1989, the Lotto Challenge in 1991 and the Tooheys Challenge in 1995
- In 1997, the Broncos played nine matches in Super League's World Club Challenge, and won them all to claim the competition.
- In 1999, Allan Langer retired after round 8 and Kevin Walters took over the captaincy.

BRISBANE BRONCOS 1988-2008

The following 163 men played first-grade premiership football for the Broncos between the beginning of the 1988 competition and the end of 2008.

Player

Isaak Ah Mau (2008)
Gavin Allen (1990–1995)
Fraser Anderson (2006)
Sam Backo (1989–1990)
Danny Bampton (1998–2000)
Berrick Barnes (2005)
Russell Bawden (1994)
Peter Benson (1988)
Barry Berrigan (2003–2005)
Shaun Berrigan (1999–2007)
Scott Blacker (1992–1996)
Leon Bott (2005–2006)
David Bourke (1988)
Darius Boyd (2006–2008)
Darren Burns (2001)
Kevin Campion (1998–2000)
Alan Cann (1990–1996)
Dane Carlaw (1999–2007)
Willie Carne (1990–1996)
Tonie Carroll (1996–2008)
Petero Civoniceva (1998–2007)
Joel Clinton (2008)
Greg Conescu (1988–1989)
Bob Conway (1990–1991)
Michael Coorey (2001–2003)
Mark Corvo (2001)
Neville Costigan (2003–2006)
Tony Currie (1989–1992)
Ben Czislowski (2004)
Michael De Vere (1997–2004)
Sid Domic (1993–1994)
James Donnelly (1989–1991)
Greg Dowling (1988–1991)
John Driscoll (1994–1999)
Shane Duffy (1988–1989)
Tony Duggan (2003)
Greg Eastwood (2005–2008)
Nick Emmett (2006–2008)
Michael Ennis (2006–2008)

Player

Jason Erba (1992)
Butch Fatnowna (1992–1993)
Craig Frawley (2003–2007)
Gary French (1988–1989)
Nathan Friend (2002)
Brett Galea (1993–1996)
Andrew Gee (1989–2003)
Keith Gee (1988)
Trevor Gillmeister (1991–1993)
Ken Gittens (1989)
Craig Grauf (1988)
Grant Graving (1989)
Brett Green (1995–1996)
Paul Green (2004)
Michael Hancock (1988–2000)
Ben Hannant (2006–2008)
Jason Hanrahan (1991)
Ashley Harrison (2000–2002)
Paul Hauff (1990–1996)
Ray Herring (1988–1990)
Justin Hodges (2000–2008)
Josh Hoffman (2008)
Mark Hohn (1988–1994)
Harvey Howard (2000)
Karmichael Hunt (2004–2008)
Ben Ikin (2000–2004)
Paul Iles (1991)
Steve Irwin (2002–2004)
Peter Jackson (1989–1990)
Chris Johns (1988–1996)
Kris Kahler (2002)
Damon Keating (2000–2001)
Shaun Keating (1992–1993)
Stuart Kelly (2001–2005)
Denan Kemp (2007–2008)
Brook Kennedy (1988–1989)
Nick Kenny (2005–2008)
Joe Kilroy (1988–1991)
Steve La Caze (2002)

Player
Ian Lacey (2006–2007)
Allan Langer (1988–2002)
Glenn Lazarus (1992–1997)
Brett Le Man (1988–1991)
Tom Learoyd-Lahrs (2004–2005)
Phillip Lee (1997–2003)
Wally Lewis (1988–1990)
Darren Lockyer (1995–2008)
Andrew Lomu (2007)
Kaine Manihera (2008)
Clifford Manua (2007)
Darren Mapp (2000–2005)
PJ Marsh (2008)
Terry Matterson (1988–1995)
Andrew McCullough (2008)
Casey McGuire (2001–2006)
Chris McKenna (1993–1994)
Keiran Meyer (1993)
Brad Meyers (2000–2004)
Steve Michaels (2005–2008)
Gene Miles (1988–1991)
Scott Minto (2002–2006)
Joel Moon (2006–2008)
Willie Morganson (1991–1993)
Paul Morris (1994)
Anthony Mundine (1997)
Bryan Niebling (1988–1989)
Billy Noke (1988)
Julian O'Neill (1991–1995)
Nick Parfitt (2002–2004)
Corey Parker (2001–2008)
Shane Perry (2006–2008)
John Plath (1990–1999)
Brett Plowman (1988–1993)
Darren Plowman (1992–1993)
Luke Priddis (1999–2001)
Scott Prince (2001–2003)
Steve Renouf (1989–1999)
Steele Retchless (1995–1996)
Grant Rix (1988–1990)
Mick Roberts (2007)
Reece Robinson (2008)
Robbie Ross (1996)

Player
Michael Ryan (2001–2004)
Peter Ryan (1991–1999)
Wendell Sailor (1993–2001)
Pat Savage (1992–1994)
Colin Scott (1988)
Dennis Scott (1996–1998)
Brett Seymour (2002–2006)
Dale Shearer (1990–1991)
Alwyn Simpson (2007)
Ashton Sims (2008)
Darren Smith (1995–2005)
David Stagg (2003–2008)
Richard Swain (2003)
Gorden Tallis (1997–2004)
Robert Tanielu (2002)
Brent Tate (2001–2007)
David Taylor (2006–2008)
John Te Reo (2007)
Craig Teevan (1988–1993)
Rohan Teevan (1988–1990)
Andrew Tessmann (1988–1992)
Brad Tessmann (1988)
Sam Thaiday (2003–2008)
Brad Thorn (1994–2007)
Grant Thorogood (1989)
Motu Tony (2004)
Scott Tronc (1989–1990)
Tame Tupou (2004–2006)
Elia Tuqiri (2002)
Lote Tuqiri (1999–2002)
Ben Vaeau (2006)
Ben Walker (1995–2000)
Chris Walker (1999–2002)
Shane Walker (1996–2002)
Peter Wallace (2008)
Kerrod Walters (1988–2000)
Kevin Walters (1990–2001)
Adam Warwick (2000)
Derrick Watkins (2008)
Carl Webb (2000–2004)
Shane Webcke (1995–2006)
Neale Wyatt (2002–2005)

Broncos State of Origin Representatives, 1988–2008 (52)

Queensland (46): Gavin Allen, Sam Backo, Shaun Berrigan, Darius Boyd, Allan Cann, Dane Carlaw, Willie Carne, Tonie Carroll, Petero Civoniceva, Greg Conescu, Tony Currie, Andrew Gee, Trevor Gillmeister, Michael Hancock, Ben Hannant, Paul Hauff, Justin Hodges, Mark Hohn, Karmichael Hunt, Ben Ikin, Peter Jackson, Joe Kilroy, Allan Langer, Wally Lewis, Darren Lockyer, Casey McGuire, PJ Marsh, Brad Meyers, Gene Miles, Julian O'Neill, Corey Parker, Steve Renouf, Peter Ryan, Wendell Sailor, Dale Shearer, Darren Smith, Gorden Tallis, Brent Tate, Sam Thaiday, Brad Thorn, Lote Tuqiri, Chris Walker, Kerrod Walters, Kevin Walters, Carl Webb, Shane Webcke

New South Wales (6): Michael De Vere, Chris Johns, Glenn Lazarus, Terry Matterson, Luke Priddis, Peter Wallace

Broncos Internationals, June 1988–May 2008 (35): Sam Backo, Shaun Berrigan, Dane Carlaw, Willie Carne, Tonie Carroll, Petero Civoniceva, Greg Conescu, Tony Currie, Michael De Vere, Andrew Gee, Michael Hancock, Paul Hauff, Justin Hodges, Mark Hohn, Karmichael Hunt, Peter Jackson, Chris Johns, Allan Langer, Glenn Lazarus, Wally Lewis, Darren Lockyer, Brad Meyers, Gene Miles, Steve Renouf, Wendell Sailor, Dale Shearer, Darren Smith, Gorden Tallis, Brent Tate, Sam Thaiday, Brad Thorn, Lote Tuqiri, Kerrod Walters, Kevin Walters, Shane Webcke

Broncos Test captains, June 1988–May 2008 (4): Wally Lewis (1988–1989), Allan Langer (1998), Gorden Tallis (2002); Darren Lockyer (2003–2007)

Player details from David Middleton,
League Information Services

INDEX

A

ACT Brumbies (rugby union) 198
Adelaide Rams 148, 201
All Blacks (rugby union) 215
All Golds (New Zealand) 323–325
Allan, Les 3, 17–18
Anderson, Chris 151–152, 261
Annesley, Graham 52
Arsenal (football) 235
Arthurson, Ken 29, 47–49, 124
Astill, Jack 9
Atlanta Falcons (NFL) 162
Auckland Warriors (New Zealand Warriors; Warriors) 144, 146, 168, 229, 246, 266, 297, 324, 348
Australia (Kangaroos) 34, 51, 66, 68, 86, 88, 105, 109, 123, 128, 140, 176, 185–186, 194, 246, 255, 261, 263–265, 269–273, 282–284, 332

Australian cricket team 196, 340
Australian Football League (AFL) 234
Australian Rugby League (ARL) 47, 123–124, 129–135, 138, 140, 146, 155, 170, 171, 177, 179, 283, 339
Australian Rugby League Foundation 335
Australian Rugby Union (ARU) 241, 276

B

Backo, Sam 19, 49–50, 59–60, 68, 70, 88
Bailey, Trevor 42
Baker, Dan 290
Balkin, Gary 23, 40, 69, 124, 218, 350
Balmain (Tigers) 45, 52, 88, 109, 128, 171, 203

Bampton, Danny 211
Barnes, Berrick 276
Baskerville, Albert 323
Bax, Bob 6, 9, 13, 32, 113–115, 199
Beattie, Chris 224
Beattie, Dud 24
Beetson, Arthur 14, 33, 225
Belcher, Gary 19, 278, 280, 303
Bella, Martin 46, 49–50
Bellamy, Craig 177, 239, 278, 331
Bennett, Justin (Wayne's son) 6, 17, 23, 156–160, 337, 351
Bennett, Katherine (Wayne's daughter) 17, 23, 192–193
Bennett, Pat (Wayne's mother) 34, 188–190, 248, 249, 337
Bennett, Trish (Wayne's wife) 6, 17, 23, 26, 27, 158, 159, 187–188, 191, 192, 193, 198, 199, 222, 243, 285, 299, 317–318, 333, 335, 351
Bennett, Wayne
   Australian coach 185–186, 203, 260, 261, 262–264, 268–272, 281–285, 286
   Australian player 249
   Broncos Life Membership 313–315
   Brothers coach 8–9
   Brothers player 2
   Canberra Raiders coach 16–17, 19, 21–22, 27–29, 31–32, 33, 42, 44, 53, 141, 299, 338
   Coach's notes 1993 111–112
   Coach's notes 1995 129–132, 136–137
   Coach's notes 1996 143–145
   Coach's notes 1997 166–167, 168–169
   Coach's notes 1998 176–186
   Coach's notes 1999 204
   Family support 22–23, 26, 33, 137, 187–193, 335
   Fined $10,000 242
   Joins Broncos 22–29, 218–219
   Leaves Broncos 288–289, 300, 308–310, 325–336
   Loyalty 36, 132, 149–150, 228–229, 329–330
   Meaning of Anzac 262, 263–264, 269
   Media 19–21, 50, 67, 80–81, 85, 126, 227, 229, 259–260, 268, 282, 283–285, 290, 316–319, 329, 332, 349–350
   Police Academy 2–7, 60, 209
   Policeman 2–5, 13, 17–18, 37, 48, 209, 218
   Ponders leaving Broncos 137, 205, 294–295, 296–297, 300, 326
   Queensland coach 13–15, 21, 25, 26, 29–32, 42, 46–50, 131, 133, 176, 178–184, 203, 221–227, 237–241, 254–257
   St George Illawarra coach 334–335, 351
   Souths (Brisbane) coach 7–8, 9–13, 301
   Upbringing 1–2, 16, 247–249, 336–337, 345
   Women in life 187–193
Benton, Dean 279, 287, 299
Berrigan, Barry 279
Berrigan, Shaun 260, 271–272, 279, 292–293, 298, 301, 312, 313

Berry, Tom 6
Best, George 347
Big League 196
Bourke, David 12
Bowen, Matt 255
Braybrook, Dennis 46
Brennan, Mitch 19
Brennan, Rowan 19
Brisbane Broncos
    Captains 48, 68, 71–73, 79, 86, 96, 99–100, 148, 196, 198, 212, 215, 225, 245, 261, 274, 288–289, 299
    Culture 39–40, 61, 85–86, 98–99, 103, 114, 207, 215, 239, 242, 278, 287, 300, 307, 313–314, 325–326, 333, 350–351
    Formation 22–29, 39–42, 44, 218–219, 325
    Jersey 43
    Impact of State of Origin 103, 109, 177, 186, 211, 215, 223, 227–228, 237, 242, 252–253, 275, 290, 311
    Move to ANZ Stadium 108–109
    Reopening of Suncorp Stadium 254
    Red Hill 37, 41–42, 72, 80
    Super League 63–64, 130–136
    1988 season 43–46, 50–53, 66, 342
    1989 season 52, 59–63, 66, 68–73, 77
    1989 Panasonic Cup 62, 66–67
    1990 season 74, 78–82, 84–88
    1991 Lotto Challenge 92
    1991 season 91–97
    1992 season 98–107
    1992 Grand Final 104–105, 186
    1992 World Club Challenge 105–107, 186
    1993 World Sevens 108
    1993 Tooheys Challenge 108
    1993 season 108–116
    1993 Grand Final 110, 111, 113–115, 301
    1994 season 123–128
    1994 Tooheys Challenge 125–126
    1995 season 130–131, 136–137
    1996 season 143–146, 148–151
    1996 end-of-season tour 161–162
    1997 season 161–171
    1997 World Club Challenge 161, 168, 169, 177
    1997 Grand Final 164, 169, 177
    1998 season 176–177
    1998 Grand Final 177
    1999 season 194–199, 201–205
    2000 season 2006–216
    2000 Grand Final 215, 217
    2001 World Club Challenge 217, 223
    2001 season 221, 222, 223, 227–230, 252
    2002 season 237, 242–245
    2003 season 252–254
    2004 season 258–259, 264–268
    2005 season 274–281
    2006 season 286–288, 290–294, 295–296, 298–302, 318–319

2006 Grand Final 301–302, 318–319
2007 World Club Challenge 310, 328
2007 season 215, 310–313, 317
2008 season 330–333, 342–351
Brisbane (Combined) 24
Brisbane Lions (AFL) 328
Brisbane State High School 40, 117, 219, 220
Brosnan, Eddie (Wayne's uncle) 34–38, 103, 248
Brosnan, Eddie jnr (Wayne's cousin) 34, 36
Brosnan, Winifred (Wayne's grandmother) 188
Brother Bible 209
Brothers (Brisbane) 2, 5, 8, 37, 42, 76, 152
Brown, Nathan 334
Buderus, Danny 263, 268
Bunn, Paul 286
Burchett, Justice James 146, 155
Buttigieg, John 224

C

Calder, Steve 81, 139
Campion, Kevin 201–202, 211, 216, 224
Canavan, Brian 41, 296, 336
Canberra (Raiders) 16–17, 19, 21–22, 27–29, 31–32, 33, 42, 44, 50, 53, 59, 62, 65, 66, 68–69, 86, 87, 95, 96, 102, 104, 109, 110, 112, 128, 135, 141, 143, 144, 159, 165, 167, 211, 260, 290, 299, 312, 338, 347
Cann, Alan 113, 148–149

Canterbury (Bulldogs) 22, 51, 52, 68, 75, 78, 108, 110, 112–113, 136, 143, 151, 177, 183, 228, 260, 265, 273, 279, 293, 295, 298, 311, 318, 327
Canterbury Crusaders (rugby union) 215
Canungra Army Camp 147, 208–210, 286–287, 305–306
Carlaw, Dane 211, 240, 313
Carne, Willie 76, 79, 80, 102, 126, 148, 213
Carr, Norm 12
Carroll, Tonie 167, 211, 216, 236–237, 273, 277, 312
Chegwyn, Peter 236
Chelsea (football) 234
Civoniceva, Petero 118, 121, 200–201, 211–212, 214, 224, 225, 253, 265, 273, 292, 293–294, 304–307, 312, 313, 315, 330, 346
Clark, Helen 323
Cleal, Noel 46
Clifford, Frank 5
Close, Chris 183–184, 186, 237
Clyde, Bradley 135
Collegians (Warwick) 2
Colwell, Marshall 7
Conescu, Greg 48, 51, 58, 68
Connell, Cyril 19, 117–122, 139, 200–201, 280
Coote, Ron 262
Corcoran, Peter 63
Cornell, John 41
Costigan, Neville 291–292
Courier-Mail 20, 179
Cowley, Ken 123, 169
Coyne, Gary 19

Coyne, Mark 42
Crocodile Dundee 41, 220
Cronin, Mick 56
Cronulla (Sharks) 21, 46, 69–70, 108, 109, 144, 150, 157, 164, 167, 168, 177, 205, 206, 213, 214, 229, 265, 288, 290, 295, 338, 347
Cross, Tony 2
Cullen, Bruno 266, 288, 290–291, 297, 313–315, 326, 333, 335
Cullen, Wayne 12
Currie, Tony 31–32, 68, 79, 88
Cuthbert, Betty 248

D
Daley, Laurie 135
Daley, Phil 48–49
Dallas Cowboys (NFL) 23, 328
Dallas, Brett 120
Daly, Fred 141–142
Davidson, Les 46, 49, 126
De Vere, Michael 167, 247, 250, 265, 274
Denver Broncos (NFL) 161
Dick, Barry 20
Docking, Jonathan 46
Dolan, Frank 8–9
Donnelly, James 85–86
Doubell, Ralph 41
Doust, Peter 335
Dowling, Greg 10, 12, 24, 42, 43, 49, 51, 64–65, 78, 79, 85, 141, 265, 301
Doyle, John 224
Driscoll, John 167
Drugs 78, 81–82, 223, 268, 291–292, 321–322
Duff, Noela (Wayne's aunt) 189–190

Duggan, Irene 192
Duke Of Edinburgh 323

E
Eade, Rodney 181
Eastern Suburbs (Brisbane) 9, 273
Eastern Suburbs (Sydney Roosters) 24, 42, 62, 63, 109, 126, 206, 207, 215, 228, 242–243, 245, 289, 294–295, 296–297, 308–309, 326, 330, 344, 347
Eastwood, Greg 287
Edwards, Shane 245–246
Elias, Ben 45, 88
Elias, John 12
Endacott, Frank 186
Ennis, Michael 333
Essendon (AFL) 309, 327
Ettingshausen, Andrew 46

F
Fans 52, 79, 99, 126, 149, 150, 171, 181, 204, 239, 256, 261, 314, 316, 318–319, 327, 342, 348
Federer, Roger 196
Ferguson, John 19
Ferguson, Sir Alex 234, 328
Finch, Robert 244
Fittler, Brad 84, 227
Fitzgibbon, Craig 268
Folkes, Steve 46
Fox, Andrew 19
Frail, Holly 43
Friis, Dr Peter 43, 202
Fulton, Bob
Furner, Don 19, 20, 22, 27–29, 33, 44, 59, 118

G
Gardner, Bill 127
Gasnier, Mark 241
Gasnier, Reg 199–200
Gates, Bill 221
Gee, Andrew 76, 107, 144, 164, 178, 184, 197, 198, 226, 247, 250, 254, 304, 307, 315, 330
Geyer, Mark 51
Gibson, Jack 8, 22–23, 338–340
Gidley, Kurt 260
Gidley, Matt 263
Gilbert, Ashley 19, 21
Giles, Kelvin 74–76, 101, 102, 107, 122, 149, 278, 279
Gill, Peter 42
Gillmeister, Trevor 31, 92–94, 114, 116, 124, 149
Glanville, Jerry 162
Gold Coast (Giants, Seagulls, Chargers) 23, 42, 47, 86, 95, 164, 170
Gold Coast (Titans) 311
Golden point extra-time 240, 260–261
Gould, Phil 103, 127, 140, 186, 237–238, 254–257
Gower, Craig 263, 268
Gray, Nola 191
Green, Paul 224
Greene, 'Joe' 166

H
Hagan, Michael 261
Halifax 161
Hancock, Michael 68, 76, 79, 87–88, 128, 144, 148–149, 163, 198, 207, 212, 213, 216, 315
Hannant, Ben 333, 349
Harrigan, Bill 182, 184, 225, 238, 243–244
Harrison, Ashley 211, 229
Hartigan, John 288–289, 300
Hatcher, Bruce 25–27, 218
Hauff, Paul 79, 80, 211
Hazard, Dr Hugh 223
Hayne, Shayne 348
Healy, Ian 316
Henjak, Ivan 19, 21, 69, 279–280, 287, 297, 309, 331
Henry, Neil 332
Hickman, Jeremy 279, 287, 336
Hill, Scott 270
Hindmarsh, Nathan 270
Hodges, Justin 211, 228–229, 239, 242, 243–244, 275–276, 298, 311
Hoffman, Jay 19
Hogan, Paul 41, 220
Holyfield, Evander 161
Houston Oilers (NFL) 162
Howard, Harvey 216
Howard, John 309, 327
Huddersfield 2, 265, 271
Hunt, Karmichael 118, 264–265, 295, 311
Hunter Mariners 168, 170
Hutchinson, Gary 2

I
Ikin, Ben (Wayne's son-in-law) 159, 211, 214, 252, 300
Ikin, Elizabeth (nee Bennett; Wayne's daughter) 23, 192–193
Illawarra (Steelers) 50, 62, 65, 104, 109, 130
Ipswich 24, 57–58

J

Jackson, Peter 16–17, 19, 28, 46–47, 59–62, 67, 68, 70, 79, 81–84, 85, 87, 175, 182, 196
Jackson, Siobhan 61
Jackson, Steve 19
Jauncey, Phil 197–198
Johns, Andrew 241, 261–262, 281, 296, 320–322
Johns, Chris 42, 62–63, 76, 79, 88, 100, 110, 115, 134–135, 148–149, 163, 184
Johns, Lisa 115
Johnston, Brian 46
Jones, Stacey 323
Jordan, Michael 265

K

Kavanagh, Lawrie 20
Keating, Sean 103
Kelly, Noel 33, 262
Kelly, Peter 49
Kenny, Brett 66
Kilroy, Joe 46, 76–78
Kim Walters Choices 175
Kimmorley, Brett 211

L

Lamb, Terry 46
Lance, Dean 19, 21
Lancini, Laurence 333–334
Landry, Tom 22–23, 328
Lang, John 9
Langer, Allan 24, 45–46, 47, 49, 57–59, 62, 63, 66, 68–69, 76, 85, 86–87, 88, 94, 99–101, 115, 126, 128, 132, 139, 144, 150–151, 163, 165–166, 167, 178–186, 194–198, 201, 202, 216, 225–227, 242, 245, 273, 303, 336
Larson, Gary 184
Lazarus, Glenn 95–96, 109, 110, 113, 124, 127–128, 131–133, 144, 164–165, 167, 198, 280, 304, 307
Lee, Phillip 208, 210, 238, 254
Lewis, Luke 262
Lewis, Wally 7, 10, 12, 14, 24, 29, 30, 42, 43, 46–49, 51, 65, 66–74, 78, 79, 85, 86, 88, 94, 102, 149, 245, 301
Lillee, Dennis 160
Lindner, Bob 47, 55
Lindsay, Maurice 135
Livermore, Ross 13, 14, 133, 221–222, 227
Liverpool (football) 328
Lockie, George 220
Lockwood, Warren 335
Lockyer, Darren 67, 87, 118, 138–140, 159, 165, 167, 186, 225, 226, 239–240, 245, 253, 254, 258–260, 261, 263, 264, 268–272, 274–275, 277, 282, 288–289, 295, 297, 299, 301, 303, 309–310, 311, 330–332, 346
London Broncos 63
Lyons, Cliff 46

M

Magic Millions 234
Manchester United (football) 196, 234
Mander, Tim 253

Manly (Sea Eagles) 32, 44, 51, 84, 85, 109, 110, 112, 128, 143, 177, 265, 275, 311
Mapp, Darren 211
Maranta, Barry 23, 40, 41, 44, 124, 218, 314, 350
Maranta, Robyn 41
Marshall, Benji 159, 276
Mason, Willie 270, 298
Massey, Paul 341
Massey, Ron 8, 182, 277, 338–341
Masters, Roy 334
Matterson, Terry 42, 62–63, 85, 100, 110, 114
Matthews, Leigh 328
McAuliffe, Ron 13, 18
McCabe, Paul 7
McCarthy, Bob 9
McDonald, John 133, 304
McDonnell, Professor Bill 271
McGaw, Mark 25, 46
McGuire, Casey 243
McIlwain, Peter 250–251
McIntyre, Les 16, 23, 27–29
Melbourne (Storm) 157, 165, 202, 203, 211, 228, 253, 266, 276, 290, 292–293, 298, 301, 306, 312–313, 331, 342
Meninga, Mal 5–6, 14, 19, 66, 165, 303
Messenger, Dally 323
Meyers, Brad 224, 265
Miami Dolphins (NFL) 328
Miles, Gene 10, 12, 24, 29, 30, 42, 43, 51, 61, 65–66, 68, 72, 75, 79–80, 85, 86, 88, 95–97, 141, 222, 301

Minichiello, Anthony 268, 271–272
Mirren, Helen 323
Mitchell, Darcy 41
Mohr, Clinton 42
Moimoi, Fuifui 276
Monday Night Football 317
Moore, Peter 32, 48, 120
Morgan, Paul 23, 24–29, 39, 40–41, 42, 43–44, 50–51, 63, 70, 80–81, 95, 115, 117, 120, 122, 124, 125, 135–136, 173, 217–220, 231–232, 234, 235, 236, 245, 294, 299, 314, 342, 347, 350
Morris, Des 9, 10, 14
Morris, Rod 10, 12
Morrissey, Les 19
Mortimer, Steve 127
Muir, Barry 11
Mullins, Brett 135
Mundine, Anthony 151–152, 166
Murdoch, Lachlan 288–289
Murdoch, Rupert 63, 125, 171
Murray, Graham 333
Murray, Mark 14–15, 30, 126–127
Myers, Dr Peter 43, 86, 266

N

Nadruku, Noa 195
Nance, Steve 278
National Rugby League (NRL) 222, 223, 230, 266, 276, 316, 321
Newcastle (Knights) 45, 65, 77, 78–79, 102–103, 109, 177, 227–228, 260, 265, 296, 298, 321

News Limited 123, 125, 129–136, 169, 170, 236, 288–289, 326, 334
Newtown (Bluebags, Jets) 142, 231
Niebling, Bryan 49
Nissen, Don 236–237
Noke, Bill 42
Nolan, Ged 73
Nolan, Rebecca, 73
North Queensland (Cowboys) 132, 141, 151, 175, 194–195, 224, 266–268, 287–288, 290, 311, 333–334
North Sydney (Bears) 22, 40, 45, 51, 68, 84, 95, 109, 128, 144
Northern Eagles 229
Northern Suburbs (Brisbane) 8, 12, 76
NSW Rugby League (NSWRL) 29, 46, 218

O
O'Connell, Wally 262
O'Connor, Johnny 247
O'Connor, Michael 46
O'Davis, Robbie 140
O'Neill, Julian 128
O'Sullivan, Chris 19
Obstruction 230
Olympic Games (1956) 248
Operation Harden Up 286–287

P
Packer, James 132
Packer, Kerry 129, 138–139, 142, 171
Parker, Corey 228–229, 306–307
Parr, Peter 333

Parramatta (Eels) 12, 22, 45, 62, 67, 95, 108, 139, 159, 177, 207, 214, 242, 253, 295, 303–304, 312
Paterson, David 19
Paul Morgan Medal 307
Peachey, David 164
Pearce, Ian 'Bunny' 6
Pearce, Wayne 46
Penrith (Panthers) 24, 45, 51–52, 84–85, 92, 95, 101, 103–104, 109, 126, 127, 157–158, 211, 253, 264, 265, 275, 276, 306, 330
Peponis, George 327
Perry, Shane 295
Perth Reds 170
Petrie, Greg 5, 17–19
Phelan, Basil 38, 190–191
Phelan, Betty 38, 190–191
Phelan, Brian 247
Phelan, Chris 8, 12, 165, 303–304
Phelan, Max 247
Phelan, Pat 8, 12
Piggins, George 126
Pittsburgh Steelers (NFL) 166
Politis, Nick 294, 297
Power, Bernie 138
Presley, Elvis 162
Price, Ray 55
Prince, Scott 252, 254, 277
Pryor, Graham 43

Q
Quayle, John 29, 124, 132
Queen Elizabeth II 322–323
Queensland Academy of Sport 119, 221

Queensland Police Academy 2–6, 8, 17–18, 60, 209, 250
Queensland Rugby League (QRL) 13, 47, 119, 133, 179, 180, 221, 237, 304

R

Ragh, Kenny 43
Raudonikis, Tommy 24, 231
Redcliffe (Dolphins) 40, 152, 218, 279, 295, 305
Reddy, Rod 201
Regan, Terry 19
Renouf, Steve 44, 79, 88, 105, 110, 112, 128, 132, 144, 161–164, 166, 178, 184, 198, 199–200, 202, 213
Referees 48, 52, 126, 157, 182–183, 225–226, 238, 242, 243–244, 253–254, 279, 348, 349
Ribot, John 25, 29, 41, 43, 63, 70, 73, 75, 80, 85, 92, 94, 95, 115, 123, 125, 129–136, 140, 151, 155, 172–174, 245–246, 325
Riddell, Mark 253
Roach, Steve 45, 46, 47–48, 265
Rogers, Mat 222
Rogers, Steve 66
Rugby union 148, 198, 215, 222, 223, 228, 230, 241–242, 261–262, 276, 314
Ryan, Peter 116, 144, 164, 198, 230, 280
Ryan, Warren 22, 45–46, 127
Rynne, Frank 17–18

S

Sailor, Wendell 121–122, 123, 128, 159, 207, 213, 222, 230
Salary cap 115–116, 123–124, 165, 197, 199, 216, 221, 222, 246, 252, 276
Seymour, Brett 260, 279, 291–292
Shankly, Bill 328
Shearer, Dale 85, 88, 102
Sheedy, Kevin 309, 327, 328
Sheens, Tim 59, 75, 159
Shula, Don 328
Simmons, Royce 46
Sing, Matt 271
Singleton, John 43, 231–235, 294
Smith, Brian 113–115, 159
Smith, Cameron 255
Smith, Darren 144, 186, 226, 273–274, 276
Smith, Jason 181, 273
Somerville, Darryl 291, 308–309, 326
South Queensland Crushers 127, 130
South Sydney (Rabbitohs) 50–51, 62, 103, 108, 125–126, 233, 265
Southern Suburbs (Brisbane) 6, 7–8, 9–13, 40, 57, 102, 104, 301, 303, 304
Spencer, Tom 43
Spina, Laurie 24
St George (Dragons) 42, 50, 63, 72, 103, 104–105, 109–110, 112, 113–115, 140, 148, 151–152, 171, 233, 301
St George Illawarra (Dragons) 213, 214, 225, 228, 229, 238,

253, 265, 275, 295, 296, 301, 334–335, 351
St Helens 217, 273, 310
Stagg, David 201
Stanthorpe 87
Stanton, Frank 32
State of Origin 14–15, 21, 24, 25–26, 29–32, 46–50, 63, 66, 68, 109, 128, 176, 178–184, 186, 221–227, 237–241, 253, 254–257, 288, 311, 316, 331–332
Sterling, Peter 46
Stone, Mick 48, 182
Strudwick, Ross 10, 42
Stuart, Ricky 94, 112, 135, 294
Sunday Sun 8
Sunday Telegraph 170
Super League 63–64, 123, 125, 129–136, 140, 146, 149, 151, 152, 155, 161–164, 166–171, 173, 177, 179, 199, 201, 246, 339, 345
Sydney Swans (AFL) 181

T

Tallis, Gorden 140–141, 146–148, 151–152, 164, 181, 200, 207, 211, 224, 225, 226, 238, 245, 254, 267–268, 288, 307, 334
Tate, Brent 228–229, 239, 263, 277, 279, 311, 313
Tessman, Andrew 52
Testa, Tony 6, 7–8, 9–10, 11
Thaiday, Sam 307
The Man in the Mirror ix
The Queen 323
There is No Indispensable Man 353

Thompson, Duncan 33
Thorn, Brad 228–229, 239, 263, 277, 279, 311, 313
Todd, Brent 19, 21
Toowoomba All Whites 2, 218, 249
Toowoomba Clydesdales 238
Trewhella, David 46
Tunks, Peter 49
Tuqiri, Lote 121, 213, 222, 224, 230, 237, 238, 240, 241–242
Tune, Ben 223
Turner, Dick 30, 47, 68, 97, 222
Tyson, Mike 161–162

V

Valleys 10, 41
Van de Velde, Darryl 197
Vautin, Paul 7, 30, 31
Veivers, Jean (Wayne's mother-in-law) 10–11, 191
Veivers, Greg 201

W

Wagon, Daniel 224
Walker, Ben 139, 148, 195, 211
Walker, Chris 224
Walker, Shane 229
Walters, Kerrod 57–59, 76, 85, 88, 114, 132, 148–149, 303
Walters, Kevin 19, 24, 57, 57–59, 63, 72, 85, 87–88, 100, 105, 106, 109, 113–115, 128, 132–133, 139, 144, 163, 165–167, 175, 178–184, 201, 202, 207, 211, 212–213, 214, 216, 226, 267, 273, 280, 303, 336
Walters, KG 175

Walters, Kim 175, 196
Walters, Sandy 175
Walters, Steve 19, 179, 285, 304
Ward, Chris 239–240, 243
Warne, Shane 347
Warrington 197
Webb, Carl 224, 229, 265
Webcke, Shane 56, 96, 118, 152, 153–154, 164, 165–166, 167, 186, 214–215, 223, 224, 225, 253, 260, 263, 265, 266–267, 269, 276, 282, 292, 296, 297, 300–301, 304–307, 310, 330, 346
Welsh, Pat 20
Western Suburbs (Brisbane) 22, 35, 40, 41
Western Suburbs (Sydney; Magpies) 45, 51, 95, 109, 127, 164, 295
Wests Tigers 159, 238, 239, 253, 276–277, 290
White Kessinger, Saxon N. 351
Whitrod, Ray 5
Wigan 95, 105–107, 164, 165, 167, 169, 197, 198, 199
Wiki, Ruben 323
Williams, Steve 22, 24–25, 40, 44, 124, 218, 327
Williams, Terri 40
Wimbrow, Peter 'Dale' ix
Wockner, Trevor 2
Woods, Tiger 196
World Expo '88 245
Wrestling 230, 278
Wynnum-Manly 5, 9, 10, 12–13, 14, 301

Y
Young, Mike 258

Photograph Sources

Section One
Page 1 — Newspix/David Kapernick
Page 2 — All pics: Wayne Bennett Private Collection
Page 3 — Both pics: Wayne Bennett Private Collection
Page 4 — Both pics: Wayne Bennett Private Collection
Page 5 — All pics: Wayne Bennett Private Collection
Page 6 — Top left: Wayne Bennett Private Collection; Top right: Newspix/David Kapernick; Bottom: Newspix
Page 7 — Top: Newspix/David Kapernick; Middle: Wayne Bennett Private Collection; Bottom: Newspix/David Kapernick
Page 8 — Top: Broncos Archives/Bob Jones Photography; Bottom: Newspix/Patrick Hamilton

Section Two
Page 1 — Top: Newspix; Bottom: Wayne Bennett Private Collection
Page 2 — Top left: Newspix; Top right: Broncos Archives/Bob Jones Photography; Bottom: Wayne Bennett Private Collection
Page 3 — Top left: Newspix/Mark Evans; Top right: Newspix; Bottom: Newspix/David Kapernick
Page 4 — Top: Broncos Archives/Bob Jones Photography; Bottom: Newspix
Page 5 — Top: Wayne Bennett Private Collection; Middle: Newspix; Bottom: Broncos Archives/Bob Jones Photography
Page 6 — Top left: Wayne Bennett Private Collection; Top right: Newspix; Bottom: Wayne Bennett Private Collection
Page 7 — Top: Broncos Archives/Bob Jones Photography; Middle and bottom: Wayne Bennett Private Collection
Page 8 — Top: Broncos Archives/Bob Jones Photography; Bottom: Newspix/Bruce Long

Section Three
Page 1 — Top: Newspix/Tim Marsden; Bottom: Wayne Bennett Private Collection
Page 2 — Top: Newspix/Laffan Grainger; Bottom: Newspix/David Kapernick
Page 3 — Top: Newspix; Bottom left: Newspix/David Kapernick; Bottom right: Newspix/Mark Evans
Page 4 — Top: Newspix/Brett Costello; Bottom left and right: Newspix/David Kapernick
Page 5 — Both pics: Getty Images/Michael Steele
Page 6 — Top: Newspix/Nathan Richter; Bottom: Newspix/Patrick Hamilton
Page 7 — Top: Newspix/David Kapernick; Bottom: Newspix/Graham Crouch
Page 8 — Top: Newspix/Gregg Porteous; Bottom: Newspix/David Kapernick

Back cover photograph
The Broncos celebrate their victory in the 2006 Grand Final (Action Photographics/Colin Whelan)

The great leader speaks little. He never speaks carelessly. He works without self-interest and leaves no trace. When all is finished, the people say, 'We did it ourselves.'

— LAO-TZU, CHINESE PHILOSOPHER AND TEACHER